CLOTHED
WITH
CHARITY

Other volumes in the Women's Conference Series

CLOTHED

WITH

CHARITY

TALKS FROM THE 1996
WOMEN'S CONFERENCE

EDITED BY
DAWN HALL ANDERSON
SUSETTE FLETCHER GREEN
AND DLORA HALL DALTON

DESERET BOOK COMPANY
SALT LAKE CITY, UTAH

Library of Congress Cataloging-in-Publication Data

Women's Conference (1996 : Brigham Young University)
   Clothed with charity : talks from the 1996 Women's Conference / edited by Dawn Hall Anderson, Susette Fletcher Green, and Dlora Hall Dalton.
      p.   cm.
   Includes bibliographical references and index.
   ISBN 1-57345-240-8 (hard)
   1. Mormon women—Religious life—Congresses. 2. Charity—Congresses. 3. Church of Jesus Christ of Latter-day Saints—Congresses. 4. Mormon Church—Congresses. I. Anderson, Dawn Hall. II. Green, Susette Fletcher. III. Dalton, Dlora Hall. IV. Title.
BX8641.W73   1996
289.3'32'082—dc21   96-53165
                                                                          CIP

Printed in the United States of America

10   9   8   7   6   5   4   3   2   1   72082

CONTENTS

CONTENTS

THE WORKS OF GOD

AWAKENINGS

PREFACE

This book is the eleventh in a series from the annual Women's Conference sponsored jointly by Brigham Young University and the Relief Society of The Church of Jesus Christ of Latter-day Saints. The essays and poems in this volume were drawn from presentations given at the 1996 conference. In their humor and openness, these essays and poems reflect the lively Women's Conference tradition of conversation. We are especially grateful to our authors for the courage to tell their own life stories as well as for their insights and expertise on the topics they address. We greatly appreciate their extra effort and cooperation in shaping oral presentations into written essays.

Our special thanks go to the 1996 conference chair, Kathy D. Pullins, assistant dean of the J. Reuben Clark Law School at BYU; her executive assistant, Vicki M. Huebner; and their energetic committee of BYU faculty members and Relief Society representatives. These women prayerfully planned and coordinated a complex, multisession, two-day conference.

And finally, we are grateful to Suzanne Brady of Deseret Book for creating the final product out of the manuscript we submitted.

"FILLED WITH ALL THE FULNESS OF GOD"

PATRICIA T. HOLLAND

> *[Christ is] the light of the sun . . . the moon . . . the stars . . . and the earth also, . . . which light proceedeth forth from the presence of God to fill the immensity of space. . . . The day shall come when you shall comprehend even God, being quickened in him and by him. Then shall ye know that ye have seen me, that I am, and that I am the true light that is in you, and that you are in me; otherwise ye could not abound.*
>
> *—Doctrine and Covenants 88: 7–10, 12, 49–50*

Every human heart desires to "abound" in God. That can come only through the light by which God quickens us. Illuminated hearts become filled with charity—for ourselves, for others, and for God, who perpetuates that cycle until charity fills the emptiness of any space. Therefore the Lord tells us, "Above all things, clothe yourselves with the bond of charity" (D&C 88:125).

Our sisterhood in this dispensation began with Emma Smith and the Relief Society. If we are to grow in charity and spirituality, we will have to do as the Lord counseled Emma: "Thou

---

Patricia Terry Holland, a native of southern Utah, attended Dixie College and studied voice and piano in New York City. A homemaker and educator, she has served in the Young Women General Presidency and on the boards of Deseret Book Company and Primary Children's Medical Center. She and her husband, Jeffrey R. Holland, a member of the Quorum of the Twelve Apostles, are the parents of three children and the grandparents of two.

shalt lay aside the things of this world, and seek for the things of a better" (D&C 25:10). The difference between our present world and the better one that we all yearn for lies within our hearts. We cannot give love or strength that we do not ourselves have. So if we expect to clothe ourselves with the bond of charity—if we hope to bless others with God's truths and compassion and sustenance—then we must spend more time with God in a very direct way. We do not have to rely on anyone else's witness of the Father. We can have direct encounters of our own. As Paul told the Ephesians, we can literally be "filled with all the fulness of God" (Ephesians 3:19). Those encounters can fill and refill our cups every day of our lives.

Paul's promise seems especially relevant because more and more we live in a world that can be frighteningly empty. Those who don't have the gospel, both near home and around the globe, often create ineffective communities, work in stress-filled professions, have declining morals, ruined health, failing families, and in the end, failing hope.

One especially troubling complaint of our time is there is no commonality among women. Across cultures and countries and even in our own neighborhoods, women have become so diverse and so separated in their lifestyles, interests, and preoccupations that rarely is there a friend such as our mothers had over the back fence, a neighbor to visit, to love, and to listen. But we still need someone to listen when our joints ache, our children squabble, or (perhaps even more urgently) when we wish we had squabbling children or loved ones nearby to nurture. We must not let the modern world isolate, fragment, or distance us from those we can love and serve.

Isolation can be one of the most frightening and stressful circumstances of the human heart. We all need other people and strong, sweet relationships if it is possible to have them. The Church helps us with that. Relief Society offers us a sisterhood that we can cherish and association with others who believe what we believe, hope what we hope, and who love the things of God.

To receive the fulness God has intended for us, to offset the emptiness of isolation or hurt or sorrow, to clothe ourselves "with the bond of charity, as with a mantle" (D&C 88:125), we are all going to have to reach out with our hearts and let down some barriers. Most of us protect ourselves from pain—hurtful experiences and words that come from our friends, our ene-mies, and sometimes from ourselves—by building walls or emotional defenses around ourselves.

The same walls we build to protect us can also isolate us, and that isolation leads to the problems we see so many others struggling with. Can we let down a few walls and find that we are in the embrace of God? Let's receive the spirit of holiness and let our cups be filled with living water. Let us receive in order to give.

One of my foundation stones for trusting that this can hap-pen is a powerful statement from President George Q. Cannon: "No matter how serious the trial, how deep the distress, how great the affliction, [God] will never desert us. He never has, and He never will. He cannot do it. It is not His character. He is an unchangeable being; the same yesterday, the same today, and He will be the same throughout the eternal ages to come. We have found that God. We have made Him our friend, by obeying His gospel; and He will stand by us. We may pass through the fiery furnace; we may pass through deep waters; but we shall not be consumed nor overwhelmed. We shall emerge from all these trials and difficulties the better and purer for them, if we only trust in our God and keep His command-ments."[1]

I would place that theology right at the heart of the gospel. We have every right to be hopeful. We have every right to have faith. God lives and loves us. He will not desert us. We can let down a few of our defenses against a faithless world, and we can, with Emma Smith, concentrate on the things of a better.

Paul wrote, "*Be not conformed to this world:* but be ye transformed by the renewing of your mind, that ye may prove what is that good, and acceptable, and perfect, will of God" (Romans 12:2; emphasis added). To connect with God and be filled with his fulness, to resist conforming to the world, and to discover "that good, and acceptable, and perfect, will of God" *for us* requires a settled, calm mind, a "renewed mind" as Paul says, a spirit of contentment, a divine trust and serenity, and a willingness to surrender to God's will. A renewed mind is one that has been illuminated by a new spiritual perception—revelation. When our mind has been illuminated to see as God sees, it becomes a joy to accept his will.

Recently I was anxiously pleading with the Lord to bless my oldest son. My request was very specific; I knew what my son needed. As I was pleading (with an eye fixed on *my* needs and *my* anxieties), asking the Lord to please bless him, the words came so resoundingly into my mind, "I *am* blessing him. Be patient with *my* plan." I was stunned—moved to tears. I realized I had been commanding heaven, saying, "Lord, here is your work as I have outlined it. Please notify me when you have bestowed my blessings, pursued my plans, and carried out my will."

In sweet reply comes the mild rebuke, "If you don't mind, Patricia, I prefer to bestow *my* blessings and to do it in *my* way." When we can feel sure that God has not forgotten us— nor will he ever—and that he is blessing us in his own way, then the world seems a better, safer place. If we can be patient with his process—which simply means having faith—if we can commune personally and often with him, we can spare ourselves the emptiness and frenzy we feel if we are "conformed to the world": fainthearted, impatient, troubled by envy or greed or pride of a thousand kinds. We can keep our minds fixed enough on eternity to remember that God's ways are not our ways (see Isaiah 55:8–9).

We then are enabled, as the Savior told his disciples, to

"take no thought for your life, what ye shall eat, or what ye shall drink; nor yet for your body, what ye shall put on" (Matthew 6:25). We have to worry about some of those things, but we don't have to worry about them too much. Competing for these things damages our unity and our charity. We can be consumed by "things." You know, "What am I going to wear today, and I hope they don't notice my nails!"

If the Savior had been speaking in Provo in the 1990s rather than in Jerusalem in the meridian of time, he might have said, "Sisters, be peaceful. Be believing. Live close to God. You are silly to spend so much time worrying about temporal, often petty things because you can't do very much about them anyway." That is my loose translation of what he said. What he *really* said was, "Which of you by taking thought can add one cubit unto his [or her] stature?" (Matthew 6:27). Why waste time worrying that we are 4'11" and, well, "solid" when we would like to be 5'9" and slinky. It is the wrong concern about the wrong things, and we can't really change much of it anyway.

Let's put our arms around the 4'11"s and the 5'9"s, and around those who have degrees and those who don't, around those who are married and those who aren't, and let's keep striving for the fulness of God and the charity of Christ. Let's not be conformed to this world.

Isn't it sometimes discouraging to see just how easily the adversary uses such earthly issues as vanity and worry, envy and pettiness to distract us from our divine mission and the unity we could enjoy in the Church? We all get discouraged and distracted—caught up in the thick of thin things—no matter how good we are. But do we have time, energy, or emotion to waste on what dress to wear or whose living room is the loveliest? We have real things to think about, things of the kingdom of God. We need to drink more deeply and be filled more fully for the work that lies ahead of us.

Let me suggest some ways that this fulness can come. Often when I face difficulties, I need to turn off the phone, lock the door, kneel in earnest prayer, and then curl up in a chair and meditate, contemplate, search the scriptures, and cry out again and again in my heart, completely focusing my mind on the mind and will and presence of God until I can see a clear picture of him. I like to think of him with loving, outstretched arms. With such a loving image, I begin to feel my connection with him and a confirmation of his love. Sometimes we may have to work at this for hours, for a significant portion of the day, or for several days.

Now I can hear every one of you saying, "Pat, get real. We don't have five minutes to do that, let alone an hour or two. We are exhausted now just trying to keep up with things." I know all about your life because it is my life, too. I am busy also, and I have been for as long as I can remember. I know what it is like to chauffeur teenagers, face the laundry, serve in the Church and in the community, and be married to one of the Lord's equally busy servants. But that has *everything* to do with the point I wish to make.

I realize that life has to go on and that you will not be able to pursue this heavenly communication in a completely uninterrupted way, but if it is a high priority and a fundamental goal in your life, you will find ways, early or late, to be with God. If the key to your car or your mortgage payment check or a child were lost, would you take time to find them? Wouldn't finding them provide the peace you need to then go about your day? If God is lost in your life and you are not going to be strong or stable without him, can you be focused and fixed enough to find him?

I know many of you have had loving fathers on this earth. If you believed your earthly father could comfort any heartache, heal any illness, solve any problem, or just be with you through the crucibles of life, wouldn't you call to him constantly? I am just childish enough to believe that our Father in Heaven can bless us in all those ways. The price to be paid for this kind of communion is time and your best powers of concentration, but by that investment you may offset untold hours—or days and weeks and months—of struggle or sorrow or pain.

For me, sometimes this has to be early in the morning— that is my best time—when I am fresh and revelation is strong. Occasionally it has to be at night before I go to bed. In any case it has to be when things are still, when the house is quiet and my mind is calm. I have the good fortune on those early mornings or late nights to have an unobstructed view of the beautiful Bountiful Temple just three-quarters of a mile from my home. As I look at the temple I see first its holiness, its brightness, beauty, and light. Whether rain or snow is falling, whether the clouds are low and hovering or the sun is bright overhead, the temple is lovely and firm. Its immovable quality steadies my soul particularly on those days when I seem so very movable and so very drawn and driven in many direc- tions. Its strong, straight spires remind me that unlike the tem- poral things in my life, my health, and the demands of the day and the laundry waiting to be done, the real me—the spiritual me, the real Pat Holland, the divine in me—is firm and fixed and stable and settled, like that temple on that hill. I take great comfort in the thought that the things that swirl around us are *not* us and that the demands on our life are *not* life itself.

President Gordon B. Hinckley has spoken often lately of meditation. My husband has commented on how often, in speaking to the First Presidency and the Quorum of the Twelve, he has asked that they make sure they take time for thoughtfulness, for pondering, for introspection, for meditation. He often refers to a statement of President David O. McKay: "Meditation is the language of the soul. It is defined as 'a form of private devotion, or spiritual exercise, consisting in deep, continued reflection on some religious theme.'"[2]

Somewhere in our lives there must be time and room for such personal communion. Somewhere in our lives there must be time and room for the celestial realities we say we believe in—or when will millennial peace be ours?

The kind of contemplation, reflection, and yearning for God I am speaking of can't be accomplished very handily in competition with cellular phones, computers, or a blaring TV. God can enter our realm only at our invitation. He stands at the door and knocks always, but someone has to hear that knock and let him enter. In this effort we ought to do whatever we can to make our homes—or our apartments or our condominiums—the temples, quite literally, that God intends them to be. Places for the Spirit of the Lord to dwell. Places for meditation, contemplation, prayer, and study. Places where good conversation and charity out of a pure heart can be present. Places where we find the fulness of God.

We need to simplify and spiritualize and celestialize. If most of what we are doing doesn't fit these categories, if at least some portion of our day is not turned to heaven, then we have a wrenching, rending emptiness awaiting us—isolation of the first order—and we will find no cloak of charity with which to protect ourselves or our sisters. We simply have to see what we can eliminate, what we can replace with something higher and holier, more reflective, compassionate, and eternal. Second only to dedicated temples, our homes are to be the sacred edifices of the Lord, places of peace and holiness and sanctity.

I am not being Pollyannish about this. I have already said that I know very well the demands upon a woman's time. It is because I know them oh so well that I am speaking as I am. I am speaking not only out of the depths of my heart but also out of the depths of my experience. You can say, "It can't be done. There is too much to do. It takes too much energy." Yes, you *can* say that—but you may miss forever the divine knock at the door. Or as the scripture says even more poignantly, "The harvest is past, the summer is [over], and [our souls are] not saved!" (D&C 56:16).

I believe a woman seeking the cloak of charity, a woman

desiring with all her heart to receive the fulness of God, has a chance to break through these telestial, temporal trappings we hang onto. I believe she can find special powers, sacred powers, to bring to latter-day tasks. Through God she can receive the power to serve and sustain and sacrifice.

Most of us are well acquainted with the responsibilities of service. I am sure many of you have baked cookies until your spatulas melted or baby-sat your neighbor's children until your brains sputtered. Occasionally when I am in such situations I fear my fatigue will slip into resentment, and then I wonder if being stretched so thin may not only prevent my developing new charity but actually diminish the supply I thought I had. I have learned, however, that though we may not have a completely willing heart every time we serve, such service molds our heart, blesses us, and does enlarge our capacity to give. We must remember, too, during periods of our lives in which we feel that all we can do is keep our own immediate circle of families or friends afloat, that *emotional* and *spiritual* service to others can sometimes be as important as physical acts.

My daughter Mary Alice tells of being assigned to visit teach a friend but procrastinating the visit because her friend, who had three preschoolers and was pregnant with a fourth child, always seemed frazzled and frustrated. Mary Alice knew she would want to shoulder some of her friend's tasks, but she also felt stretched to the limit with two preschoolers of her own, a husband in graduate school, and a demanding Church calling.

The idea of having three more children in her two-room apartment adding to her own children's chaos, even for only a few hours, seemed overwhelming. Yet, partially out of duty, but mostly out of love and a desire to lift her friend's spirits, she regularly offered to tend, clean house, and relieve her of some of her other burdens. Occasionally those offers were accepted; more often they were declined. Even when her friend accepted help, Mary Alice could see little difference in her friend's mood.

One day, when Mary Alice herself was having a particularly exasperating day, she called her friend—in the spirit of good visiting teaching—just to tell her that she couldn't help thinking of her and empathizing with her struggles. During that conversation, Mary Alice sensed a gradual change in that sister's attitude, a kind of happiness she hadn't sensed in her very often.

Near the end of the conversation, her friend admitted to feeling nearly ecstatic to realize that Mary Alice, who seemed to be able to handle everything with grace and goodwill, was having a miserable day. The sister explained, "Mary Alice, I am so grateful. I've never had anyone share their frustrations with me. They are always terribly concerned about mine, and they just know I can't handle any others. Your honesty has made me feel so much better. I didn't think you ever felt frazzled like I do. I have always thought you were perfect. But today I see that you are not so different from me. Maybe I am doing just fine. I don't really need help as much as I just need to know that I am normal. Thanks!" Offering someone our companionship and our honest shared sorrows as well as joys is as important as quickly finishing a physical task for them.

What I wish to affirm is that we do need to charitably share and serve—emotionally and spiritually as well as temporally—but we must fill ourselves at the fountain of living water, at the feet of our Heavenly Father himself, or we have nothing of real strength to give. When we connect with God, then we will connect with others honestly and compassionately. When we pay the price to see God, we become aware of how closely connected we are to each other.

One bright crisp British morning in Solihull, England, as I was sequestered with my scriptures trying to practice exactly what I am preaching, I read this verse in the book of Revelation: "And there appeared a great wonder in heaven; a woman clothed with the sun, and the moon under her feet, and upon her head a crown of twelve stars" (Revelation 12:1).[3]

There must be profound purpose in the Lord's selecting a woman to symbolize something of glory and grandeur in God's power and influence in these last days. As I read that scripture that morning, the sun shining brilliantly upon the written page, suddenly the glory and beauty and blessings of womanhood were illuminated in my heart. In my mind's eye, I saw a woman—a woman like you—clothed with the sun, the moon under her feet, wearing a crown of stars. And the glory around her from all these celestial sources was light. To my limited view, I could see "woman" as a transmitter, a conveyor, a conduit of light and love. I could see that a woman can, if she lives for it and wants it and asks for it and seeks it, be the medium through which gospel light and truth can pass or be conveyed from one person to another.

In this same scriptural description, John, the writer of the book of Revelation, says that the woman fled into the wilderness. God prepared a place for her, a place of safety and strength and protection.[4] In dark and dangerous days, God will provide for us safe places, even wilderness places (I take that to mean sacred places undefiled by worldly civilization) where he protects us against evil and nourishes us with strength. Please allow yourself to take the time to go to that wilderness retreat now, that sanctuary, if you will—the temple, your own home, places of privacy and revelation, places filled with prayer and meditation and scriptural truths. Allow yourselves to turn a few things down and turn a few things off. Seek to position yourselves prayerfully in some solitude and serenity to receive the mind of God. Stop what you are so frantically doing and go into your private wilderness. Shut the door, turn out all earthly lights, set aside all earthly sights. Position yourself calmly, quietly in humble serenity until your prayer flows naturally, lovingly. When you feel God's presence, when you feel he is with you, you will be filled with a wonderful strength that will allow you to do anything in righteousness.

Thus filled and strengthened, we can return to the battle, to some inevitable noise and commotion and, yes, even some drudgery. But we do it more happily, more hopefully, more optimistically because we have communed with God and been filled with his joy, his charity, and his compassion, and we bear something of his light as we return. And because we are filled and strong, we can be a source of light, life, and love for others.

NOTES

1. George Q. Cannon, "Freedom of the Saints," in *Collected Discourses Delivered by President Wilford Woodruff, His Two Counselors, The Twelve Apostles, and Others (1890–91)*, comp. Brian H. Stuy, 5 vols. (Burbank, Calif.: B. H. Publishing, 1988), 2:185.

2. David O. McKay, in Conference Report, April 1946, 113.

3. I know that the book of Revelation is filled with allegory and symbolism and that several interpretations are given to the woman in this passage, including a very important one from the Prophet Joseph Smith. I acknowledge those multiple meanings.

4. It is important to note that the woman is also a symbol for the Church, suggesting that as a group, as well as individually, we will need our places of communion, safety, and strength in the last days.

PRINCIPLES AND PREFERENCES

BRUCE C. HAFEN

The gospel teaches all of us to develop a strong sense of the difference between right and wrong and to pay attention to that difference when making choices. We can learn right from wrong through our blessed access to scriptures, revelation, and prophetic guidance. These sources of truth give us an incalculable advantage over the masses of modern society, who are drifting ever more aimlessly in a sea of moral and intellectual confusion. Moreover, many people today compound the harm of this general aimlessness by insisting that no one should sit in judgment on anyone else's "lifestyle." Being tolerant—leaving other people alone—has become for some not only the highest virtue but the only virtue. These people are forgetting or do not know Elder Neal A. Maxwell's insight that a "society that permits anything will eventually lose everything."[1]

Some of us in the Church, however, have the opposite problem: we aren't tolerant enough of other people. Our very confidence in the correctness of the Church's positions on numerous lifestyle issues leads some of us to become opinionated and judgmental about other people's choices. As we resist the permissiveness in the world around us, we sometimes have

Bruce C. Hafen was sustained as a member of the First Quorum of the Seventy on 6 April 1996. A native of St. George, Utah, he earned a juris doctor degree from the University of Utah. He has served as president of Ricks College, dean of Brigham Young University Law School, and provost at BYU. He and his wife, Marie K. Hafen, are the parents of seven children and the grandparents of ten.

difficulty sensing where our religious principles end and our personal preferences begin. When that happens, we might unintentionally defend our personal interpretations in such narrow, dogmatic ways that we assume anyone who disagrees with us or doesn't do things our way not only is wrong but is rejecting the Lord's will. At that point, we may wrongly assume that our personal perspective is also the Lord's perspective and that our preferences reflect his principles.

The kind of self-righteousness this attitude can produce reminds me of a cartoon I saw on the Brigham Young University campus some years ago. A gaunt, long-haired, and bearded young man in sloppy clothing stood, all scratched and beaten, amid a pile of rocks in a BYU campus street. Talking to a campus police officer who was writing down his statement, the beaten-up young man said, "Officer, all I said was, let him who is without sin cast the first stone."

Sometimes we sit in harsh judgment on those closest to us, such as our spouses, family members, or fellow Church members. Precisely because these are the people who typically share our convictions about lifestyle principles, we may think they need our unsolicited advice when their ideas and preferences differ from ours.

The very intimacy of family bonds can make us be tough on each other when we differ on choices ranging all the way from the teams we cheer for and the cars or clothes we buy to our choices about careers, colleges, and companions. One man I knew admitted he got downright angry with his son when they disagreed about which route along the city streets was the quickest way to drive downtown from their house.

Young married couples may encounter such friction when they discover differences in the lifestyle traditions of their two families, whether in their approach to vocations or vacations. I have recently seen instances in which differences in personal approach between a husband and a wife led to harsh judgments that needlessly damaged a relationship. In one case, the

14

young husband is a fanatic about avoiding fatty foods; his wife is more pragmatic, eating what she feels like eating, subject to her quite mature instincts about moderation. She is healthy and looks fine, but he is so nervous about her becoming over-weight that his constant complaining about her eating habits has rubbed their relationship raw.

In a more serious case, a woman in the midst of a divorce told me how her husband's continual criticism of her choices ultimately destroyed not only their marriage but her funda-mental sense of self-worth. Increasingly over several years, he complained about her cooking, her housecleaning, how she used her time, how she talked, looked, and reasoned. This tor-rent of criticism escalated until, as she told me through her tears, she became convinced that she was utterly inept and dysfunctional, unable to do anything right. Obviously, the reverse is equally possible: a wife may also inflict serious emo-tional abuse on a husband.

I have learned from a variety of Latter-day Saint women that this tendency to judge other people's choices can become emotional and ugly among LDS women. A woman who writes for a Church-owned publication reports that no matter what feature stories her publication runs on LDS women, she receives angry mail from women readers who disapprove of the messages they think are hidden in the stories. Stories about women doing professional work may prompt the complaint that such features undermine the Church's counsel that a wom-an's first priority is her family. Stories about women doing domestic work provoke the response that such features improperly exclude all LDS women from higher education and meaningful careers. According to this woman, the people who are hardest on LDS women are other LDS women.

One experienced LDS woman writer I know believes that this tendency reflects the adversary's attempt to neutralize women, isolating and alienating them from one another. The evil one tempts them to compete with each other rather than connect with each other, because women's interconnectedness is such a force for good that it undermines his work.

LDS men can be equally judgmental. I remember my astonishment as dean of the BYU law school when I learned that some male law students were leaving hate mail in the carrels of women law students, telling them they ought to leave the law school and make room for a man, who, they said, would need the education more than they did.

Family size is another subject about which women or men in the Church occasionally but unfairly judge others, simply because the number of children in a home is so visible. I know of a young LDS couple who sought prayerfully for five years to have a child. They wanted a whole houseful of children but were unable to conceive. Then one day an LDS neighbor left in their mailbox a copy of a Church leader's talk encouraging couples to begin having children early in their marriage. This thoughtless act only compounded the disappointment and frustration the young husband and wife had long been feeling.

I've been grateful for women who have with skill, love, and gentle humor tried to awaken their sisters to the perils of forcing all LDS women into the same mold of personality and preference. For example, a few years ago Sister Patricia Holland expressed her concern that women are "getting away from that sense of community and sisterhood that has sustained us." She said, "There seems to be an increase in our competitiveness and a decrease in our generosity with one another." She spoke of women who "can their fruit and vegetables" and then "look down their noses at those who buy their peaches, or who don't like zucchini in any of the thirty-five ways there are to disguise it, or who have simply made a conscious choice to use their time and energy in some other purposeful way."

Sister Holland then confessed her own lack of interest in sewing: "Imagine my burden over the last twenty-five or thirty years, faking it in Relief Society sessions and trying to smile when six little girls walk into Church all pinafored and laced and ribboned and petticoated—identical, hand sewn—all trooping ahead of their mother, who has on the same immaculate outfit. Competitive? I wanted to pull their pleats out. . . . I have grown up a little since those days in at least two ways—I now genuinely admire a mother who can do that for her children, and I have ceased feeling guilty that sewing is not particularly rewarding to me. We simply cannot call ourselves Christian and continue to judge one another—or ourselves—so harshly. No Mason jar of Bing cherries is worth a confrontation that robs us of our compassion and our sisterhood."[2]

That does not mean, of course, that there is no place for needed advice shared in the right spirit between people who depend on each other. Good marriages, for example, thrive on a couple's ability to share gentle and loving correction with each other when it is needed. I can think of a few husbands—and wives—who are innately insensitive to the way they affect other people. These people need help to see how they come across to others, what they're forgetting or missing. Each of us needs corrective vision for our blind spots, especially when the correction is given with affection and humor. Single men and women can sometimes find this blessing in a close friend or family member.

Our son Jon's wife, Joy, has learned this skill of giving sweet counsel. On a bitterly cold day last winter, she hauled pail after pail of hot water from the house to the driveway, where she melted a pile of ice and snow to free her husband's car from a frozen curb. When she called him at work to report that he could now drive his car, he said, "Thanks, Joy—I owe you one." She replied with her gentle laugh, "Jon, you know why we're married for eternity, don't you?" He asked, "Why are we?" Said she, "Because that's how long it will take for you to pay me back all the ones you owe me."

Against the background of these examples, I'd like to offer four ideas on the general problem of our trying to judge how other people apply the gospel to their lives. Some of these ideas also apply to the related issue of judging ourselves. First, some choices are matters of *principle,* but others are matters of *preference;* and when dealing with the legitimate realm of personal preference, we should not expect everyone to like the same things we do. I'm glad we don't all have the same favorite color! In an essay entitled "Decisions of Principle and of Preference," Elder Richard L. Evans once wrote: "As to decisions of principle, we shouldn't really waste much time on clear-cut questions of right and wrong," such as stealing, lying, or adultery. Our decisions about such things should be "more or less automatic." He continued, "And now as to decisions of preference—as to what suit we should select, or what course we should study, what job we should take: For such decisions we have to consider ourselves, our qualifications, our personal preferences, and those of others."[3]

Elder Boyd K. Packer once talked about the interaction between our preferences and the Lord's direction when he discussed with BYU students the topic of spiritual self-reliance. In one example, he described the process of building a house. He said suppose you pray endlessly whether to build "early American style, a ranch style, Modern style architecture, or perhaps Mediterranean style. Has it ever occurred to you that perhaps the Lord just plain doesn't care? . . . Build what [you] want to build. . . . In many things we can do just what we want." What the Lord does care about is that when you "build that house, then be honest and pay for the material that goes into it and do a decent job of building it. . . . [Then] live righteously in it." Elder Packer added: "On occasions I've had to counsel people that the Lord would probably quite willingly approve the thing they intend to do even when they want to. It's strange when they come and almost feel guilty about doing something because they want to, even when it's righteous."[4]

Elder Bruce R. McConkie once gave BYU students similar advice about choosing a marriage partner. In choosing his own wife, he said, "[I] went out and found the girl I wanted. . . . All

I did was pray to the Lord and ask for some guidance and direction in connection with the decision that I'd reached. A more perfect thing to have done would have been to counsel with him relative to the decision and get a spiritual confirmation that the conclusion, which I by my agency and faculties had arrived at, was the right one."[5] The application of principle in choosing houses or marriage partners is fundamental, but there is considerable room for differences in taste and style.

These insights about agency and spiritual self-reliance call to mind the uplifting promise found in many patriarchal blessings that if we are faithful, the Lord will grant us our righteous desires. *We do not, nor need we, all desire the same things.* Doctrine and Covenants 7 describes the differing but righteous desires of Peter and John at the close of the Lord's earthly ministry. John desired to remain on the earth that he might live to bring souls unto Christ. Peter preferred to be in heaven with the risen Lord, but he seemed to feel guilty that perhaps he wasn't as brave as John. Apparently sensing that, the Savior said to Peter: "If I will that [John] tarry till I come, what is that to thee? For he desired of me that he might bring souls unto me, but thou desirest that thou mightest speedily come unto me in my kingdom. I say unto thee, Peter, this was a good desire. . . . Ye shall both have according to your desires, for ye both joy in that which ye have desired" (D&C 7:4–5, 8).

Second, even when we apply true principles to our lives, variables of personality, circumstances, and needs can lead different people to different outcomes. As a missionary, I had three different mission presidents, with three widely varying personalities and approaches to Church leadership. I wondered which was the correct approach. Then I discovered the wonderful news that the Lord has more than one cookie cutter. I recently sought counsel about my new Church assignment from one of the senior Brethren. I was feeling, and still feel, enormous inadequacy in contemplating responsibilities that often seem overwhelmingly out of reach for me. Listening to

19

my feelings, this wise leader said, "Bruce, the Lord didn't call you to this position so that you'd go try to be like Elder So-and-so. He called you to be you—your best self. Trust your own best instincts." I once heard this same leader quote these verses: "Ye have an unction from the Holy One, and ye know all things. . . . But the anointing which ye have received of him abideth in you, and ye need not that any man teach you: but as the same anointing teacheth you of all things . . . ye shall abide in him" (1 John 2:20, 27). I understood him to mean that all of us who are called to positions of responsibility in the Church, men and women, are entitled to personal revelation to fit the unique needs we encounter. Such inspiration comes only after we follow faithfully every true principle. But when it comes, inspiration can be very personal, as the Lord "teaches" us in a firsthand way.

Doctrine and Covenants 46 makes clear that the Lord gives every person a spiritual gift. We all have different gifts, interests, and backgrounds. The Lord is likely to give us what we uniquely need. Other people can't and won't know our needs. We ourselves often won't know what challenges and trials would stretch us in the most needful way. Paul's analogy between the Church and the body is an eloquent reminder that some of us function best as eyes and others as hands or feet or ears (see 1 Corinthians 12).

For writer Louise Plummer, the difference is between ants—who are task oriented and well-organized—and grasshoppers—who are spontaneous, creative, and sometimes chaotic. As a grasshopper, she wondered if there was room for her in a church of ants. Her fear was that the ants would not accept her unless she was just like them. Then she realized—it isn't that ants work *harder* than grasshoppers; it's just that grasshoppers work *differently* from ants.[6]

I once saw how much Church members can differ when I interviewed two couples for a temple marriage one evening in a BYU stake. Following my interview with the first prospective bride, a quiet and thoughtful person, I asked if she had any questions about going to the temple or becoming married. She expressed honest concerns about the whole subject of marital intimacy, and I felt prompted to encourage her warmly about the naturalness, the goodness, and the sacredness of that dimension of marriage. When the second couple sat down in my office, they remained so literally wrapped up in each other that I felt like an intruder even to say hello. I soon found myself giving them very different premarital advice from what I'd given the first young woman.

Third, even when we eliminate differences of preference, personality, and circumstance so that we're talking only about principles, all situations will not yield the same results because of the natural and often unavoidable paradox of competing true principles. When Joseph Smith was asked in Nauvoo how he could govern so many people and preserve such perfect order, he replied, "I teach them correct principles, and they govern themselves."[7] His response clearly implies that people must exercise some judgment in governing themselves by the application of correct principles—in part because true principles are often in tension with one another. Think of married LDS students trying to finish school in four years while avoiding debt, having their children early, and having the mother stay home if children have already come. Talk about competing principles! But is this so unusual? The gospel is full of paradoxes that arise from tension between true principles.

For example, the Lord said he cannot look upon sin with the least degree of allowance. Yet elsewhere he said to the adulteress, "Where are those thine accusers? . . . Neither do I condemn thee: go, and sin no more" (John 8:10–11). Justice and mercy are both correct principles.

The Savior once said, "Do not your alms [to the poor] before men to be seen of them" (3 Nephi 13:1). But he also said, "Let your light so shine before men, that they may see your good works" (Matthew 5:16). Further, on one occasion he said, "In me ye might have peace" (John 16:33). And the angels who announced his birth sang, Peace on earth (see Luke 2:14). Yet elsewhere he said, "Think not that I am come to send peace on earth: I came not to send peace, but a sword" (Matthew 10:34).

Each of these statements expresses a true principle. But together, the statements can seem inconsistent until we assume the responsibility of governing ourselves by prayerful, diligent application of the principles to a given situation. Think of priesthood leaders who hear confessions of wrongdoing. Some bishops say they always seek justice; others may think mercy the more important principle. The fact is that every truly faithful bishop is committed to both justice and mercy. And the Brethren don't tell local leaders how to apply those principles to specific situations precisely because the judgment must be made by a judge in Israel who sees all the circumstances, knows the people, feels their hearts, discerns the depth of their repentance, and seeks pure revelation in accordance with the higher principle of the Atonement, which reconciles mercy and justice as particular needs require.

President Harold B. Lee loved to quote the Lord's words: "Wherefore, now let every man learn his duty, and to act in the office in which he is appointed, in all diligence" (D&C 107:99). And he would always put the emphasis on "let," as he encouraged Church leaders to "let" or *allow* people to learn their duty as they act in the particular office of their appointment. How equally essential it is for us to "let" people govern themselves and be themselves in circumstances in which they apply competing principles and consider appropriate matters of preference.

Fourth, consider how we judge ourselves. The more we learn to distinguish principles from preferences and the more we appreciate the delicate process of applying competing principles to life circumstances, the more reluctant we will be to judge another person's righteousness. These perspectives also inform the process of self-judgment, because we often judge others as part of pulling ourselves up, or putting others down, by comparing ourselves with other people. So all of the arguments against judging others also apply to judging ourselves by making comparisons with others. At the same time, freedom from self-judgment and comparisons allows us to study out in our minds our own righteous desires and preferences; then we are fully entitled to the inspiration of heaven to reconcile competing principles as we seek to govern ourselves.

We must resist the natural urge to take too seriously both the positive and the negative judgments others make about us. When those who love us choose not to condemn us, even though we're doing something wrong, we must be careful not to infer from this silence that our behavior is acceptable. Sometimes our loved ones, the Church, and even the Lord *expect* more than they *require* of us, which means they may tolerate conduct they would never encourage. This approach leaves upon our shoulders the heavy burden of agency—and the Lord *expects* us to self-correct. If we make corrections only when we're required to, or coerced, we are slothful servants who refuse to grow spiritually (see D&C 58:26).

In a more general sense, someone said we wouldn't worry so much about what others think of us if we realized how seldom they do think of us. Popular opinion is too fickle and fleeting to be a reliable guide for measuring our self-worth or the soundness of our self-judgments—again, whether positive or negative. Others cannot know enough about our circumstances and our hearts to judge us fairly. Other people also lack the perspective on our nature and character that only the Lord has. The Holy One of Israel is our judge, and for better or worse, we cannot deceive him. But most significantly of all, the Savior's grace made possible by his atonement compensates for all our failings, as Nephi put it so clearly, "after all we can do" (2 Nephi 25:23). When we have in good faith done all within our power to do, there is a success that compensates for all our failures—the infinite and eternal success of Christ's holy

23

atonement. Our self-judgments must not underestimate that part of our self-worth.

When we sit in judgment on other people, even if their lives aren't fully in order, we are violating the Lord's commandment against judging others. "Judge not, that ye be not judged," the Savior taught (Matthew 7:1). The point here is not that those we might judge aren't doing anything wrong, nor is it that wrong-doers won't be judged. Rather, the question is, Who has the right to judge, and why do we lack the capacity to judge? Most historical uses of the verb "to judge" in the English language link judging with condemning, sentencing, pronouncing judgment upon, or otherwise acting with special judicial authority. These terms imply that a true judge must be authorized to affect another person's life with a costly sentence of judgment. As Eliza R. Snow wrote in "Truth Reflects upon Our Senses,"

> Jesus said, "Be meek and lowly,"
> For 'tis high to be a judge.[8]

That is why those whom the Lord appoints as judges, such as bishops, have such a high and holy calling.

In addition, our human limitations render our judgments inherently unfair. Eliza R. Snow echoed this point, based on the Savior's teachings against judging:

> Once I said unto another,
> "In thine eye there is a mote;
> If thou art a friend, a brother,
> Hold, and let me pull it out."
> But I could not see it fairly,
> For my sight was very dim.
> When I came to search more clearly,
> In mine eye there was a beam.
>
> . . . .
>
> Others I have oft reproved,
> For an object like a mote,
> Now I wish [my] beam removed,
> Oh, that tears would wash it out![9]

An old Indian proverb states, Don't judge another until you have walked a mile in his moccasins. As the Lord has said, "I, the Lord, will forgive whom I will forgive, but of you it is required to forgive all men" (D&C 64:10). Thus in all of our relationships with other people, we must rise above the temptation to compete, to criticize, and to condemn.

The Lord himself is the ultimate judge of our transgressions, and he personally will meet us at the gate to his kingdom. Said the prophet Jacob, "The keeper of the gate is the Holy One of Israel; and he employeth no servant there; and there is none other way save it be by the gate; for he cannot be deceived, for the Lord God is his name" (2 Nephi 9:41). How sublimely reassuring—and for some, how terrifying—to know that we will finally be judged by the impartial fairness of him who cannot be deceived, who expects more than he requires, and who gives us more than we could ever earn without him.

NOTES

1. Neal A. Maxwell, "Deny Yourselves of All Ungodliness," *Ensign*, May 1995, 67.

2. Patricia Terry Holland, "Many Things . . . One Thing," in *A Heritage of Faith: Talks Selected from the BYU Women's Conferences*, ed. Mary E. Stovall and Carol Cornwall Madsen (Salt Lake City: Deseret Book, 1988), 15–16.

3. Richard L. Evans, "Decisions of Principle and of Preference," *Improvement Era*, December 1956, 969.

4. Boyd K. Packer, "Self-Reliance," *Ensign*, August 1975, 89.

5. Bruce R. McConkie, "Agency or Inspiration?" *New Era*, January 1975, 40.

6. Louise Plummer, "Thoughts of a Grasshopper," in *Heritage of Faith*, 185–91; or Louise Plummer, *Thoughts of a Grasshopper* (Salt Lake City: Deseret Book, 1992), 7–15.

7. Joseph Smith, *Millennial Star* 13 (15 November 1851): 339.

8. "Truth Reflects upon Our Senses," *Hymns of The Church of Jesus Christ of Latter-day Saints* (Salt Lake City: The Church of Jesus Christ of Latter-day Saints, 1985), no. 273.

9. Ibid.

FITLY FRAMED AND BUILDED TOGETHER

CAMILLE FRONK

In his epistle to the Ephesians, Paul described the collective membership of the Church of Jesus Christ as a temple built on a sure foundation: "the foundation of the apostles and prophets, Jesus Christ himself being the chief corner stone; in whom all the building fitly framed together groweth unto an holy temple in the Lord: in whom ye also are builded together for an habitation of God through the Spirit" (Ephesians 2:20–22).

Individual Church members in the analogy make up the stones which are "builded together" to form the walls of this "holy temple" of believers. The stones reflect unity of purpose, although individual expression, creativity, and varied application of gospel principles add dimension and character to the whole. For illustration, consider the stones of the Salt Lake Temple. They were cut from huge boulders of granite in Little Cottonwood Canyon some twenty miles from the temple site. The temple architect sent specific instructions to the quarry superintendent describing the various sizes and shapes of stones required for the temple walls.[1] Each stone's unique characteristics and strengths—in both the Salt Lake Temple and the

Camille Fronk is an assistant professor of ancient scripture at Brigham Young University and a Relief Society teacher in her ward. She has served as a member of the Young Women General Board, as dean of students at LDS Business College, and as a seminary and institute instructor.

metaphorical temple composed of a Zion people—were "fitly joined together" with other unique stones "and compacted by that which every joint supplieth" (Ephesians 4:16) to eventually contribute to the enduring beauty of the whole.

Critics would try to convince us that any population built on a single foundation is bound to promote cookie-cutter dimensions among its individual members. They would say that the stones or bricks that make up the walls of this "temple" must surely come from the same mold and allow for little or no individuality or agency.

But recall the familiar account of Mary and Martha when Jesus came to visit at Martha's house (Luke 10:38–42). While Martha is occupied in serving her guest, perhaps preparing a meal, Mary is at Jesus' feet, feasting on his word. The account depicts a lovely scene, doesn't it? But who is uncomfortable with this situation. Who feels something is not right? Is it Jesus? Certainly Jesus cautions Martha, but he does so only after Martha first objects to the situation? Catherine Corman Parry, a professor of English at Brigham Young University, examines the Savior's words from a new perspective. She says: "Those of us with more of Martha than of Mary in us have long felt that this rebuke is unjust. While we do not doubt the overriding importance of listening to the Lord, does the listening have to be done during dinner preparations? Would it have hurt Mary to have joined us in serving, then we all could have sat down to hear the Lord together? And furthermore, what about the value of our work in the world? If it weren't for us Marthas cleaning whatever we see and fussing over meals, there would be a lot of dirty, hungry people in this world. . . . Why, oh why couldn't the Lord have said, 'You're absolutely right, Martha. What are we thinking of to let you do all this work alone? We'll all help, and by the way, that centerpiece looks lovely'?

"What he did say is difficult to bear, but perhaps somewhat less difficult if we examine its context. . . . The Lord acknowledges Martha's care: 'Martha, Martha, thou art careful and troubled about many things' (v. 41). Then he delivers the gentle but clear rebuke. But the rebuke would not have come had Martha not prompted it. The Lord did not go into the kitchen and tell Martha to stop cooking and come listen. Apparently he was content to let her serve him however she cared to, until she judged another person's service: 'Lord, dost thou not care that my sister hath left me to serve alone? bid her therefore that she help me' (v. 40). Martha's self-importance, expressed through her judgment of her sister, occasioned the Lord's rebuke, not her busyness with the meal."[2]

Sister Parry's suggestion increases in merit as we note that, first, the Savior's final recorded words on the occasion do not compare the acts of service of the two sisters; rather, he points out that what Mary is doing is service and should not be discounted. His words are not, "Mary hath chosen the better part" or even "Mary hath chosen the good part." Rather, the scripture reads, "Mary hath chosen that good part, which shall not be taken away from her" (Luke 10:42). There is no measure of comparison in the Lord's statement, only validation of Mary's service.

Second, consider these two sisters on a later occasion, again in association with the Savior. This time, they are not at Martha's house but at the home of Simon the leper. Notice what Mary and Martha are doing. "Then Jesus . . . came to Bethany, where Lazarus was . . . whom he raised from the dead. There they made him a supper; and Martha served . . . Then . . . Mary . . . anointed the feet of Jesus, and wiped his feet with her hair: and the house was filled with the odour of the ointment" (John 12:1–3). Even when the gathering is not at her house, Martha is still serving the food, and Mary is at the feet of Jesus. Their roles are exactly the same as before. The difference this time is that no one seems to be upset about the manner in which the other has selected to serve the Lord. We would do well to learn what Martha apparently discovered— that each of us offers service, to each other and to the Lord, in a variety of ways, using our diverse talents and gifts. The Lord in turn accepts our devotions in the spirit in which they are offered.

In reality, it is not the Lord but Satan who entices us to be carbon copies of those around us. Elder Dallin H. Oaks suggested that when Jesus warned Peter, "Satan hath desired to have you, that he may sift you as wheat" (Luke 22:31), he was telling Peter that the adversary's goal was to make Peter common. Satan wants to make us just like everyone else in the world in much the same way that particles of wheat are so uniform that they can be sifted and exchanged for one another without distinction.[3]

If Satan cannot make us common, he will try to divide us, to use our uniqueness against us. Consider this tactic employed among the Corinthian Saints. These early Christians appear to have been ranking each other according to each one's gift of the Spirit. In his first epistle to them, Paul taught the futility of such comparisons because all the gifts come from the same Spirit (1 Corinthians 12:4). None of us serves in the same Church calling and, as Paul points out, no Church calling is more important than any other because all rely on the same Spirit for fulfillment. Certainly the Lord doesn't deem one who serves as Beehive advisor to be less worthy than the Young Women president. That is ridiculous! And yet, often without intention, we assume the importance of an individual to be directly related to her current Church calling.

Similarly, different individuals will appropriately magnify the same Church calling in diverse ways. Hundreds of members of the Church are called to teach the fourteen-year-olds in Sunday School, and hundreds of others conduct singing practice in Relief Society; yet no two perform either of these services exactly alike, and all may have the Spirit to sustain their efforts. We are given guidelines, but individually we have the privilege of receiving inspiration to use our God-given gifts and talents to bless the lives of those we are called to serve. Simply

29

because someone else leads the music in sacrament meeting differently from the way we would lead it does not mean the Spirit is offended or that the message of the hymns is lost.

Sister Chieko Okazaki has reminded us that our differences of culture, race, marital status, or place of employment should *strengthen* our unity rather than encourage us to find fault with each other. "The ideal family for raising children, we believe, is a stable, loving, two-parent family where young children receive full-time parenting. But not all situations are ideal. Not all women are mothers, and not all mothers have children at home. Furthermore, not all mothers can make the choice to be home with their children all of the time. . . . Let us trust the Lord, trust ourselves, and trust each other that we are trying to do the best we can. We need all the strength we can find for our daily trials. Let us not add our disapproval to a sister's burdens. And as we struggle with our own burdens, let us not diminish our strength by accepting the perhaps thoughtless judgments of others."[4] As we learn to appreciate the challenges that others face, it is suddenly easier to see life from their perspective and refrain from judging their manner of coping. In most cases, we gain increased respect for their faith and endurance.

Think of the temple again. Does your eye focus on its sturdy foundation? the angle of its walls? the diverse colors and shapes of each stone? Or are you more likely to stand back and exclaim over the beautiful appearance of the temple as a whole? We can see that the whole becomes more important than any of its parts. And the parts become stronger and more dynamic as part of the whole than they are when seen in isolation.

We have covenanted to remain grounded and rooted on a firm foundation whose cornerstone is Christ's perfect atonement. What a reason to rejoice, to be of good cheer! Truly the Redeemer of Israel has overcome the world. He is our cornerstone. He restored his everlasting gospel through the Prophet Joseph Smith. He speaks to a prophet today, namely our beloved President Gordon B. Hinckley. What a sacred foundation we share. Let us therefore press on, reaching out to our brothers and sisters throughout the world, secure in our testimony of Christ and the restored gospel. I bear witness that as we remain true to covenants made with him who is our Father, ever anchored on that sure foundation, we truly have no need to fear. This is his Church, we are his children, and his promises will not fail.

NOTES

This selection has been excerpted from "Anchored in Sacred Ground: Building Unity amid Diversity," the closing address of the BYU–Relief Society Women's Conference, 3 May 1996.

1. Each stone in each course, or layer, was listed on an order sheet by a number and size specification and often included scale drawings illustrating the patterns for the more difficult cuts. When the stones were sent down the mountain to the temple site, the architect noted the number engraved in each stone and knew immediately where that stone would fit in the overall temple construction (Wallace Alan Raynor, *The Everlasting Spires: A Story of the Salt Lake Temple* [Salt Lake City: Deseret Book, 1965], 65; Paul Smith Collection, University of Utah Institute of Religion, slides).

2. Catherine Corman Parry, "'Simon, I Have Somewhat to Say unto Thee': Judgment and Condemnation in the Parables of Jesus," in *Brigham Young University 1990–91 Devotional and Fireside Speeches* (Provo: Brigham Young University, 1991), 116.

3. Dallin H. Oaks, BYU 9th and 17th Stake Conference, Provo, Utah, 24 March 1996; notes in possession of author; used by permission.

4. Chieko Okazaki, "Rowing Your Boat," *Ensign,* November 1994, 92–93.

THE WIDOW'S MITE FROM RUSSIA

NINA BAZARSKAYA

I am a humble Russian woman who feels blessed and privileged to communicate with you on behalf of my Russian sisters. I come from Voronezh, a city of about a million people in central Russia. When in January 1993 the first three missionaries came to open my city for missionary work, only three Latter-day Saints met them at the railway station. They were the only three members in the city. Now, three years later, there are about one hundred families. I was baptized in December 1992, and two months later those first missionaries who came to Voronezh baptized my son. A year after that, my son baptized his father, my husband. It was very hard for my husband to join the Church. His way was from being a committed atheist to becoming the branch president. I just thank the Lord for the blessings of a baptized family.

Every Russian sister has one great priority: missionary work in our families. Russia is deeply troubled right now. We are in the bottom of deep economic depression. Our political situation is also very unstable. A terrible war continues in Chechnya, but even worse, we have lost our moral bearings. The old Communist ideology has passed away, but we don't have a new one to replace it. People are searching for moral integrity.

Nina Bazarskaya serves as Relief Society president of the Voronezh branch of the Russia Moscow Mission. She was baptized in Moscow by a visiting Brigham Young University student on 15 December 1992, a month before Voronezh was officially opened to missionary work.

Russian women are the first who come to the gospel. Shortly after they find this narrow road that leads to the tree of wisdom and to the tree of life, their primary concern becomes bringing their family to the Church. I can't tell you how happy we are when we see our husbands and our children sitting side by side with us in Church meetings.

The traditions of sisterhood are very young in my city. We sense the tremendous opportunity available to us through sisterhood and are making fledgling efforts guided by the words of Jesus Christ: "A new commandment I give unto you, That ye love one another; as I have loved you, that ye also love one another. By this shall all men know that ye are my disciples, if ye have love one to another" (John 13:34–35). Following this commandment, we use the very modest financial resources of our Relief Society to support families who are in need, to make Christmas gifts for our children, to visit our orphanage, to cook Easter food for the soldiers who are wounded in Chechnya and for those in the local hospitals, and to support the many missions of our younger members. These are, of course, very modest projects.

I asked the sisters of my Relief Society to think of at least one episode in their lives when this sisterhood helped them. Their answers differed. One sister remembered how happy she was to find a food package on the doorstep of her house when her family didn't have money. Another remembered medication brought to her to relieve her fever. The third remembered a funny birthday gift that made her smile. One story, however, touched me by its simplicity. It happened because many sisters remembered that moral support is perhaps the best help we can offer each other.

Valentina is a very nice, pretty, twenty-nine-year-old woman in our branch. She is also terribly sick. While she was in the hospital, her husband divorced her. Both her disease and her divorce broke her down completely, because the dream of her life was to have a baby. She loved her husband very much,

33

and his betrayal nearly killed her. When she was released from the hospital, her doctors sent her to a distant resort to recuperate. There she felt lonely and homesick. Surrounded only by sick women, whose constant talk was only about her disease and its terrible consequences for her health, she cried day and night, and very soon the people in the resort started to call her not "Valentina" but "the woman who is always crying." This very difficult period in her life tried both her patience and her faith.

One day she wrote to me, sharing her doubts and her disappointments. I knew she needed help. I contacted sisters who cared about her in the Relief Society, and we responded immediately. She received our letters regularly for the remainder of the four months she stayed in the resort. We shared with her our love, our hope in her recovery. We tried to strengthen her. We wrote to her our city news, our branch news, and tried to support her in every possible way. One day she realized that these four months were not a trial for her but rather a great blessing given to her so she could concentrate, think about her life, read the scriptures, and be a missionary to the other women who hadn't heard anything about the gospel. The day she realized this, her life changed completely. When she returned home, she was a totally different person with a very strong testimony.

Missionaries who come to Voronezh often say that we have a special branch. Many of our members are young—girls and boys. That's not a great surprise because the gospel was first brought to us by young people, young ambassadors, young teachers from Brigham Young University who came to Voronezh to teach English in our nurseries. We see how the seeds planted by these young people grow. Now we have our own missionaries, five from just our branch. Two of them have already returned, and three are still teaching in different cities of our country. A young and new generation of young people is growing up before our eyes—one reared on the principles of the Word of Wisdom, of eternal love, of faith, and of following the commandments of our Heavenly Father. Though our branch is not very large by American standards, we feel ourselves a community, a family in which everybody loves each other and tries to support each other. And we also feel ourselves under the protection of our Heavenly Father. We are not lost in this world; by a million ties, we are connected with the sisters throughout the world. We receive letters from America, from the United Kingdom, from Switzerland, and from Lithuania, where our missionaries serve right now.

Often mothers of the missionaries who serve in Voronezh write to us, even after their children return home, and we become good friends for the rest of our lives. These women send us materials necessary for our Relief Society activities, for our homemaking activities. Sister Jeppsen, the mother of one of our first and one of our most respected and most beloved branch presidents, came to Voronezh and got acquainted with Valentina, our sick sister. Back in America, Sister Jeppsen started a charity project, seeking donations to provide her with special treatment in a Utah hospital. We know that such things do not happen very quickly or easily, but we pray and hope that one day our sister will come to America, receive this special treatment, recover, and the dream of her life—having a baby—will still come true.

"And Jesus sat over against the treasury, and beheld how people cast money into the treasury: and many that were rich cast in much. And there came a certain poor widow, and she threw in two mites, which make a farthing. And he called unto him his disciples, and saith unto them, Verily I say unto you, That this poor widow hath cast more in, than all they which have cast into the treasury: for all they did cast in of their abundance; but she of her want did cast in all that she had, even all her living" (Mark 12:41–44). As I read this scripture, I suddenly thought about Russian women, Russian sisters. Our input into the treasury of international sisterhood is very humble, very small, but it's all we can cast in. What we give is our respect to your historical heritage, our appreciation for all your achievements, for your wonderful example for us. It's our love for you and our faith in our Heavenly Father, in the truthfulness of our Church and the Book of Mormon. It's our faith that Jesus Christ is alive and that he brought the gospel into our country to make us happy and to make our families happy. As I think about each Latter-day Saint woman united in sisterhood, worldwide, I realize that yes, we are a great strength. The international sisterhood is a great strength. We can make miracles if we unite and share love with one another.

FROM CRITICISM TO COOPERATION TO CHARITY

MARIE K. HAFEN

A well-informed Latter-day Saint woman asked me, "I guess you know who's the hardest on Mormon women, don't you?"

I shook my head.

"It's other Mormon women. They often judge each other, and sometimes they're not very nice about it."

Surprised by that response, I began thinking of my own experience. Yes, I thought, but we also sing gratefully "Each Life That Touches Ours for Good," which includes the lines:

> What greater goodness can we know
> Than Christlike friends, whose gentle ways
> Strengthen our faith, enrich our days.[1]

If we believe the words of this song, why do some of us gossip judgmentally about each other? What drives us to pick at and on each other? Isn't it ironic that sometimes the relationships that could most enliven us are the very ones we undercut with negative criticism?

Marie Kartchner Hafen has served on the Young Women General Board and on the board of the Deseret News. She holds a master's degree in English from Brigham Young University and has taught courses at Ricks and at BYU in composition and Shakespeare. She and her husband, Bruce C. Hafen, a member of the First Quorum of the Seventy, are the parents of seven children and the grandparents of ten.

Further, we don't fully satisfy Christ's injunction to "judge not" (Luke 6:37) by simply *not* judging. Refraining from harsh judgment is a step in the right direction, but being neutral and tolerant is not enough.

In a recent dinner-table conversation, for example, a young woman's parents were trying to teach her to use her judgment skills to decide which of the diverse young men who showed interest in her she should get to know better. When asked what she saw as distinctions between young men who chose to serve missions and those who chose not to, the young woman indignantly squared her shoulders. "I don't judge people! I don't compare guys. That's not Christian. I should go out with anyone who asks me." For her, the idea of judging carried only negative connotations; there was no difference between discerning judgment and harsh judgment. In her mind, the choice was either to be overly critical and hurtful or to accept everything and everybody regardless of any personal risk involved.

Rightful judgment is necessary. Mormon cautioned, however, "And now, . . . seeing that ye know the light by which ye *may* judge, which light is the light of Christ, see that ye do not judge wrongfully" (Moroni 7:18; emphasis added). One way to judge "rightfully" I will call "cooperation." Cooperation in this sense is using rightful judgment to work with another person for everyone's benefit—for hers, for mine, for both—asking for heaven's help along the way.

How can we move from judging wrongfully, to not judging at all, and then to judging with enough discernment to cooperate with others? What about a major leap beyond that—to becoming not only cooperative, but even charitable toward others?

Three short examples will show this progression from criticism (wrongful judgment), to cooperation (rightful judgment), to charity (Christ's pure love).

First, consider a young wife who consciously decides not to criticize but to cooperate in her marriage. Picture her leaving

Provo to drive thirteen hundred miles to her new home in Chicago. In the back of the family station wagon, along with the usual luggage, is a huge box filled with her husband's aquarium equipment. The box is so large that it pushes her seat as far forward as it will go. Her knees are crunched up under the steering column, her shoulders hunched over the steering wheel, and her back scrunched through the seat against the sharp corner of the aquarium box. She has no real interest in aquariums or saltwater fish herself but is willing to cart the huge apparatus all the way across the country. Why? For her it's simple: "Because it means so much to him." She knows that bringing the aquarium along will make him happy, so she never says anything about the weight, the smell, or the discomfort. Is she just being naive? Shouldn't she stand up to him and point out the negative aspects of hauling the fish tank, perhaps putting her foot down and flat-out refusing? Of course, she shouldn't just submit to his every whim; but when love and a desire to cooperate motivate action, then both partners benefit.

The second example is a husband whose cooperation in a marriage helped his wife to love and respect herself in new ways. Recently a BYU student was killed in an accident. In her talk at the funeral, the young widow, Tiffany, told how her husband had radically changed the way she lived by changing the way she looked at herself. For her whole life before her marriage, Tiffany had judged herself harshly.

"When Tyler and I got married," she said, "I didn't have a very high opinion of myself. But Tyler had confidence in me. He believed in me. We were married only three years, but in that short time I began to believe in myself. I began to know that I could do things and do them well. Now, he's gone; but the confidence that he gave me will always be with me. Nobody can take that away from me."

Her relationship with Tyler had lightened her countenance and demeanor. Where before she was timid and shy, she now stood erect, confident, and looked people in the eye. Through giving specific, deserved appreciation, he helped her to erase her wrongful judgments of herself and encouraged her to catch glimpses of the woman she could be. Tyler saw her with a cooperative vision. Because he loved her and actively supported her, she began to see how she could love herself. More than that, she began to understand how much God loved her. Tyler's encouragement and her trust in God caused Tiffany to become "lighter" until she could say, "Nobody can take that away from me."[2]

Third, I know a couple whose marriage completely changed when one partner ceased a long-standing pattern of wrongful judgment and allowed God more deeply and more intensely into her life. This woman longed for love in her marriage, yet she found herself judging her husband, and being judged by him, in ways that chilled their marriage. Rather than feeling appreciated, she felt both judged and emotionally neglected by the man she had married.

In her anger and frustration, she decided to "pour it all out" in a letter for her husband to read—all her intense longing for love, all of her emotional deprivation. She said, "The longer I wrote, the more I began to have a feeling come over me that what I was writing was false. The feeling continued growing until I could no longer squelch it, and I knew intuitively that the feeling was coming from God, that He was telling me that what I was writing was false. 'How could it be false?' I asked angrily. . . . But the feeling became so powerful and overwhelming that I could no longer deny it or fight against it. So I tore up the pages I had written, threw myself down on my knees and began to pray, saying, 'If it is false, show me how it could be false.' And then a voice spoke to my mind and said, 'If you had come unto Me, it all would have been different.'

"I was astounded. I went to church; I read the scriptures often; I prayed pretty regularly; I tried to obey the commandments. 'What do you mean, "Come unto You?"' I wondered. And then into my mind flashed pictures of me wanting to do things my own way, of holding grudges, of not forgiving, of not loving as God had loved us. I had wanted my husband to 'pay' for my emotional suffering. I had not let go of the past and had not loved God with all my heart. I loved my own willful self more.

"I was aghast. I suddenly realized that I was responsible for my own suffering, for if I had really come unto Him, as I outwardly thought I had done, it all would have been different. . . . I . . . did not mention to my husband anything of what had transpired. But I gave up blaming. . . . And I tried to come unto God with full purpose of heart. I prayed more earnestly, and listened to His Spirit. I read my scriptures and tried to come to know Him better.

"Two months passed, and one morning my husband awoke and turned to me in bed and said, 'You know, we find fault too much with each other. I'm never going to find fault with my wife again.' I was flabbergasted, for he had never admitted he had done anything wrong in our relationship. He did stop finding fault, and he began to compliment me and to show sweet kindness. It was as if an icy glass wall between us had melted away. Almost overnight our relationship became warm and sweet. Three years have passed, and still it continues warmer and happier. We care deeply about one another and share ideas and thoughts and feelings, something we had not done for the first sixteen years of marriage."[3]

After they stopped judging each other wrongfully, stopped "finding fault," this couple began to "share ideas and thoughts and feelings." In other words, they began to cooperate—to think and feel together. This woman had needed to connect her heart in her marriage to her heart in the Lord. Her own sense of stifled spiritual growth dissipated as she opened her heart to the Lord and then to her husband. When she formed bonds that went from the Lord through herself and then to her husband, both hearts were melted. The very moment she came to Christ "with full purpose of heart" was the same transforming moment that brought her closer to her husband (Mosiah 7:33). Because of her own strengthened relationship with the Savior, she began to reflect the spiritual gift of charity in her relationship with her husband. Christ's love flowed through her to her companion.

If in the midst of our own often-difficult, sometimes wrenching, maturing process, we make the Savior the center of our lives, we can leave behind frailties and imperfections—such as wrongfully judging others—and we can also have the Savior's love flow through us to others.

Making Christ the center of our lives reminds me of the flying saucer at Utah's Lagoon Amusement Park. As children, my friends and I would go to the Fun House and clamber onto the saucer, shaped like an upside down plate, crawling and scrambling to get to the middle so we wouldn't be thrown off as the saucer spun faster and faster. Often someone nearer the edge would grab a friend who was closer to the middle and pull her, sliding and sprawling, completely off the saucer. But if I could struggle and strain to make it to the very center, without getting shoved or pulled off, the centrifugal force didn't affect me. I could stay there solidly, even as the saucer spun. I discovered that the most fun was to help someone climb onto the center with me. Of course, I had to be vigilant to keep my place because stretching hands and feet were constantly trying to knock me from my secure perch. So it is with keeping the Savior in the center of our lives. We must be vigilant in holding on to the Savior and staying with him in the center. When Christ is the focus of our lives, we know he will help us if we have the spiritual maturity to stay with him no matter what is swirling around us. And when we are secure and watchful in the center, we can stretch out our hands to pull others, in charity, into the center with him, too.

When we have a secure relationship with Christ, we cannot help loving others: in our family, our ward, and beyond. Alma says to those at the waters of Mormon who are thinking about being baptized, "And now, as ye are desirous to come into the fold of God, . . . and are willing to bear one another's burdens, that they may be light; yea, and are willing to mourn with those that mourn; yea, and comfort those that stand in need of comfort, and to stand as witnesses of God at all times and in all things, and in all places, . . . what have you against being baptized?" (Mosiah 18:8–10).

Like those Nephites who "clapped their hands for joy" at this prospect, we consecrate ourselves when we are baptized, to "bear," to "mourn with," to "comfort," and to "stand as witnesses of God" with and for those who are part of the "body of Christ." At baptism we commit ourselves to become charitable.

A young mother in France was forced to confront her baptismal covenants—her call to charity—after experiencing frustration at the apparent disunity and lack of caring in her small branch. Collette and her family were the only members in their town. The branch, an hour away in another town, was composed primarily of members of the Poulet family. The branch president, the Relief Society president, the elders quorum president, and the Primary president were all part of the Poulet clan, a wonderful family who worked hard to keep the Church alive in that area.

Collette spent two days a week working with the sister missionaries—tracting, taking them to see her friends, even introducing them to people she knew only slightly, such as her baker. She tried to be obedient to her leaders but couldn't help feeling that the one dominant family made it difficult for new members to feel needed or included in the branch. She scarcely dared to speak about her feelings for fear of seeming disobedient or controversial, yet she wanted to serve in her branch and make a difference.

One day while talking about her baptismal covenants and Mosiah 18 with one of the sister missionaries, Collette burst out, "I look around the branch, and I don't see anyone who is truly willing to comfort those who stand in need of comfort or cry with those that cry. I don't see anyone coming to mourn with me when I'm mourning. How am I supposed to feel a part of a unified Church when no one will support me in my efforts? I know the Church is true, but it's almost impossible to live as I would like to in this branch." She sighed and threw her hands in the air in frustration.

The missionary looked at her sympathetically but asked some searching questions. "Wait a minute. You know that scripture you quoted in Mosiah 18? Let's look at it. I've never really noticed it before, but who does it say will 'bear,' and 'mourn,' and 'comfort,' and do all of those other wonderful things? It doesn't say, 'And *you* will be comforted; and *you* will be cried with; and *you* will be mourned with.' The scripture says that *you* will covenant to help *them*. Are these conditional or unconditional covenants?" Collette suddenly realized that she was so intent on keeping tabs on other people's covenants that she had almost lost sight of her own.[4]

If we sit and wait for others to come and wipe our tears, we may miss the opportunity to wipe the tears of a neighbor or a friend. We can sit at home behind seemingly safe walls, or we can push beyond our comfort zones and break through our walls of judgment and criticism to someone else who needs us but who may also be hiding behind heavy bricks of negative thought. We can cooperate with others if they will let us; but if they will not, the only remedy that will heal our own hearts and the hearts of others is the gift of charity. As gifted at cooperating as Collette was, as willing to work and to contribute, she still had to progress until she could let the Lord influence her attitudes and motivations. It was at this point that she began the process of becoming charitable.

The Lord invites, even requires, us to keep growing up— even though we already think we are grown up—first in our marriage and family relationships and then in our relationships with others. Mere cooperation isn't enough; we must push ourselves to develop a dependence upon the Lord so that he can mold us spiritually into the kind of people we must become to "be like him" (Moroni 7:48). Whereas cooperation involves mostly our own power to love, charity is a combination of our own desires and energies coupled with the Spirit and the healing power of God. Whereas cooperation may be action-centered, charity is motive-centered.

With our covenant "to remember him always" comes the covenant to remember each other always, in the same way he remembers us, through charity. Even then, this charity is a "gift" to us, "which he hath bestowed upon all who are true followers of his Son, Jesus Christ" (Moroni 7:48). I desire that gift. I am willing to be a "true follower." Instead of sprawling off the saucer from the centrifugal force of daily temptations and distractions, I desire to move myself more completely toward the center. I am finding that coming to Christ in the center and remaining steadfast in that focus requires constant vigilance—constant faith, constant prayer. Yet as I seek to love him more fervently, I feel myself loving others without constraint. "O to grace how great a debtor / Daily I'm constrained to be."[5] I thank God daily for those who love me with charity.

Over the last few months, my faith in Christ's atonement has increased. I seek to understand his atonement through deeper faith, prayer, and study. I seek charity, "the pure love of Christ" (Moroni 7:47). I seek this gift, a gift that comes to us only because of the atonement of our Savior. Without his atonement, we would not have the power to love as he loves. "Wherefore, my beloved brethren, pray . . . with all the energy of heart, that ye may be filled with this love, . . . that when he shall appear we shall be like him" (Moroni 7:48). I believe we will not have the capacity to see him or withstand his presence until, as our charity increases, we have begun to be like him.

When we come so fully to Christ that we have true charity, his pure love will flow through us into other people. We will become conduits for his grace and mercy. As Karen Lynn Davidson wrote:

> Each life that touches ours for good
> Reflects thine own great mercy, Lord;
> Thou sendest blessings from above
> Through words and deeds of those who love.[6]

I pray that "we may have this hope; that we may be purified even as he is pure" (Moroni 7:48).

NOTES

1. "Each Life That Touches Ours for Good," *Hymns of The Church of Jesus Christ of Latter-day Saints* (Salt Lake City: The Church of Jesus Christ of Latter-day Saints, 1985), no. 293.

2. The names in this story have been changed to protect privacy.

3. As quoted in C. Terry Warner, "Honest, Simple, Solid, True," *Brigham Young Magazine,* June 1996, 36–37.

4. The names in this story have been changed to protect privacy.

5. "Come, Thou Fount of Every Blessing," *Hymns* (Salt Lake City: The Church of Jesus Christ of Latter-day Saints, 1948), no. 70.

6. *Hymns,* 1985, no. 293.

SPIRITUAL MATURITY

ELAINE L. JACK

During the past six years as Relief Society General President, I have seen a strength in women—a charity almost beyond expression. I have seen the women of this Church "follow after charity" and receive spiritual gifts as they are needed (1 Corinthians 14:1).

Some time ago we received a letter from Marilyn Smolka, a member of the Monument Park 20th Ward in Emigration Canyon in Salt Lake City, who told of a Relief Society meeting in which a sister rose to her feet to describe an incredibly difficult challenge. With tears streaming down her cheeks and her hands shaking, she asked the sisters to pray in her behalf. Another sister stood, walked over, and, putting her arms around the first sister, said, "We'll all join in prayer for you."

Marilyn's ward was small and newly formed at the time but richly blessed with some qualities that would make any ward effective. The ward members shared a high level of trust. Marilyn's description of her ward reveals some reasons why they have developed a distinct identity with feelings of love and unity among members:

"We had always been a part of a larger, more affluent ward in the midst of a thriving, active east bench stake, when an

---

Elaine L. Jack grew up in Cardston, Alberta, Canada. She attended the University of Utah as an English major and is an avid reader. She and her husband, Joseph E. Jack, are the parents of four sons and have thirteen grandchildren. Sister Jack serves as general president of the Relief Society of The Church of Jesus Christ of Latter-day Saints.

inspired stake president created a ward composed only of members living within our canyon. Many said, This will never work. We don't have enough active families to fill positions. Our ward budget won't be large enough to cover our activities. But to everyone's amazement, it did work.

"For almost ten years, from a nucleus of only about twenty-five active families, people jumped in feet first to respond to callings from the new bishop, who was my own husband. They accepted jobs they might never have filled in a larger ward. They developed skills and talents and matured spiritually because in a smaller setting they were willing to risk. Our young people, instead of becoming lost, found that they liked each other across age-group boundaries, unconcerned about whether they were Beehives or Mia Maids or Laurels. Activities were planned that included all ages. We welcomed new folks with open arms. No one could slip in unnoticed and sit on the back row. In fact, we were small enough that for many years we held activities in our home. We absolutely needed everyone.

"On Sunday mornings, Relief Society sometimes was a group of only ten or twelve sisters, including the presidency, but we developed a warm, supportive atmosphere. There was no judging. It was safe—safe to share, safe to be honest. And we found that when people are willing to share their innermost feelings, their fears, and their failings, a wonderful thing happens. People reach out to you from the reservoirs of their souls to fill you with strength and counsel and courage. I was deeply grateful for my share in the blessings of being in this loving ward.

"When a man is serving as bishop, there is no promise that his own family will be protected from problems. During this time we discovered that our fourteen-year-old son was heavily into drugs. I chose to be honest in Relief Society with what was going on in our family, with the pain, and the process. In response, I received hugs, encouragement, and acceptance as we worked through my son's rehabilitation with him. The spirit of honesty and love permeated the entire ward. It felt like family.

"An honest, supportive sisterhood is harder to accomplish in a larger setting, but it boils down to an individual willingness to risk and share. If one person reaches out, it spills over to others who want and need to share but are too timid to start the process. The reaching out eventually forms a circle that connects everyone. In 2 Corinthians 4:6, Paul describes what that connection feels like and what its source is: 'God, who commanded the light to shine out of darkness, hath shined in our hearts, to give the light of the knowledge of the glory of God in the face of Jesus Christ.' It seems to me that we are all striving to reach out to each other with the light of Christ in our own faces."

The sisters in Marilyn's ward are close to each other and close to the Lord because they have sought the gift of charity—the pure love of Christ. Though a young ward, they are mature in their thinking. At the end of Paul's marvelous discussion of charity in 1 Corinthians 13 is a compelling statement about maturity: "When I was a child, I spake as a child, I understood as a child, I thought as a child: but when I became a man, I put away childish things" (v. 11). To some, this passage may refer to maturing in the things of the Spirit. I think Paul is saying that maturity enhances his charity. Maturity anchors our lives to the important principles governing daily living.

I remember so clearly when Barbara Bush, wife of George Bush, spoke on national television at the time of her husband's inauguration as president of the United States. It was an auspicious occasion. "See this styled hair?" she said. "See this designer suit? Take a good look because you probably won't see them again." Women loved Barbara Bush because she was able to say, "There is no artificial standard. I am comfortable with myself as I am, and I want you to know it." That's maturity—the ability to happily face yourself.

49

Maturity allows us to accept ourselves even when we're not all we want to be. Maturity allows us to accept who we are and where we are. We should never abandon the quest for a better self, but neither should we allow ourselves to become immobilized, thinking we are nothing. Accepting ourselves, knowing we are progressing, frees us to reach out to others in charitable ways.

As you take stock of yourself and your situation, base your evaluation of where you are on your own criteria, not that of another person. In visualizing the maturing process, I think of it as comparing: checkers to chess; commentaries to the actual scriptures; short-term satisfaction to long-range goals; self-centered ego needs to bonding together for the good of the whole. Are you thinking and acting inclusively? Are you appreciating another's best efforts? It is so easy to notice what people do wrong and what we would do differently. Can you imagine how different our world would be if we concentrated instead on what all of us do right, on the positive acts of ourselves and others? That's maturity.

There are times when all of us are not at our best—perhaps we have different communication styles, or maybe we're just feeling cranky. Whatever the reason, we may, at times, give or take offense. If that happens, it is so helpful, even soothing, to consider the character of the woman who may have spoken impatiently or bluntly disagreed with you. When a friend whom I know and trust speaks a little harshly, first I think, "Maybe she is having a bad day. Maybe I misunderstood her. Maybe something is troubling her." I'm not easily offended. My advice is, "If people drop an offense, don't pick it up!" I always expect the best from people. In our dispensation, the Lord said, "And by their desires and their works you shall know them" (D&C 18:38). I rejoice when I work with women who have righteous desires and do good works. I can be very patient with them. In turn, I hope they will understand my desires and be patient with me. Charity, after all, "suffereth long, and is kind" (1 Corinthians 13:4). That's maturity.

And we must recognize that becoming mature is a process. As we mature, we "put away childish things" and begin to recognize the Lord's hand in so many simple but significant ways. Charity is the ability to rejoice in the accomplishments and the gifts of others, to forget about competing—over money, house size, success of children, or anything else. Charity—mature, pure Christlike love—is an arm that reaches out to encircle and reassure; it is a willingness to forgive—and forget—an unkind remark; it is the faith that we can do what the Lord has asked; it is the humility to take direction and the strength to lead.

I don't think age is the key to maturity. We don't simply mature as we grow old. We have to work at it. I wonder how King Solomon became so wise. His startling judgment in the case of the squabbling mothers—"Divide the living child in two, and give half to the one, and half to the other" (1 Kings 3:25)—is recognized for its depth of wisdom and maturity. How did he reach such a level of maturity? As a young man he said to the Lord, "I am but a little child: I know not how to go out or come in" (1 Kings 3:7). He needed to grow. It wasn't the physical process that concerned him, however, but the maturity that refines the feelings of the heart. He turned to the Lord for guidance. We put away childish things as we use Christ as our guide, for he, too, had to "increase in wisdom and stature and in favour with God and man" (see Luke 2:52).

I firmly believe that "charity never faileth"—unless it is never tried. In Paul's letter to the Corinthians, he promises to tell the Saints of "a more excellent way" to be one in Christ. Then, in 1 Corinthians 13, he describes the way of charity: "Charity suffereth long, and is kind; charity envieth not; charity vaunteth not itself, is not puffed up, doth not behave itself unseemly, seeketh not her own, is not easily provoked, thinketh no evil . . . Beareth all things, believeth all things, hopeth all things, endureth all things. . . . When I was a child,

I spake as a child, I understood as a child, I thought as a child: but when I became a man, I put away childish things. . . . And now abideth faith, hope, charity, these three; but the greatest of these is charity" (1 Corinthians 13:4, 5, 7, 11, 13). These are the gifts of the Spirit I have seen demonstrated by the women of Relief Society. They provide the "more excellent way" that Paul promised.

Mature people, regardless of age, are able to face themselves and act in positive ways despite flaws they may see. We all have parts of our character we are working on. Mature people "press forward with a steadfastness in Christ, having a perfect brightness of hope, and a love of God and of all men" (2 Nephi 31:20). As we put away childish things, as we mature spiritually, as we develop charity, we understand what we see, we know who we are, and we act upon what we believe.

NOTHING EXCITING EVER HAPPENS TO ME—AND OTHER MYTHS

CAROL CLARK OTTESEN

Speaking of myths, let me tell you right off about a monster named Moleman invented by my son Eric to keep his younger sister in bed when he was baby-sitting her. Luckily for him, I was ignorant of this story until they were all grown and I read of Moleman in my now-adult daughter's journal: "Moleman lived in the large bushes just below our bedroom window, and he only came out at night. Then, according to Eric, he'd scratch on the window to signal that he was starting to dig a hole to come up through the floor of our bedroom. When he got there he'd stare at you for a long time, so close you could feel his breath before he attacked. When we heard that scratching on the window, we were paralyzed and, of course, never, never got out of bed. The image was so vivid, that hot breath so real, I was scared until I went to college."

I bring up this journal entry for two reasons. One is to give you an example of reaching back in your life and recording those seemingly childish incidents that are certainly not a contributing factor to the spiritual giant you have become, yet which add color and interest to your story. The other reason is

Carol Clark Ottesen, a writing instructor at Brigham Young University in the honors department, is a published poet and the author of a recently published nonfiction book. She and her husband, Sterling E. Ottesen, are the parents of six children. She serves as ward organist.

53

that Moleman also represents for me the false fears and myths that keep us from doing personal writing.

One of those myths is that we have nothing extraordinary to write about. The poet Rilke says, "If your daily life seems poor, do not blame it; blame yourself . . . *[for you] must call forth its riches*" (italics added).[1] My father, who grew up in Mesa, Arizona, wrote a book of stories about his life for his grandchildren. One of the stories begins like this: "'NOTHING EXCITING EVER HAPPENS TO ME,' and especially to a nine-year-old boy in a small town like Mesa on a boring hot summer day—that's what I *thought*. Up on the roof of our house, two men were painting it green. . . . I had a piece of bread and butter and was walking under the eaves of the house. I heard a rattling sound like an empty bottle coming down the roof. 'Look out,' a man shouted. I took a bite of bread and looked up—then five gallons of green paint came over my head and eyes and ears. My muffled cry brought my mother running. She stripped all my clothes off and scraped, dug and wiped paint out of my ears, eyes and hair. When I could open my eyes, some neighbors were there including a girl I liked pretty well, so I closed my eyes quick for I was naked. I was glad I had paint all over me. I tried to imagine that she didn't recognize me. . . . In a week or so with my hair all cut off, . . . I thought about how I wished I could live in New York where exciting things happen. I thought exciting things happen in Mesa to a small boy if you're in the right place at the right time when someone says, 'Look out!'"[2]

Even if your life does not spill over you greenly or may seem to be a mere waiting for that wonderful "New York day" to come, your inner life is full of fire and fascination. Writer Eudora Welty, who never married, never had children, never ventured more than a few miles from her hometown, says, "I am a writer who came of a sheltered life. A sheltered life can be a daring life as well. For all serious daring starts from within."[3] And it is when we dare to write about the truth that we begin to enjoy writing. And then we begin to see meaning in the things that have happened to us.

A former student of mine at California State University, an African-American woman of about forty, walked into my office one day and sat down beside my desk with a great sigh. Her face was passive, her sweat suit had holes in it, and her corn-row braids were gray at the roots. Her assignment was to write a twenty-five-page autobiography, but she couldn't think of anything to write. "My life is boring," she said. I ventured some provocative questions, but she only shrugged her shoulders, and I began to believe her life *was* boring. Finally she said grudgingly, "I have three kids. I work. Why would anybody want to read about my life?" But ultimately she began to open up. It seems she was born in poverty in a little town in Georgia. Her mother went away to work and left her to live with her grandmother. "It isn't worth talking about. Lived in a shantytown, so poor I'm not going to tell you about it. Thirteen kids. I was in the middle. . . . Nothing more, really. I did leave, though, when I was thirteen . . . .

"Had to. I saw what I'd have to do. All my other sisters, well, my grandma gave them to white men for money. She came to get me one day when I was thirteen. Had a man for me in the barn. She nearly caught me, but I got away. She ripped my dress, but I started running and I never came back. No matter what, I wasn't about to do that. No way. I got a job working for folks and then I hitched a ride to California.

"I knew my daddy was there, and I wanted to see him. But I found he didn't want anything to do with me. I got a job working in a motel and met Leroy. First time anybody showed me any attention.

"Then we had this retarded daughter. She's both mentally and physically handicapped. And then had two more kids real quick. He couldn't take it and left. My mom called and said she didn't have anywhere to go and could she come and live with me. So I went to work to support all of us and got my high

55

school diploma at night. I was the first one in all my family to graduate from high school. Now there'll be another first. I graduate from college in June."[4]

I wanted to shout, to dance her around the room, to embrace her, but said more sedately than I would have liked, "LaWanda, you are the heroine of a great story." She wrote her story and received an overwhelming ovation after she read it to the class. She was shocked. Later she came to me with a new air of confidence, "You know, writing this made me see what I actually did." LaWanda did not write as a victim *or* as a heroine but merely documented without judgment the events of her life.

I read many such stories from students of culturally diverse backgrounds at California State University, and I noticed that as the students shared these stories with one another, the hostility between ethnic groups lessened; the groups began to mix, and the students began to realize what it's like to be inside a certain skin color, or to be forced into a gang, or to be handicapped. And though we may not have had those particular experiences, we have not been without our own struggles. We need to share our stories as parents and children, as husbands and wives, to be understood and to understand. Does your family really know you?

In workshops I have heard many women voice another fear: "Does my family really want to know me? Who will ever read this stuff?" We may feel as Mormon pioneer Margaret Judd Clawson felt: "And now that I have written this long, disconnected, rambling remembrance of the past, I Scarsly know what to do with it For who Can be interested in the little things of [the] Common, everyday life of another?"[5] Let me share a personal experience that says to me graphically: someone will read with hunger what you record.

Because my mother died when I was a teenager, I didn't have the luxury of asking her all those questions you want to ask after you get married and have children. At age thirty-two she contracted cancer. As a mother of five little children, she seemed to be almost canonized for her courage and faith in the face of eight years of suffering. For years, I lived with the shadow that I could never be *that* loved, *that* beautiful, *that* good. Years later when my father was moving, he found in the bottom of an old trunk the diary she had written as a teenager up to age nineteen. I read it voraciously, puzzled at first by this new image of an immature, volatile, boy-crazy teenager. I was amazed at the depth of her down times, the sentimental ecstasy of her discovery of the physical, the absence of the spiritual impulse that so permeated her maturity. And the puzzlement turned to a redemptive weeping—here was a human being in process, a real person I could love and forgive—not an impossible icon of perfection that made me want to give up before I began. Did I love her less to discover her struggle? Just the opposite. I loved her—perhaps even more because she was now accessible to me, and suddenly we walked hand in hand, joining with that continuum of mothers and daughters who strive together to meet the challenges particular to being a woman. If only one person reads your story, honestly written, and finds in it a personal revelation, your time is well spent.

We have all written some hogwash—trying to make our lives more acceptable—but journal writing should not be fiction. My belief is that if we reach into those places in us that cannot lie, if we see clear to the bottom, truth will be there and our view will be wide and revelatory, like God's.

I'd like to share a revelatory experience from my history. When I was about twelve, I had a friend, an only child who had everything materially that any child could want. I came from a large family, and we did a lot of sharing. I loved to play at my friend's house because it was so quiet and her mother served us lunch on placemats. Besides all that, she was beautiful. I thought she was the luckiest girl in the world. One Sunday, we both had to speak for the first time in sacrament meeting. My mother made me a dress for the occasion, in the era when homemade was definitely second class. On that Sunday, I put the dress on, arrived early with my talk perfectly memorized, and was sitting on the stand when my friend walked in the door. I watched her as she floated up the aisle in the most beautiful yellow dress I had ever seen, definitely store-bought. Her curls bounced; a gold bracelet shone on her wrist; her black patent-leather Mary Janes shone. She sat down by me, and I became brown-gray against the floating yellow dress. I was first to speak and, consumed with the comparison, I forgot the end of my talk. I sat down humiliated. At the end of the meeting, I headed for the side door and ran to the car, jumped in the back seat, and burst into hot tears. My mother came to the car, slipped into the back seat, and put her arm around me. But I pulled away and lashed out, "Did you see her? The dress? She was so beautiful! Why do I have to wear homemade dresses—why are we so poor?" She could have told me how ungrateful I was, how superficial, but instead she turned to me with tears in her eyes. "You know, Carol, I would give you the world if I could." She embraced me, and I wept for my own folly. I knew then she had clothed me in love like a princess, and I have never forgotten the warmth of those arms, the sense of what is ultimately important.

Perhaps you can think of an incident in your life in which you were disappointed or shamed, in which perhaps you came to an awareness of what is truly important. You can begin by writing that one story. Time yourself to see how much you can record in just five minutes. Allowing yourself a limited time compresses your thinking and lends spontaneity and vigor. Don't take time for issues of grammar: Kick that impertinent Moleman! Don't let him keep you under the covers.

The poet May Sarton said, "The senses are the keys to the past."[6] Give detail so the reader can see and feel your experience. Don't just say, "I went to the prom," but "I wore a rose chiffon dress with tatting on the collar and little pink rosebuds embroidered on the edge." Relax your body in the chair; let your muscles sag. Close your eyes; breathe deeply. Forget your present surroundings and enter this memory. Feel it. Remember colors, sounds, smells, impressions, and begin to write. Write without stopping, no matter what, for five minutes. You'll be amazed at what you can do. Ultimately you will have a collection and can piece these together into the complex quilt that is your life.

Another myth is that writing is what we do when we have completed all other tasks. But if we view writing as MaryJan Munger suggests, as a service—a "communal and spiritual action"—then writing becomes a more justifiable choice.[7] Writing is not just the act of expressing ourselves but is an ultimate act of charity. I'm grateful that my mother, in the last days of her life, spent her limited energy writing with a shaky hand, propped with a pillow, only a few minutes at a time, recording the important stories of her life so that we might know her and that her written testimony might stand as a witness of God's goodness. I'm indebted to the young Alma, who heard Abinadi in the court of King Noah and, at the peril of his life, hid himself away to record the words for me to read as a model of fearlessness and consummate faith.

Sisters, do not respond to self-negation or false fears, but test the deeps from which your life takes rise. Write about your workaday world as well as your peak experiences to help those who come after you who may feel constricted, doubtful, lonely, misunderstood. Though you may feel like writer Virginia Woolf, that rather than write in a journal you'd like to "roll up the crumpled skin of the day . . . and cast it into the hedge,"[8] write to find that in exhaustive dailiness is power, courage, a bringing forth of the highest consciousness of what it is to be a woman. Write.

NOTES

1. Rainer Maria Rilke, trans. M. D. Herter Norton, *Letters to a Young Poet* (New York: Norton & Co., 1934), 19.

2. Harold Glen Clark, "Nothing Exciting Ever Happens to Me," *Tell Us Another One, Grandpa,* privately published, 1986, 11.

3. Eudora Welty, *One Writer's Beginnings* (Cambridge, Mass.: Harvard University Press, 1995), 104.

4. Carol Clark Ottesen, *L.A. Stories: The Voices of Cultural Diversity* (Yarmouth, Maine: Intercultural Press, 1993), 22–23.

5. Maureen Ursenbach Beecher, "In Search of Spirit: Life Writings of Latter-day Saint Women," in *Hearts Knit Together: Talks from the 1995 Women's Conference,* ed. Susette Fletcher Green, Dawn Hall Anderson, and Dlora Hall Dalton (Salt Lake City: Deseret Book, 1996), 146.

6. May Sarton, quoted in *Barnet and Stubbs's Practical Guide to Writing,* 4th ed. (Boston: Little, Brown and Co., 1983), 342.

7. MaryJan Gay Munger, "Creating Zion: Why Write in the Household of Faith," *Annual of the Association for Mormon Letters,* ed. Lavina Fielding Anderson (Provo, Utah: Association for Mormon Letters, 1996), 58.

8. Virginia Woolf, *A Room of One's Own* (San Diego, Calif.: Harcourt, Brace, Jovanovich, 1929), 24.

SOUL STORIES

NATALIE CURTIS McCULLOUGH

I believe it was Mark Twain who gave my favorite reason for keeping a journal when he said something to this effect: The older I get, the more clearly I remember things that never happened.[1] One of the things that never happened to me which I remember well, but have not told many people about, is that I grew up crossing the plains with Mormon pioneers in their exodus to the Salt Lake Valley. Night after exhilarating night, I battled rattlesnakes, recovered missing cattle *before* they required blessings for health, fought in Indian raids, and single-handedly delivered babies in rain-soaked tents.

All I needed to transform the end of my bed into a high-performance covered wagon on the Mormon Trail was a pillowcase. I needed a pillowcase because my mother had seven children and no interest in hair. Every several months, whether my hair needed attention or not, I was taken to Bob's Barbershop in Foothill Village to submit to Bob's shears for what my mother called "a cute little pixie haircut." In today's vernacular, a pixie would be a near miss with a buzz. Pioneer women did not wear pixies. So, I bobby-pinned my pillow case to my head each night after the lights went out. Suddenly, I had long blonde ringlets falling into golden tresses that I

Natalie Curtis McCullough and her husband, James R. McCullough, are the parents of four children, with whom they hike, boat, camp, and ski. Natalie enjoys public speaking and teaching writing projects in her children's classrooms. She volunteers as an English tutor for middle-school students taking English as a Second Language (ESL) courses and is a substitute seminary teacher.

61

tossed from shoulder to shoulder. No sooner did the hair fall down my back than I could hear the lowing of oxen, the creaking of wagon wheels, and sometimes, the menacing hiss of a rattlesnake.

The stories of my childhood are more than valued bridges back to my children. They are pioneer pathways leading to my own emotional frontier. I want them recorded, in all their simplicity, because my experiences and stories become my history, and it is from my history that I form my identity.

I married a man with a list of goals as long as my arm. For every one checked off, he adds another. He has never left the house without a destination. He knows the date we were married. I, on the other hand, remember being moved out of my bedroom the night before my wedding to make way for another child, sleeping on the couch, bawling the entire night. My husband remembers the weight of our children at birth. I remember the sound of nursing babies in the night and learning to turn my rocker into the corner of the room so my scratchy lullabies would echo back sounding fuller and more soothing. I can close my eyes at any moment and feel the thrill of the sink and rise of cutting figure eights in wilderness powder, skiing with my sweetheart for my fortieth birthday. My sweetheart has calculated how big a profit percentage the helicopter pilot made and how many calories he burned per turn. Jim has always known where he is going. I know where I have been.

One of the compelling images of journal writing has its roots in the early Saints of the Restoration. These were pioneers in the literal and symbolic sense of the word. Theirs were the diaries and letters and journals to record the epic Latter-day Saint events from conversion to purification. They pushed the frontier in every conceivable way, from groundbreaking religious ideals to backbreaking temple building to heartbreaking exodus. Their stories have become our identity as a faithful people, a temple-worthy people, a missionary people. Their stories teach us where we have been and inspire us to continue onward. It is from the lives of Emma, Eliza, and Emmeline that we know to value our own Elaine.

My adult life has been shaped by my adolescent experience of watching my mother die from the metastasis of cancer over a period of seven years, from the time I was ten to the time I was seventeen. Many are the vague, sacred fears I have lived by that were cultivated in my mother's garden. At the time, I imagined my experience to be so rich and painful that I would never forget it. And yet, I have relatively few specific memories of my mother in all those days we shared around her sickbed. I have already lost touch with the teenage Natalie, pioneering the wilderness of a loved one's death, because I protected her pain, unexamined and unrecorded. When Joan Didion says in her book, *Slouching towards Bethlehem,* "I have already lost touch with a couple of people I used to be," her imagery haunts me.[2]

Whether or not they blossom in the garden of our life's history, all our experiences enrich the soil. I have no words to tell my sorrow that my mother's thoughts and feelings went unrecorded. Because she did not keep a journal and she died young, I lost her twice. Writer Alice Walker said: "And when we go in search of our mother's gardens, it's not really to learn who trampled on them or how or even why—we usually know that already. Rather, it is to learn what our mothers planted there, what they thought as they sowed, and how they survived the blighting of so many fruits."[3]

In other words, the stories and feelings recorded in our journals are about soul work. In that sense, maybe *Star Trek* has missed the mark, entirely overreaching: maybe our journals are the last great frontier. My mother's illness, my fear of her death, the actual loss of her, and the fear of my own early death have had singular impact on me. As I approach and then pass some of Mother's significant dates—her first mastectomy at age thirty-seven and so forth—I find myself reexperiencing the emotional trauma, which resurrects all my regrets for Mother and my fears for myself. My journal is the garden of refuge where I turn to have my heart really known, my cancerous fears validated, and my adolescent self understood and thus liberated. It is through my own midlife journal that I begin to understand "what my mother planted, what she may have thought as she sowed, and how she survived the blighting of so many fruits." In a very real sense, my journal acts as surrogate mother.

In the children's book *Are You My Mother?* by P. D. Eastman, a baby duck quacks around asking all the different farm animals, "Are you my mother?" No, the cow won't take responsibility for the little duckling, neither will the pig nor the dog, and so forth. I can't remember how the story ends. Maybe because I am still mired in asking the question of assorted women in my life, Will you be my mother? Will you take responsibility for knowing and loving me? So far, many women have blessed my life with significant nurturing. And through the arduous soul work of my journal, I slowly emerge as more able to love and value myself.

The bulbs along my front border blossomed early last spring. I worried over them in February when they burst from the earth too soon, fearful they would be crushed by the late spring snows. I anguished they would be shredded before Easter, and Mother's Day brought them into full bloom. My daughters daily reported the coming of the tender green shoots, while I wished they would retreat back into the safety of the earth's womb. We learn humility through the early blooming of late February and early March thaws. Who are we to schedule the moments most convenient to have our flowers bloom? Their motion is upward towards the sun and whatever fate awaits them. My job is to admire them, appreciate them when they come. I marvel that my bulbs risked coming forth in January to be loved by the sun.

Perhaps it is not so different with our creative, pioneering energies. I have spent fruitless energy repressing thoughts that appear at random, inconvenient, or emotionally unsafe times. A journal can be the welcoming garden where the heart's seeds come to fruition.

One summer, I preferred to spend time writing with my children rather than driving them frantically to lessons. The first week of summer found us working in the garden, so we naturally studied "seeds" as a writing concept.

We learned that every seed contains the beginnings of a root and the beginnings of a stem. A seed can weigh as much as the double coconut tree seed, which tips the scale at fifty pounds, or as little as orchid seeds, which require eight hundred thousand seeds to make an ounce. There is no apparent relationship between the size of the seed and the size of the plant that develops from it. We learned that seeds may remain dormant for varying periods of time until the most favorable conditions for germination occur. The general span for viability is from a few weeks to fifty years, but ten-thousand-year-old lotus seeds have germinated under the right conditions.[4] With these facts in mind, my daughters set out to write about themselves as if they were a seed, soil-surrounded and ready to struggle for light and air and space.

Some cousins were staying with us on that particular morning. One of them, eleven-year-old Catherine, wrote, "I was finally pushing my way up through the soil. It was comforting to know that part of me was staying in the place I loved and part of me was going to somewhere new. I would expand, share my secret beauty, and offer my seeds."

Isn't that a lovely idea? A germinating seed feels both the pull of the womb, wanting to sink and stay soil-surrounded, and the hope of breaking into a new identity, experiencing change and hoping to bear seeds of its own. The metaphor is not too simple for us all to imagine that we are seeds, wanting to express rootedness and adventure. I always wanted to participate in the "roots and wings" idea, but for me it is awkward imagery. Roots and wings are not features of the same thing. But a root to push down and a stem pulsating up, that is an image to ponder. That is what writing in a journal feels like to me.

I understand myself as a seed with immature root and stem, a stored supply of food, and, unfortunately, a protective seed covering that often keeps me from exposing my real feelings. I write in my journal to shed the protective seed coat that holds me compressed and dormant. Sometimes it is a long stretch skyward. Writing, like gardening, is risky business. It is not only about cultivating the soil and planting seeds. It is about thinning, weeding, and the sometimes sickeningly successful bounty of harvest.

Not all our gardens have to be public. There is no answer to the question, "Why write in a journal?" that does not begin with the inestimable joy of seeing my name at the top of a piece of white, blank paper. There is no understanding the answer short of the metaphor of bulbs and blossoms. Seeds long buried and not intentionally nurtured come forth into ideas and stories of such presumptuous beauty that I must concede credit to the Spirit and congratulate myself, simultaneously. I keep a journal to discover what I know, how I know it, and why it matters. I write to unearth treasures and mysteries buried in my heart. Writing the tender stirrings of my heart is the act of spring on my subconscious. It is not always a blossom that rises up to be shown, but it is always important.

Most of what I write is not to share or show. Few are the flowers of my thoughts that are destined for a crystal vase on the piano. But the thoughts are vibrant, growing things and are welcomed in privacy as well as for public display. I keep a journal to witness the miracle of sitting to an empty page and watching the soul fill it.

Some people keep a journal for the factual accounting of their whereabouts. Others resist writing for the invasion of privacy they feel. Many complain that they have nothing to record. Maybe it is the little lost details of our lives that make the richest compost for our gardens. Thomas Moore said: "To live with a high degree of artfulness means to attend to the small things, . . . [for they are] the very heart of soul-making. From some grand overview of life, it may seem that only the big events are important. But to the soul, the most minute details and the most ordinary activities, carried out with mindfulness and art, have an effect far beyond their apparent insignificance. . . . Art is not about the expression of talent or the making of pretty things. It is about preservation and containment of the soul. It is about arresting life and making it available for contemplation."[5]

Preservation of the soul is the point of journal writing. Nephi said, "Behold, I write the things of my soul" (2 Nephi 4:15). The Savior told Joseph Smith to "care for the soul and the life of the soul" (D&C 101:37). Journal writing is one way to record and remember your developing soul. A journal becomes personal scripture, in this sense.

If soul work is the point of journal keeping, why do we squander ourselves on things that diminish our spirit? Maybe the Lord is interested in what we have learned, what we hope, how large our soul has grown, and what we value.

In rereading my journals of many years, I see that I chose my life for the very privileges that overwhelm and discourage me. I treasure my children, but none of them self-clean. I'm grateful for a yard and garden, but they won't vacation when I do. I value friendships, but I am a largely interior personality. A journal gives me the perspective to embrace all of this.

Our family took a hike called "The Pioneer Register" in Capitol Reef National Park recently. My girls loved running up the sandstone and climbing into hollowed-out pockets of red rock, just their size, made by wind and rain. A short way into the walk we encountered the Pioneer Register on the steep, smooth canyon wall, where pioneers who traveled the then-treacherous road etched their names into the rock. The beautifully inscribed signatures with their curlicues and graceful lettering inspire belief in the nineteenth-century men and women who settled the harsh desert area, planting orchards that still produce fruit, nudging space from grudging sage, cedar, and cactus.

The next mile or so was filled with recent graffiti from those who read the register and felt the desire to leave their own name somewhere on the canyon walls. Of course, my children wished to leave their names, and it was no small task to explain why the signatures and symbols of the past were both artistically and historically significant, but alas, our names did not belong on the walls. They could not understand why their name would deface the rock, but the name of a passerby a century removed was a thing to treasure. Wouldn't someone a distant century from now value our names as we did the pioneers'—and the Anasazi markings a thousand years before that? they asked. I tried to reason that part of the wonder in reading the pioneer names came from the fact that they were first in their era to enter-to-stay in this remote area. They were first to build the road, to cultivate and value the harsh land. But we came later, by their fruits, and must have a higher vision for our names than so much graffiti on the walls of life. Then, children satisfied, I wondered if what I told them was true.

Implicit in the desire to etch our names is the belief that others will follow and find our lives as curious and interesting as we have found those of others who went before us. We learned on our petroglyph hike the day before that the Anasazi markings may have been not so much attempts at important messages as just a way of leaving their mark, of saying, "We were here and found deer," or "We worshiped here," or "This is our territory. Trespass and we will fight." Why were these messages of greater historical significance than the one which might read, "The McCulloughs passed this way and were happy" or "It is a pleasure to watch my daughters climb the red rock with grace and agility"?

Walking out of the canyon we noticed a wooden stand with a register and a sign inviting all park visitors to leave their name and comments. It doesn't matter that no one reads them. They are an attempt to replicate the park's bathroom stalls, pine signs, and historic canyon cliffs. Maybe that accounts in small part for the step from historic graffiti to spray paint on freeway signs and business buildings. The point is, the register was filled. It is the modern equivalent of the petroglyph.

Some intrinsic part of the human experience makes us want to communicate what we are feeling. We all experience some degree of desire, at some time, to leave our mark, telling the world that we accomplished something of note, that we passed by, that we were here.

Whether people sneak their names as a scrawled blemish on an obscure wall in a remote canyon in the central Utah desert, make pencil marks in a register no one will read, or sprawl them across the cover of *Time* magazine, our names belong somewhere.

By our interest in and preservation of a journal, we all place our names on our own "pioneer register." We have all felt the desire to leave our name, our story, our message to the next traveler. We enrich and enlarge our souls by the expression of our fear, hope, wonder. That truth best addresses my interest in journals. They are one more place where pioneers may come to see themselves in a larger context, one more register in which people may come to be valued. We write the things of our soul so that they may be called sacred records by our children and our children's children. We must write the things that have been, the things that are, and the things we hope for. In the great tradition of the early Saints who gathered to Zion, we can plant seeds for the next wagon train of pillowcase pioneers to harvest.

NOTES

1. "When I was younger I could remember anything, whether it happened or not; but I am getting old, and soon I shall remember only the latter." Albert Bigelow Paine, *Mark Twain, A Biography* (1912), quoted in *Bartletts' Familiar Quotations,* 16th ed. (Boston: Little, Brown and Company, 1992), 528.

2. Joan Didion, *Slouching towards Bethlehem* (New York: Noonday Press, 1990), 139.

3. Alice Walker, quoted in foreword to *Their Eyes Were Watching God,* by Zora Neale Hurston (Urbana: University of Illinois, 1978), viii.

4. *World Book Encyclopedia,* s.v. "seed."

5. Thomas Moore, *Care of the Soul: A Guide for Cultivating Depth and Sacredness in Everyday Life* (New York: HarperPerennial, 1992), 285, 303.

THERE'S NO SUCH THING AS A MID-LAUGH CRISIS

LOUISE DURHAM

I learned to laugh in the back seat of a Ford station wagon as a seven-year-old traveling to Denver with my nine brothers and sisters. At least two of us were carsick at any given moment. I remember looking from face to anxious face wondering who would need the bucket next. Only my older sister, Janice, seemed full of disdain rather than worry. Four years older than I but acknowledged by all as the ranking authority in the family, she looked on as each new victim succumbed and muttered, "That's disgusting." So when Janice's face finally whitened and then took on the familiar green around the eyes and nose, I couldn't restrain myself; I giggled. It was a chain reaction: nine of us in various stages of misery laughed out loud. And then, almost as instinctively, we bellowed in unison: "Ooh, that's disgusting." More laughter. That drew the attention of even my parents, who were in another country—the front seat.

"What's so funny?" they asked.

"Janice is throwing up." The poetic justice overrode sympathy. They laughed, too.

Louise Durham received her bachelor's degree from the University of Utah and teaches English at Timpview High School in Provo, Utah. A homemaker, she and her husband, W. Cole Durham Jr., are the parents of four children. She teaches the home and family lessons in her ward Relief Society.

I suppose I had laughed a lot before this particular instance, but it is my earliest lasting impression. My family still laughs about that trip, although each of us remembers it differently.

Even though she doesn't admit it, my sister Janice needed our laughter. Without a word, we communicated valuable information to her. We told her, "Hey, Janice, nobody likes to be yelled at for something entirely out of their control when they don't feel well" and "Hey, Janice, watch out. What goes around comes around. Now take some of your own medicine."

Even more, we needed to laugh with each other. Packed together so tightly we stuck to each other's skin, our laughter said worlds to us: "We're all in this together. No one is exempt, but we can get through this."

As far as I'm concerned, humor is serious business. It is both a salve to heal wounds and an astringent that occasionally stings in the right places. It is instantaneous perception. Sometimes humor declares to the world, "I understand how little this matters." Laughing often clears vision and can put things back into focus. When my son was a baby, I worried about his drooling. Some mothers put bibs on their children when they eat. That's when I took Michael's bib off. It was the only time he didn't drool. I researched drooling in all the children's medical books I could find, but I unearthed remarkably little information. I asked my pediatrician about drooling. He only stared at me. Time didn't diminish the problem. Finally, I confided my worst fear to my husband: "He's going to drool at his missionary farewell," I lamented.

"We'll cross that bridge when we come to it," my husband replied.

Somebody should have laughed. I should have been shown right then—even in my pre-varicose-vein innocence—that my fears were foolish. Michael may even have drooled a bit at his missionary farewell; I don't know because I wasn't paying attention. I was absorbed in the gentleness of his spirit and the power of his testimony.

One of the most important things we can do for our children is to teach them what matters in life. Humor is an effective sorting tool, but we can't be effective teachers until we learn how to laugh at ourselves. Early in our marriage, my husband and I experienced one of those miscommunications that ends in disaster—or what seems like disaster before you know what real disaster is. As we attempted to sort things out, we found ourselves disagreeing hotly about who was at fault. Neither of us remembers what we were arguing about, but we were definitely angry with each other. I wanted to get to the bottom of the situation and lay the blame where it belonged—squarely in my husband's lap. But he's a lawyer. He kept finding ways to implicate me. Our discussion grew more heated. Finally, weary of the fight to be right, my husband looked at me kindly. "Louise, there's no question that this was my fault. In fact, let's just stipulate here and now that whatever happens in the future is also my fault. That way we won't have to fight about it." I accepted the offer. For years afterward, misunderstandings and disagreements melted away as we acknowledged Cole as the source of the problem and then burst out laughing. Our partnership has benefited from the shared belief that there's no such thing as a mid-laugh crisis.

Anna Tueller, a friend and master teacher, tells how her own mother conceded with flair to a superior opponent, her recalcitrant teenage daughter. In one exchange, the daughter blurted out angrily to her mother, "Go soak your head in the toilet." A few minutes later, Anna's mother appeared in the room with her long hair sopping wet. "Is this what you wanted?" she asked. The conflict was forgotten in the ensuing laughter.

My children have also helped in my education. One day I was fixing dinner when my high school senior walked in and said, "Hi, Gunther."

Gunther? What does that mean? Is it dirty? I tried to act non-chalant, knowing that if I appeared to be bothered by the name, it would stick.

"Why do you call me that?" I asked casually.

"I don't know," Emily said. "You just look like a Gunther."

Bethany walked in. "Who's Gunther."

"Mom is."

"Yeah, she looks like a Gunther."

I smiled and was particularly entertaining at dinner, hoping to deflect attention from my new name. I made it almost halfway through the meal when I made the mistake of asking for the peas. Emily boomed out: "Pass the peas to Gunther." I knew it was over.

"Who's Gunther?" This time it was my ten-year-old.

"Mom."

"Oh. Why?"

"It just fits her."

"Okay."

That was almost four years ago. Last night before I went to bed I left a note on the kitchen counter for Emily. "You got three phone calls. Dinner is in the fridge. Don't forget to lock the door. Love, Gunth."

My children love to hear the story of how I didn't get into Pep Club. It was the most important thing in my life, the symbol of all that matters when you're sixteen: acceptance, valida-tion, popularity, attention, uniforms. After a week of marching, posters, skits, and interviews, the newly selected members were notified with signs and balloons decorating the fronts of their houses. At the appointed time, I went outside. Nothing. Not a balloon, not a note. It must have fallen down, I thought. I looked behind the bushes. Then I crawled behind the bushes. They were prickly bushes. Still nothing. I called my mother frantically: "Did anyone take down any signs from the front of the house?"

"Sorry."

I went back inside, heartbroken. Mother read my face. "I know why you didn't make Pep Club," she said. "The judges knew you are strong enough to take defeat. Some other girls wouldn't have been able to handle it as well."

Do you have any idea how much I wanted to believe my mother? I was looking for a way out of my humiliation. Now whenever any family member suffers horrendous, humiliating defeat or rejection, someone invariably says, "I know why you weren't chosen; it's because the judges know you can take it. Others might not be able to handle being a loser as well as you can." Then we laugh. I love sharing life with my children, the successes as well as the failures. My miscues make them laugh. They also carry a comforting message: If Mom can laugh at such losses, so can we.

With humor, our shortcomings are no longer debilitating weaknesses but common bonds that link us together. Think about it. The one trait we all share is imperfection. If we laugh at them, the flaws aren't threatening. My daughter Bethany is almost six feet tall, a fact that wouldn't bother her if she weren't convinced that boys by definition are 5'10" or shorter. Bethany has lived all her life with tall jokes: "Bethany, what's the weather like up there? Any ships on the horizon?" She must have become immune to these barbs, because when she ran for junior class vice president, she came up with slogans that laughed at her height. "As Tall As a Tree, Only Nicer"; "As High As a Mountain, but Easier to Talk To"; "As Long As a River, Only Friendlier"; and so on. I loved the campaign. It was a big success. She lost the election. After a few tears, we laughed and kidded, "As tall as a tree, only less popular." Bethany's own joke allowed her to bridge the gap from realization of the loss to acceptance and also to understand how little the election mattered in the long run—or even the short. Our joking with Bethany said, "You haven't let anybody down. This loss doesn't diminish your worth. You don't have any reason for regret or reproach." Children need such messages in times of disappointment just as they need the disappointment. They must be able to recognize trivia so that it will not ultimately obscure what really matters.

Humor in a family says, "All is well—or it will be eventually. Even if times are tough, even if you messed up, even if pain is required, all is well. You don't have to face this alone." Humor is often a way of getting through an uncomfortable or disappointing experience, of coping with the adversity that threatens to break us.

My father-in-law had multiple sclerosis. In his final years, it was difficult and then impossible for him to speak. Although the disease was the source of much pain and frustration, one of my favorite memories is of him and my mother-in-law doubled over in laughter because no one could understand what he was trying to say. He made a series of attempts to articulate, each more ludicrous than the last. They laughed until the tears filled their eyes. Although tears in those days were close to the surface, it took laughter to release them.

Laughter brings a feeling of well-being to a family. My husband's grandfather used to ask, "Are you happy? Then notify your face." It's good advice.

One day my young daughter asked me, "Do you like being a mom?"

I was surprised. "Why do you ask?"

"You don't look happy," she said. Children are sensitive to slight changes in countenance, an important lesson I learned from a five-year-old who stopped me mid-chore and began rubbing the skin on my forehead.

"What are you doing?" I asked.

"I'm getting rid of your mad."

My "mad," as she called it, was a wrinkled forehead, which apparently is my unconscious reaction to stress. "Mommy, don't show your mad," my children used to plead when they were young. It has been a poignant reminder to me. Children ought to know that being a mother is a joyful experience. They deserve to hear it, too, but they ought to be able to read it on our faces as well. Laughing eyes or smiles say, "I'm happy. I like what I'm doing." If we're joyful mothers, we need to notify our faces. Our children will get the message either way.

I like the advice of British poet Matthew Green. "Fling but a stone, the giant dies. / Laugh and be well."[1] Humor is such a stone. With so many giants confronting our children, we do well to make sure they don't leave home without it. We can be sure that the scorners, the mockers, and the scoffers will come. Those who can laugh at themselves will be impervious to the world's weapons.

NOTE

1. Matthew Green, *The Spleen* (1737), line 69, quoted in *Bartlett's Familiar Quotations,* 16th ed. (Boston: Little, Brown and Company, 1992), 307.

ROLLER-COASTER PARENTING

JANENE WOLSEY BAADSGAARD

Can you remember your first time on a roller-coaster ride? I remember too well, especially that first big hill. I clenched my teeth, held on so tight my knuckles went white, and wondered hysterically, "Why did I ever want to go on this ride? I must be crazy. I know I'm going to pass out, throw up, fall out, and die!"

I was terrified, and it must have shown, because my mother took one look at me and yelled, "*Scream,* Janene, *scream!*" I followed her advice and let out a blood-curdling scream. A strange thing happened. The ride didn't suddenly become any less scary, but I started having a good time because I quit trying to hide my fear. Family life is like that. You find yourself laughing one minute, screaming the next. Motherhood especially is one colossal, wild journey full of ups and downs, twists and turns. One of the important quests in life is to discover what frees us up to enjoy the ride.

Most of us are like my young son Joseph. One day after he had been caught punching his brother and I plastered him with a reprimand, he lowered his eyebrows and grumbled back at me, "Why did we have to come down from heaven anyway?"

"Why, Joseph," I answered, "when you were in heaven,

Janene Wolsey Baadsgaard, a homemaker and freelance writer, is the author of several books on family matters. She has been a columnist for the *Deseret News,* written articles for the *New Era* and the *Ensign,* and taught at Utah Valley State College. She serves as the home and family education teacher in her ward Relief Society. She and her husband, Ross, are the parents of nine children.

you shouted for joy because you were so happy about the chance to come down to earth and get a body and experience everything here."

"Oh yeah?" Joseph answered. "Well, if I did, I was just teasing."

Joseph expresses well what many of us feel when we're faced with life on the uphill side. Like that first big hill on the roller-coaster ride, we find ourselves wondering, "Why did we have to come down from heaven anyway?" In 2 Nephi 2:25 we learn why: "Men are, that they might have joy." Do we really believe that? Do we really believe that the reason we exist— men, women, and children—is to have joy? Then why are all of us so serious so much of the time?

Feeling joy and finding humor can be learned, practiced, reinforced, and internalized just like any other skill. Humor is not just telling jokes but a way of looking at life and responding to it positively. When we decide to respond to life this way in spite of our circumstances, it's easier to find the silly or absurd around us. Take, for example, the church bulletin board notice announcing: "There will be meetings in the north and south ends of the church. Children will be baptized on both ends." Or the sign on a hospital bulletin board: "Research shows that the first five minutes of life can be the most risky." Someone alert to absurdity had penciled underneath: "The last five minutes are pretty risky, too."

Humor's lenses allow us not only to see what's funny around us but to deflate a bit of life's very real troubles. One concentration camp survivor advised her daughter: "Take life lightly. . . . Pain is inevitable, but suffering is optional." That is a profound thought. We can't control what happens to us, but we can choose how to respond. I think of the well-known athlete being carried off the football field with a serious injury. The newspapers reported that through clenched teeth he quipped to the stretcher-bearers, "My mother was right. I'm so glad I have on clean underwear."

79

To keep healthy we not only have to exercise and eat right, we have to laugh regularly and think right. People who treat a stress or a threat as a challenge rather than as a negative event generally have more fun and energy to cope with everyday difficulties. With our families or on the job, humor can break a conflict cycle and foster cooperative solutions to problems. One wife tells of a time when she and her husband had started arguing and couldn't stop the cycle. Because they were both being dramatic anyway, she decided to play out the scene to the hilt. She clutched her heart and threw herself on the floor, yelling, "Oh you're so right it's killing me!" Her sudden burst of insanity drained the steam out of the conflict. Another wife released her resentment over her husband's too-frequent hunting trips by placing a classified advertisement: "Husband for sale cheap. Comes complete with hunting and fishing equipment, one pair of jeans, two shirts, boots, black Labrador retriever, and too many pounds of venison. Pretty good guy, but not home much from October to December and from April to October. Will consider trade." After approximately sixty-six phone calls, some of them serious, the wife placed another ad: "Retraction of husband for sale cheap. Everybody wants the dog, not the husband." Being able to laugh—instead of bemoaning our fate or resenting other people—is mentally healthy.

I admit it isn't always easy to reverse a bad mood. When I'm having a bad day or dark thoughts, I can usually change the way I feel by changing the way I think. I start that mental process by mentally finishing this thought: "I am so grateful for . . ." Joy comes when I pay attention to all the things I'm grateful for instead of all my problems. While I was in bed because of premature labor a few years ago, I became telephone buddies with Blanche, a woman who was confined to bed because of a stroke. Before her stroke, Blanche had been wheelchair bound for thirty years because of a doctor's devastating error in surgery. Her husband, unable to face the trauma, left her to raise their four children alone. Now bedridden, she had every reason to focus on what she had lost. Instead, in our telephone conversations she chose to focus on what she had retained. From her bedroom window, Blanche could see a single tree. During our conversations, she would describe in detail the intricate changes the seasons brought to her tree. "It's such a miracle to be able to see," Blanche said one day. "I have so much to live for. I am so grateful I can see."

Blanche spoke with the same detail of her grandchildren. Unable to walk, often alone, Blanche could have been miserable. Instead she chose gratitude. And her grateful heart showered her with beauty and blessings everywhere she looked, even when her entire landscape was limited to a tiny bedroom.

Over the weeks of waiting for my baby to reach end of term, I took prenatal lessons from Blanche on celebrating life: I am the only one who can give my children a mother who loves life, no matter what. I learned from watching her to see life as it really is. Life as it really is—even not at its best—is downright amazing.

I sometimes forget, however, that I don't experience true joy on a smooth celestial highway. To experience joy, I have to experience its opposite. Without sorrow and pain, like the uphill climb on the roller coaster, there is no hill to descend, no thrill or reward, no true joy.

Before I met Blanche, I had learned this lesson the hard way. One evening, soon after my husband and I moved into our first new home, we seeded our front yard with grass. The next morning my husband told me it was important to keep the dirt wet or the grass seeds wouldn't sprout. Then he kissed me on the cheek and left for work.

Since it was the middle of a hot July, this wet-dirt assignment was a full-time job. On top of that, I was pregnant and had two baby daughters to care for. I remember standing out on the front porch, feeling lightheaded and nauseated, squirting the dirt for hours while my one- and two-year-old daughters tumbled down the steps, threw their shoes in the ditch, and stuffed tiny rocks up their noses. After days and days of constant watering, our front yard began growing the biggest, greenest weeds in the whole neighborhood.

"This is my life," I remember mumbling as I sprayed the dirt. "All I do is water weeds. I feed one end of the girls and clean up the other. Nothing I do really matters. All I do is water weeds."

A few days later, I started having serious complications with my pregnancy, and late one night I began hemorrhaging. My husband quickly called a neighbor to watch our children and raced me to the emergency room of the nearest hospital. After the doctor arrived at the hospital and slowed the bleeding, he told us that our baby had died.

Leaving the hospital that night with empty arms was one of the hardest things I've ever done. When we arrived home, we found our two baby daughters asleep on our bed. Now, I'd always loved my daughters but never quite as I did at that moment.

"Thank you, God," I whispered. "They are alive. It is such a miracle to have a child who is alive."

Several days later when I went out to check on our front lawn of weeds, I found something I hope I never forget. If I got down on my hands and knees and took out a magnifying glass, I could see tiny green blades of grass so fine they looked like green sewing thread. All my watering was starting to pay off. It occurred to me that perhaps all the work involved in caring for a family was like our newly seeded lawn. It seems to be all work and weeds at first. It's hard to see the tender seedlings or take joy in their growing. But in time my children, like the lawn, will not require my constant care, and our mutual growing season in my home will have passed all too quickly.

So let's not put off living and loving and laughing. The joy of life is in the ride. So stop waiting. Eat more ice cream, go barefoot, watch more sunsets, laugh more, cry less, let out a few screams, and get into the adventure of it. Let's quit viewing life as a long, hard, uphill ride to the ultimate destination of heaven. I'm sure heaven will be wonderful, but so is life right now. There is more joy and wonder right here in our own lives than we are willing or able to enjoy. Just think . . . all this and heaven, too!

REPLY

KARROL LYMAN COREY

Can you see to drive? my son asks.
Mother, you look like an old woman.
Why don't you drive with the seat close
and the back straight?

I am an old woman:
wrinkles and eyes;
I'm last year's potato wintering
in a dark cellar.
My nine lives raising children
—one mother's life per child—
are calendars stacked and
tipping.
        I'm six hundred and sixty.
My teenagers spilled me like
a jigsaw puzzle around the TV
and by the front window.

My grandchildren find pieces of me
in sandboxes, in jump-rope chants,
and by moonlight through elm branches.

Karrol Lyman Corey, a piano and children's singing instructor, earned a bachelor of music degree from Brigham Young University and composed the music and lyrics for the recent Utah Centennial musical, *Deseret,* performed in Delta, Utah. She teaches the Gospel Doctrine class in her ward Sunday School. She and her husband, David L. Corey, are the parents of nine children.

They think they have found everything—
an eye, an elbow, a bumpy thumbnail.
I stretch and cover to make whole
the warped parts of ages.

When the car door opens and I get out,
I'll stand for a measure of time,
then my legs will muscle in to carry me.
God, with his crystal stone, has the key
to my illegible word search,
knows where the worn-away answers
and pieces of light have blown.
His breath will gather me whole.

LOOSEN UP AND LAUGH

LORI BOYER

For me, humor is the WD40™ in the grind of everyday life. Humor rescues me from friction in countless crucial ways. First, I find humor can diffuse the tension and douse the sparks in very volatile situations. My husband will always be grateful to a man who saved him with humor from a terribly embarrassing incident. Richard had been invited to his high school girlfriend's home for a formal, no-holds-barred, linen-and-fine-china Sunday dinner. For a teenage boy, fathers and fine china are unwelcome prospects. But he really liked this girl and recognized the significance of the invitation. He wanted to make a good impression, so he dressed up, sought a briefing from his mother on dinner etiquette, and arrived at his girlfriend's house reasonably well prepared.

The whole family was there, a large family. He was the only guest. After the blessing on the food, the girl's father turned to my husband and said, "Richard, please pass the salt and pepper."

Richard, praying that no one would notice his hand was shaking, picked up the crystal salt and pepper shakers, reached out to hand them to the father, but instead dropped them in a goblet of ice water. To his horror, the goblet shattered, spilling water everywhere.

Lori Duncan Boyer received her bachelor's degree in elementary education and special education at the University of Utah. A homemaker, she and her husband, Richard Boyer, have eight children. Lori serves as Relief Society president in her ward.

A long painful silence ensued during which Richard fervently wished to disappear. Then the father said amiably, "Richard, please pass the salt water."

Everyone doubled over with laughter, and the tension was broken. The father's gentle joke was a way of saying, "It's okay, Richard; we always shatter the goblets and spill our water. You'll fit right in here."

What could have been a humiliating experience is instead a funny memory. Although the daughter relinquished Richard to me, he is still very good friends with her whole family.

My brother-in-law is also a master at turning potential fiascos into fun. When he and my sister were first married, she was nervously getting ready for her first back-to-school night as a high school history teacher. She was much closer in age to the students than to the parents. Thoughts of presenting to them her teaching plan for the year thoroughly intimidated her.

For dinner she put some chicken pot pies in the oven. When her husband came home from work, she asked him to listen for the timer, get the pies out, and call her in from the other room where she would be getting dressed. After a bit, she heard the creak of the oven door, followed by a crash and resounding clatter. Already tense, she snapped, "That better not have been the pot pies!"

When there was no answer from the kitchen, she assumed Jim had knocked a pan off the counter or dropped a lid or something. She returned to mental rehearsals and distracted hair combings. When Jim called, she headed to the kitchen. On the floor in front of the oven was a modest mound of chicken pot pies. Surrounding the pies on the floor were place mats, silverware, and Jim, looking eager to eat. Not only did she laugh, but she joined him on the floor and went off to back-to-school night fortified by chicken pot pie à la linoleum and the thought that, really, very few things in life are worth getting uptight over.

Second, humor is a great attention-getter. As a parent of

eight, I find myself repeating lectures so often even I get bored with them. Often my kids are bored, too. In fact, they even have numbers for the lectures. When I begin the discourse on the dangers of leaving backpacks by the door so that a mother trips over them, they have been known to nudge each other and say, "Here goes lecture number 6." Sometimes my lectures are so memorable they can even recite them with me. I try to convince them that I give the same lectures day after day because things just don't get done. But sometimes a fresh approach gets the point across better. For example, one night at dinner everyone had forgotten their table manners. Eight hungry, grabby, gabby children proved oblivious to lecture number 3 on what napkins and silverware are for and number 11 on transporting food without injuring others at the table. By the end of the meal my husband and I knew we had to try a new tactic. The next night, dinner began as usual, but as soon as he heard the amen on the blessing, my husband yelled, "Lori, the casserole!"

I scooped out a huge blob of casserole and catapulted it down to Richard's end of the table with an overhand shot. About one-third landed on his plate, one-third on his lap, and one-third on the dog's head. Richard immediately frisbeed a tortilla to my end of the table and then dived ravenously into the Mexicali casserole on his lap. I, meantime, was shoveling food into my mouth as fast as I could and elbowing everyone around me. The children froze in horror. Then they started laughing. It was the funniest lecture they had ever seen.

Without knowing whether this tactic would prove effective in changing their behavior, we at least held their attention. They would remember what it is like to sit next to someone who chews open-mouthed. They would remember what it's like to get an elbow in the jaw as someone dives for the salad. They would remember the appetite-suppressing experience of watching food vacuumed from plate to mouth without the interference of utensils. They would remember getting tackled from behind as they reached for the salsa. Gross as we were, they recognized some similarities to their own table manners, and it shocked them a little. We noted enough improvement that we haven't yet felt a need for an encore.

In many ways, humor rescues me from insanity. In *Parenting Isn't for Cowards,* James Dobson says, "Laughter is the key to survival during the special stresses of the child-rearing years. If you can see the delightful side of your assignment, you can also deal with the difficult."[1] Humor can also soothe anxiety. It can be an important coping mechanism not only for us but for our children. Humor helps them cope with genuine fears. Halloween is a very important holiday for this reason. In an education class I took, the instructor confirmed that it is healthy for children to drag out costumes of monsters, grotesquely deformed bogeymen, and frightening spooks. Laughing at them helps keep fears manageable. If children are never allowed to face their fears and make light of them or talk about them, they become much bigger and more bothersome.

Understanding humor's role in calming anxiety guides me in handling my children's sometimes inappropriate joking. Sometimes children laugh at people who are handicapped or look different. Though this must not be tolerated, realizing that it's a way of dealing with their own fears of being injured or different helps me respond patiently. When children laugh at someone tripping or someone provoking the teacher, they may be dealing with anxieties about getting hurt or their own worries about authority.

Crude humor and bathroom talk also need not be tolerated, but it helps us correct the problem without overreacting if we understand that children are expressing concerns about bodily functions. Laughter distances children from situations and feelings that disturb them. It is a form of self-comfort.

My children are exposed to plenty of cruel, crude, and inappropriate humor away from home. I want to prepare them to distinguish between what is really funny and what is not. A

89

loving home is a safe place to teach the difference between teasing and ridicule. Good-natured kidding can be a way of acknowledging people, letting them know they are okay. But tender personal struggles such as bed-wetting, thumb-sucking, stuttering, or size are never safe to kid about. There is often a fine line between kidding and hurtful teasing or ridicule. When a child wants the joke to end, respect that wish, because the child is the best barometer of when the line has been crossed.

And finally, humor can teach humility. In fact, my parting advice on mothering is, Loosen up and laugh. If the home isn't a safe place to make mistakes, no place will be.

NOTE

1. James C. Dobson, *Parenting Isn't for Cowards: Dealing Confidently with the Frustrations of Child-Rearing* (Waco, Texas: Word Books, 1987), 101.

ON THE TAKING OF HEARTS

NANCY BAIRD

It was on a beach,
on an emerald island.
There was sun, the heat toiled.
A child came down the sand
running and leaping, arms
and legs blurring
in a weightless flash, flung—
a whippet of white flame from
some other world . . . And the people
on the beach lowered
their books of tales
to watch the child . . . Oh let it never end—
listen to the song she makes!—
her small body a perfect chord of gladness,
her fingers and toes tasseling
in the bright morning—it is never
too late . . .
But she leaves, in one heartbeat
is gone, the space
of her fills with salt spray,
the people rustle and breathe, are burned
in the bone, grieve
as the fragrance of blessedness
sweeps the beach
and the sea claims her footprints.

Nancy Hanks Baird was named Utah Poet of the Year in 1996. She received her bachelor's degree in English from Brigham Young University and has worked as a freelance writer and editor. She and her husband, John K. Baird, are the parents of five children. She is the Gospel Doctrine teacher in her ward Sunday School in Salt Lake City.

PRAY WITH ALL ENERGY OF HEART

ANN N. MADSEN

I met fourteen-year-old Julie Wang twenty-three years ago in K'Liau, Taiwan. She was a new convert to Mormonism. We corresponded, and later she came to visit America and stayed with us. I asked her to teach my Mia Maid class about prayer. She said shyly, "What can I teach them?" I said, "Just tell them how you pray." So she did. "I pray like this," she said. "I say, 'Hello, God, this is Julie Wang,' then I wait, and he says, 'Hello, Julie.'" My class and I were taken off-guard by her simple faith in a God who is alive, listening, and ready to respond. She taught all of us that day. One thing I have learned is that there are as many ways to pray as there are people. The one prerequisite is that we "pray . . . with all . . . energy of heart" (Moroni 7:48).

How does prayer work? I don't presume to offer you a paradigm, a perfect pattern for everyone. Instead, I want to examine my own prayer life, beginning with my earliest memory of my sweet father saying in our family prayers, "We come to thee on the bended knees of our body, Father." How humble that made me feel.

Today, I love to pray. Ask my husband. I'm always poking

Ann N. Madsen is the mother of four, including an Indian foster son, and the grandmother of sixteen. She teaches in the Department of Ancient Scripture at Brigham Young University and has taught at the BYU Jerusalem Center for Near Eastern Studies, where her husband, Truman G. Madsen, was director. She teaches the Gospel Doctrine class in her Provo ward Sunday School.

him and saying, "Shouldn't we pray now?" But I didn't always love to pray. Nine milestones in my own prayer history will illustrate how this process unfolded in me. I hope these will bring similar moments to your mind.

1. Under the old-fashioned, six-foot-high rose bush, which was like a cave to an eight-year-old, I made my first attempt the week after my baptism at praying for repentance. I had lied about practicing the piano. I'd messed up my music books to look like I had practiced, but I'd put in only half the time I'd claimed. Prior to my baptism, my father had done a good job of explaining personal responsibility to me. He almost scared me to death, I think, and I'm so grateful. In that solitary confinement of my rose bush, I knew enough to cry a bit, say how sorry I was, and ask for help not to tell lies ever again. I soon found that I sometimes *did* do it again and that the best of intentions wavered when friends called me to come out to play. I learned to repent until I got it right.

I've continued to learn in the fifty-plus years since my baptism. I have learned to say I'm sorry when I pray, to take my shame humbly before the Lord, to take responsibility for my actions. During the sacrament is an especially meaningful time to do this. I'm learning to forgive—everybody, everything, every time—because I truly want to be forgiven. I'm also learning to pray to love those more whom I have loved less. I understand why God requires this of us. He loves us all more. He wants us to be like him. I understand all this much better than I did that first time as a newly baptized member weeping under a sheltering rose bush.

2. Even saying the word *Brighton* stirs deep feelings in me. I was thirteen years old and just finishing an idyllic week at the Brighton MIA Girls' Camp in Big Cottonwood Canyon. It was Sunday, and sitting in tall meadow grasses on a mountainside strewn with white granite boulders on a sunny, summer day,

we had listened to an inspired Sunday School teacher bear witness to us. Then all of us knelt together in the tall grass, almost invisible to any passerby, while a young man about to serve a mission prayed in a way I had never heard before—he addressed God directly—and suddenly I didn't dare open my eyes because I knew for certain that God was a person and I felt him unmistakably near. At that moment and ever since, I have known that God is a living, loving, powerful being. After the others had wandered back down the trail, my best friend and I knelt once more, hidden under an overhanging pine bough. We didn't say much to each other, but we each knelt down and poured out our hearts in gratitude. We both knew what had happened and felt a tremendous need to tell the Lord how grateful we were that we'd come to know him.

I have learned since then that kneeling and speaking aloud to our Father in a quiet place daily gives focus to my faith. I have a window in my walk-in closet, and I pray there at dawn, each morning. I enter my closet and shut the door, exactly as the scriptures direct. I feel really good just to have done that much right each day.

We can pray any place, any time—beside a mountain trail at Brighton, kneeling in a closet, anywhere. We are the ones who choose the when and the where. No time is wrong. The only prerequisite is a broken heart and a contrite spirit. And I think *broken* can mean more than the painful process we think of in repentance. *Broken* can also mean open, not hardened and inaccessible but open and ready to receive, to make place for the Lord's direction. The scriptures teach us to "pray *always,* and I will pour out my Spirit upon you, and great shall be your blessing" (D&C 19:38; emphasis added). Does this mean keeping up a running conversation with the Lord every waking hour? Yes! He has taught, "Look unto me in *every* thought; doubt not, fear not" (D&C 6:36; emphasis added). So be informal; be formal; be all ways prayerful. Formal, kneeling prayers help us focus and cut out distractions. Consider locking the door, turning off the phone, savoring the silence. Perhaps setting your alarm for ten to fifteen minutes earlier than usual would enable you to enjoy the quiet before the three-year-old gets up or the baby cries. When we reverently enter the presence of the Lord in prayer, we can feel like guests in heaven.

3. A few months after my mountaintop experience at Brighton, well after midnight one night, I finished reading the Book of Mormon for the first time. I had been reading it in my closet, because my dad had told me to turn off the light. (I was devious then, I confess.) I had excitedly finished, anxious to put Moroni's promise to the test. My dear teacher and friend, Oscar Hunter, week after week, pleaded with a group of youth attending his weekly ward fireside not to take his word only but to find out for ourselves. He urged us to read the Book of Mormon and do exactly what Moroni invites. At last, I could ask that prayer, because I had finished the book from cover to cover—except those tedious chunks of Isaiah, which I didn't understand. (This makes my students, children, and husband smile because I now teach Isaiah classes at BYU.)

As I knelt beside my bed, I was excited, full of faith, and prepared to entertain an angel should my answer come by that means. I used Moroni's words exactly: "I am asking with a sincere heart, with real intent, having faith in Christ, if this book is not true." (I remember wondering why it said "is not true." Why don't I ask if it "is true"? But the scriptures said "is not true," and I didn't dare say any other words because I wanted Moroni's promise to be answered.) In the guileless innocence of youth I repeated that plea over and over. I resolved I would not get up from my knees until I had my answer. After what seemed a very long time, it came. In an unmistakable way I felt the Spirit from my head to my toes, filling me with a warmth I could not deny. I remember a heartfelt thank-you as I jumped to my feet, rushed to my window, and barely restrained myself from shouting to all the world, "It's true! Joseph Smith is a prophet!" Thus began a lifelong study that continues to this moment. I can never get enough of the gospel of Jesus Christ. I learned for myself about the Holy Ghost and the reality of the Restoration—and I learned that God truly answers prayers.

Since that singular day, I have learned to ask for the daily guidance of the Holy Ghost. I have experienced what Isaiah describes when he says, "Thine ears shall hear a word behind thee, saying, This is the way, walk ye in it" (Isaiah 30:21). The Holy Ghost guides us into the will of God and away from temptation. He speaks directly to my spirit. Sometimes, when I have made up my mind, he causes me to question my confidence. At other, less-certain times, when I am confused or discouraged, I have learned to ask what I should pray for—ask in a prayer what to say in a prayer. As I learned from Paul's writing to the Romans: "Likewise the Spirit also helpeth our infirmities: for we know not what we should pray for as we ought: but the Spirit itself maketh intercession for us with *sighings*[1] which cannot be uttered" (Romans 8:26).

Joseph Smith made significant changes in that verse. "The Spirit maketh intercession for us with *striving* which cannot be *expressed*."[2]

So the Holy Ghost translates and delivers our pleadings and praises to our Father even when we can't find the words to express our deepest joy or darkest sorrow. When you can't find words, trust the Spirit. Modern revelation teaches us: "He that asketh in Spirit shall receive in Spirit. . . . He that asketh in the Spirit asketh according to the will of God; wherefore it is done even as he asketh" (D&C 46:28, 30).

4. In the following years, my testimony grew, as I listened intently in seminary and then ate up every word offered me at the University of Utah institute of religion. The summer after high school I met and fell in love with a handsome young man—who was not a Latter-day Saint. We began reading the

Book of Mormon together, and I was sure he would join the Church. In the middle of this process, he begged me to marry him. I thought I would—one year to the day after he was baptized, when we could go to the temple. My prayers began to move from, "I know how great my joy will be with this one soul I'm bringing to you" to "Father, should I marry Bob?"

I was a freshman at the University of Utah, working part-time at ZCMI during the Christmas break. Almost the moment I began asking the second prayer, "Is Bob the man I should marry?" a series of experiences and thoughts cumulatively answered me a resounding no! I remember the day the thought came, "Weren't you going to marry a returned missionary?" and I wondered when I had lost sight of that goal. Probably in the moonlight at Zion National Park, where we had worked the summer before. Day after day a former goal or idea surfaced in my mind. It was as if the Lord were saying to me gently but firmly, "What is it you don't understand about 'no'?" Finally, after about eight days of asking, I owned the answer to my prayer and told Bob no. I had learned that God could communicate clearly to me on important matters and could say no.

Since that painful day when I said no, even though I was sorely tempted to say yes, I have learned to pray to recognize temptations, no matter how subtle, and for the strength to flee from sin once recognized and to avoid going counter to God's will for me. Marrying Bob would have been going against God's will, which I was tempted to do. Temptation itself is not sin. In fact, as Elder Rulon G. Craven points out, temptation serves a purpose: we learn where we truly are when we are tempted; our strengths and weaknesses become brightly apparent to us as we respond to each temptation.[3] It's hard but it's true. Life is truly a test. I have learned to pray for the strength to meet challenges, not to have them removed.

"Resist the devil, and he will flee from you" (James 4:7) is our sure promise. I teach that to my New Testament students, to my Isaiah students, to my Old Testament Roots students. In every class I teach, some time during the semester I tell them the great secret: "Resist the devil, and he will flee from you."

How grateful I am that Jesus taught us to meet temptation by paying no heed to it. I know we can lose all desire for sin. One day we will simply ignore the devil, not interested in the least in what he offers because we are so mightily interested in the promises of our Father to share all he has with us. So, I don't just pray not to be led into temptation, I pray to be led into understanding God's will for me. The basic purpose of prayer may well be to find out the will of God and then to ask for faith and strength to carry it out.

5. I told my granddaughter the other day that from the moment I broke off that "first love" relationship, I prayed about every boy I dated. It was tedious. "Is this the man I am going to marry?"—and I would supply the name of my latest date. That is when I learned to continue in prayer, using "vain" repetition. I learned a modicum of patience but got tired of repeating those same words over and over again, filling in the blank. But one night, standing with Truman Madsen on a northern hillside overlooking the Salt Lake Valley, which was a jewel box of lights, I heard the whispered voice of the Spirit, "This is the man you're going to marry"—and I didn't believe it. I remember shaking my head and scolding myself for entertaining such a notion, but then it came again with more force. And yet again. And I learned how the Holy Ghost speaks with us, Spirit to spirit, putting words not our own into our minds in the customized, unmistakable way only he can communicate to each of us individually. I learned one way God can say yes. That was one of the most pivotal yesses I was ever able to recognize.

How do we know when our prayers are being answered? Sometimes we don't. Sometimes we don't want to, like investigators who put off praying to know if the Church is true because they are not ready to shoulder the responsibility of knowing.

I am continuing to learn how to recognize answers that come in unexpected ways. Sometimes he tells us directly "in our minds and in our hearts," in words, like my answer on that breezy hilltop overlooking the Salt Lake Valley. I am learning to sort out his impressions from my own ideas. Sometimes I have a lot of great ideas. I want to do a lot of good things, and sometimes I can't tell whether it's really the Lord that wants me to do it or whether it's only my wanting to do it. It's one of the biggest problems I have. From Isaiah I've learned that the Lord's thoughts are not my thoughts—they are higher. "Neither are your ways my ways"; his are higher (Isaiah 55:8–9). That's how I can tell the difference. Sometimes a three-year-old's scripture, spoken confidently by heart on a Primary program, matches precisely my need. At times the opening hymn may tell me all he wishes to communicate to me, or the closing hymn, or the sacrament hymn. I bear you my witness that has been true for me. Often the gentle words of a friend, even the friends in my own home—my husband, my children, my grandchildren—hold the answer. And, don't forget, God has been giving answers for a long, long time and commanded those who received them to take notes. Search the scriptures. Your answer might be waiting for you there.

6. I began praying for children before Truman and I were even married, and from the moment we were married, we both prayed earnestly to begin our family. Truman was beginning his four-year Ph.D. work at Harvard. It never occurred to us to postpone our family. Kneeling at that altar in the Salt Lake Temple, we felt more than ready to welcome children into our home. (That's how young and ignorant we were—who is ever fully ready for children?) For nine months our pleading for children seemed to produce nothing, and I feared I would never have a child. Then I was pregnant! Five years later when

Truman was a bishop and we had three children under four, I was frenzied but fulfilled. We were a year into Truman's teaching career at Brigham Young University. I went to my obstetrician at this point, anticipating that he would tell me that I was expecting our fourth child. (Our third was about seven months old at this time.) Instead, he told me I was not pregnant but had a problem.

During the next few years I had tests and surgery to enable me to bear more children. But the fear I had early in my marriage of not being able to bear children was now a reality. We prayed, pleading with the Lord to enable us to have more children. Then we were called to New England, where Truman would be a thirty-five-year-old mission president and I would be a twenty-nine-year-old "mission mother" and our three children under seven would live for the next three years in a wonderful old mission home. This, of course, was an amazing moment in our little family's life. When my doctor heard we would be in Boston, he was elated: the world-renowned Dr. John Rock had established the Rock Infertility Clinic there. I felt confident that this was to be the answer to our prayers.

After a thorough course of treatment, Dr. Rock gave me the medical verdict. I had evidently gone through a very early menopause and would have no more children. I was devastated. President Hugh B. Brown was touring our mission, and I asked him for a blessing. If the best of medical science couldn't do it, I was sure the Lord could handle it and, after all, I was serving him on a mission right now. It was only logical. Right? *Wrong*. In his eloquent blessing President Brown told me to "trouble the Lord no more on this matter." After I had cried my heart out, I asked President Brown what that meant, and he explained very simply that in my prayers I should no longer beg for a child. I learned about another kind of no. I learned to obey, to endure something that was totally against my will. I was *beginning* to learn "thy will, *not mine*, be done." That day I stopped praying for a baby.

7. During the years when our children were growing up, I performed a small ritual as I lay in bed after family prayer. I would put the name of each child before the Lord so that I could analyze the unique challenges he or she faced. Then I would ask for the Lord's help in being his instrument to nurture and guide. It was such a tender task. I looked forward to it and to the mornings that followed when many of my queries were answered quietly during that clean slate time of just after awakening.

One of my great concerns during those late-night reveries was how to teach each of our children to really pray—to open conduits to their Heavenly Father. I remember thinking that this would be the best insurance we could leave them if anything should happen to us before they were grown. And so I prayed that they would learn that God hears and answers prayers.

About this time, during a severe drought, when the Wasatch Mountains had never greened through spring and summer, President Spencer W. Kimball asked us as a church to fast for rain on an appointed day. Our family did. During family home evening, we heard the rain begin to fall on the metal roof of our patio. It was an electric moment. At first it was just a few drops, but soon it was a torrent. We all ran outside, and one of our children said, "Let's kneel down here with the rain falling on us to thank the Lord." Then we all put around small bottles to catch the water. I've kept mine since that day; it's full of "holy" water. Our children learned part of the lesson then; God indeed hears and answers prayers. Their dripping faces and soaking clothes and water bottles clutched in their damp hands were tangible proof.

In addition, they learned that uniting our prayers with others changes the equation. Later, temple experiences taught them of a united upward reach, made more effective by kind feelings, full of love. Unity is powerful in prayer. Personal prayers reflected in family prayers make us one in purpose. I love to hear my husband use the exact words in our morning prayer that I have uttered in solitude just moments earlier in my own personal prayer. It is a wonderful coming together. To paraphrase a statement we all know, "If ye are one, ye are mine."

During the years since my first halting prayers, I have uttered many kinds of prayers. "Telegraph prayers" use a few, simple words to tell our urgent need or joy. I don't think the Lord expects beautiful, poetic words when we're in a crisis. I remember standing outside of a hospital x-ray room saying just, "Save her. Save her, please, save her."

Sometimes the crisis is one of personal survival. God also hears self-centered prayer, when survival is all that matters. As we work our way out of depression, we move thankfully from focusing on our own coping to noticing once more the needs of others around us. I speak from personal experience in this regard. What a blessed moment when we are able to reach out once more, stretch forth our hand in the pattern we learn from the Lord, to name the names of many others as we pray, seeking to bless their lives. One day recently I numbered the times I said, "Please bless *me*." It was appalling. I don't recommend that exercise. But if survival requires all our focus for a time, we can rejoice in the hope of a moment when we will lose our ego-centered view and see again the whole wide world who needs our ministrations. We can then fill our prayers with the names of others.

Pray from the heart, a broken heart, a contrite spirit. It's our hearts that need to change and will change.

8. It was a splendid, starry night in the Caribbean, my first and last time on a small yacht. The next day we would fly home after one of the most spiritual weeks of my life, during which we had attended the dedication of the Washington Temple. I remember it now with just as much joy as I felt then. I think of it often when I need to remember; when I need to feel the Holy Ghost telling me again that it was a high point in

my life. We were with beloved friends who had also attended the dedication, and the relaxed atmosphere and perfect weather were a great catalyst for long gospel conversations—a continuation of the Spirit we had felt at the temple.

One of those inspiring exchanges was in progress when I decided to go up on deck, just one more time, to see the stars. I climbed into a hammock and found myself totally alone under a magnificent canopy of stars. As I lay there in utter contentment, I was gradually flooded with gratitude. I began to name the individual reasons for my joy, counting stars as I did. The stars seemed endless, and so did my thanks. As I catalogued each one, beginning with Truman, I would add a sentence explaining one or more reasons for my joy. "Oh, Heavenly Father, I thank thee for Truman, for his integrity, for his patience with me, for his fidelity to me in a world where those words are almost unknown."

I warmed to the task, speaking aloud and at length about the temple, my family, my friends, each one on the boat and all over the world, my experiences one by one, and on and on, counting stars and equating them with my gratitude. What had begun as a list of blessings was continuing as a prayer. I soon realized this was the longest prayer I had ever offered, and I felt no need to stop. When I ran out of people, I counted sea and breezes and birds and flowers—I described them, and I would have included those beautiful blue flowers in England if I had known of them then. I even listed some qualities in myself, talents with which I had been blessed. Somehow it was easier to see them in this context. You can see how gratitude can be contagious.

Then I began to realize how I prized my knowledge of the Restoration and Joseph Smith. I had a lot to say about Joseph Smith. It was only natural to chronicle my joy in the Savior and his atoning for me. By then I was filled to the brim, and I didn't want to stop. I understood how Enos and others could have prayed all night. And with Enos I cried out in joy, "'Oh

Lord, how is it done?' How do you give me these feelings? How do I know the feeling of the Holy Ghost?" I wanted this feeling of love and joy never to end. But it did.

When we flew into Salt Lake the next evening, I was still trailing the clouds of gratitude I had felt. Our bishop was waiting for us in the rain. He had come to tell us that our Lamanite son had been sent home from his mission and put on Church probation. I think that after expressing gratitude for Truman, my prayer the night before had moved to this son, "Thank you that after eleven years, Larry is serving in the mission field."

I learned then that counting blessings with all energy of heart can be a glorious, communing experience and that it will fill you with love. I also learned that the love fortifies us for the pain and disappointment that are a part of this earth life. To paraphrase, after great blessings, cometh the tribulation.

On the boat, praying felt easy and natural, but I have also learned to pray when I don't feel like it. Sometimes we feel unworthy to pray; we avoid the process because we feel unclean, out of sorts, angry, hostile, or just plain tired. How Satan must laugh as we *abandon praying* instead of hurrying to our knees to be cleansed and nurtured.

"Prayer changes things" read a little sign sitting in the bookcase of my childhood home. I learned there that prayer is our pathway to mighty changes. When you don't feel like praying, read the words of the Lord. Read Jesus' tender invitation, "Come unto me, all ye that labour and are heavy laden, and I will give you rest" (Matthew 11:28). Come, he says over and over. Through Alma he implores us, "Come and fear not, and lay aside every sin, which easily doth beset you, . . . and show unto your God that ye are willing to repent of your sins and enter into a covenant with him" (Alma 7:15). The desire to pray will grow in you as you read the scriptures, and you will be able to close the book with renewed desire to speak with the author.

9. To say "Thy will be done" in matters of life and death, and mean it, requires tremendous faith and courage. Three and a half years ago our youngest daughter was literally bleeding to death just after her last child was delivered. Truman rushed to the hospital to help administer to her. I was left alone in her home with two sleeping grandchildren. Her newborn son slept in the hospital nursery. All three were oblivious to the fact that their mother was seriously at risk. But I wasn't. I paced and prayed and cried and gazed out into the black night.

"Thy will, *not mine,* be done." We mouth the words easily until someone we love deeply is at risk. I found it impossible even to mouth the words then, just in case it was *not* his will for her to live. At such moments we plead, "claiming" our imagined merit or theirs; we bargain with the Lord, not unlike Abraham as he bargained for a handful of the righteous in ancient, wicked cities. Sometimes, after the flailing around is finished, we sink again to our knees and whisper as quietly as we can, "Not my will but thine be done," barely able to muster the faith to say it.

I had not yet reached this point of submission. Instead, I paced and prayed, looked in on the children, and imagined various possible scenarios. Who could possibly love and support Grant as Mindy could? Who could rear those three little ones with the same dedication, inspiration, and flair? My agitation fed on itself, and I could see all would be better served if I focused my faith on the miracle needed. "Please stop the bleeding," I pleaded over and over, weeping as I spoke.

Then I learned what the Lord meant when he said, "Did I not speak peace to your mind concerning the matter? What greater witness can you have than from God?" (D&C 6:23). In the midst of my churning emotions, an unmistakable calm came over me. "Everything is going to be all right." It was a clear message, but I quickly inserted into my running prayer, "But will she live?" because I knew everything could be all right but she could die. No answer. That's significant. No answer, but again, and with a serenity I have memorized, "Be at peace. Everything is going to be all right." And it was. She was anemic and weak for months but today is healthy and strong.

That same coin has another side, however. Just last year our family combined our faith to pray for the healing of a beloved friend with cancer. We asked for a miracle. We pleaded for a miracle. But he died. During the long year of his illness, we exercised faith for his recovery, and at moments it seemed to be happening. But finally this strong man gave himself over to the will of the Lord. There was a purity and grace about him during his final days. I learned from him the meaning of sanctification. We prayed often together. He no longer asked for his life to be prolonged—he was forty-three years old with a wife and three young children—but he quietly assured the Lord that he wanted nothing more than to see the Lord's will done. He didn't pray for himself. He prayed for us and others whom he loved. I watched his own will being swallowed up in the will of our Heavenly Father. So I began to exercise the faith that I hoped would prolong his life to aid him in this sacred process.

It has been a year since he died. I watched and learned, but I still struggle to understand God's purposes, to align my will with his. The process continues in me. I do not doubt God's wisdom, but I struggle to understand, to make that wisdom my own. I know that bringing that struggle to the Lord in prayer is my avenue to peace.

Life-and-death experiences continue to tutor me. I learned in those crisis times to "pray with all energy of heart." What other way was there? I learned to focus in ways I had never dreamed possible. That kind of prayer takes an amazing amount of energy and endurance and patience. I don't always manage it. We "underpray" far more often than we "overpray," skimming the surface, seldom dipping heart-deep. But I know now how it feels. How we can learn to look up! Reach up! Pray through tears. Pray steadfastly, patiently, but look up![4]

The words of the prophet Micah come to me readily when

I find myself looking down. "Therefore I will look unto the Lord; I will wait for the God of my salvation: my God will hear me. Rejoice not against me, O mine enemy: when I fall, I shall arise; when I sit in darkness, the Lord shall be a light unto me" (Micah 7:7–8). Don't rejoice, Mr. Devil. I may be down, but I'm not out! We can only be defeated if we refuse to get up, to look up, to reach up!

Isaiah teaches us that the Lord constantly reaches to us as he repeats over and over again, "His hand is stretched out still"—not just "out" but "*stretched* out."[5] How often the Lord asks throughout the book of Isaiah, "Is my arm too short to save you?" and the rhetorical question is answered with a resounding, "No!" We are his work and his glory. We are his first concern. We are, after all, his children. If we stretch to him, we will reach him. I picture the hands on the ceiling of the Sistine Chapel, all but touching. He longs to touch, grasp, and lift us to him.

These are the ideas about prayer that I hoped would be most helpful to you. I could go on and tell you how my mother taught me to love the words of St. Francis: "Lord, make me an instrument of thy peace."[6] She taught me that *all* people can know how to pray and approach God, not just Latter-day Saints.

Or, I'd tell you of sublime answers when I have prayed to be an instrument in the Lord's hands. Or I would tell you about my ongoing prayers to perfect my relationship with my cherished husband so that the promises given to us would launch us from our forty-three years so far into forever. Or I would tell you about the gentle guidance that came to me in answer to my prayers about this talk.

Mormon spoke the words which are my theme. Quoted by his son, Moroni, Mormon's words are the climax of a great sermon on charity, the pure love of Christ. "Pray unto the Father with all the energy of heart, that ye may be filled with this love, which he hath bestowed upon all who are true followers of his Son, Jesus Christ; that ye may become the sons [and daughters]

107

of God; that when he shall appear we shall be like him, for we shall see him as he is; that we may have this hope; that we may be purified even as he is pure" (Moroni 7:48). I know that we receive the Spirit through prayer and are thus given access to Christlike love. Our lives—mind, body, and spirit—are renewed in this process of sacred communion, and we become like him and like our Father in Heaven who loves and reaches out to each of us.

NOTES

1. I chose to use the alternate translation from the Greek here: *sighings* instead of *groanings*. See Romans 8:26, footnote d, in the LDS edition of the King James Version of the Bible.

2. Joseph Smith, *Teachings of the Prophet Joseph Smith,* sel. Joseph Fielding Smith (Salt Lake City: Deseret Book, 1970), 278.

3. Rulon G. Craven, "Temptation," *Ensign,* April 1996, 77.

4. See Russell M. Nelson, "Thou Shalt Have No Other Gods," *Ensign,* May 1996, 14–16.

5. See, for example, Isaiah 5:25; 9:12, 17, 21; 10:4.

6. Saint Francis of Assisi, "Make Me an Instrument of Thy Peace." See, for example, *Love Never Faileth: The Inspiration of Saint Francis, Saint Augustine, Saint Paul, and Mother Teresa,* by Eknath Easwaran (Petaluma, Calif.: Nilgiri Press, 1984), 18.

   Lord, make me an instrument of thy peace.
   Where there is hatred, let me sow love;
   Where there is injury, pardon;
   Where there is doubt, faith;
   Where there is despair, hope;
   Where there is darkness, light;
   Where there is sadness, joy.

   O divine Master, grant that I may not so much seek
   To be consoled as to console,
   To be understood as to understand,
   To be loved as to love:
   For it is in giving that we receive,
   It is in pardoning that we are pardoned,
   It is in dying to self that we are born to eternal life.

AN EARTH-LIFE THING

JEANNE EDMONDSON CARRAWAY

L ast summer my fifteen-year-old son received the first serious sunburn of his life, and as he gravely surveyed his blis-
tered skin, he asked, "Mom, do you think I'll be all right?"

"You'll be uncomfortable for a while," I replied, "but you'll
be all right."

I smiled as I thought about his choice of words, remembering a time I had asked a similar question. Almost thirty years
ago, aggressive radiation therapy for Hodgkin's disease (cancer
of the lymph system) had left a deep burn on my neck. My
doctors were worried that the skin in the area had deteriorated
to a precancerous state, so they scheduled a series of three
surgeries to remove the burned tissue and replace it with skin
and muscle from my right arm. As the surgeon explained
potential complications from the painful procedure, only one
seemed of any real concern to me: I could lose the use of my
right arm.

Later, at home, I sat in terror. I am right-handed. I shud-
dered to imagine the kind of life I might have without the use
of my arm. Questions raced and tumbled through my mind.
How would I write? Carry things? Lead music? Partake of the
sacrament in the prescribed way? Raise my right arm to the

Jeanne Edmondson Carraway, a career counselor, worked for many years as a newspaper
reporter and a freelance writer. She and her husband, Jack Hal Carraway, have one child.
She serves as her ward's music chairman. She began chemotherapy two days after returning from the 1996 Woman's Conference.

square? Participate fully in temple ordinances? In tears and on my knees, I pleaded with Heavenly Father. Finally, in the midst of my anguish, I had a strong, specific prompting. I felt rather than heard, "What do you want me to do?" Surprised, I thought a while and then replied, "I just want to know that everything is going to be all right." Then came a sustaining moment of peaceful sweetness that I still carry in my heart. He had answered, in the clearest, most specific response to a prayer I have ever received: "No matter what happens, everything will be all right."

I came out of the surgery with reduced use of my arm. Since then, I have gradually lost the ability to use it for most things. Cooking, canning, cleaning, and dressing are very difficult for me. I can do them all, but very slowly. I can lead music only with my left arm. I cannot attend the temple without help. I struggle to take the sacrament with my right hand, and my right arm, raised as high as it will go, doesn't come anywhere close to being at the square.

Over the years I have come to understand the Lord's message to me. It has sustained me through subsequent surgeries and treatments for thyroid, skin, and lung cancers that resulted from that first aggressive radiation therapy for Hodgkin's. I have gained great peace in the midst of frustration, turmoil, and uncertainty because those trials have taught me that truly, no matter what happens, everything will be far better than just "all right" if I trust the Lord and work to keep the challenges of earth life in perspective.

Elder Russell M. Nelson has said, "With celestial sight, trials impossible to change become possible to endure."[1] Celestial lenses, I have found, reveal things that are invisible to the earthbound eye. Through them, we can see what we can become, and what it will take to get there. As Paul told the Corinthians: "Our light affliction, which is but for a moment, worketh for us a far more exceeding and eternal weight of glory; while we look not at the things which are seen, but at the things which are not seen: for the things which are seen are temporal; but the things which are not seen are eternal" (2 Corinthians 4:17–18).

I served in the Indiana-Michigan Mission with a companion who inevitably responded to less-than-pleasant experiences by saying, "Well, it's just an earth-life thing." What she meant, of course, is that rocks and thistles are part of our earth experience, but they are temporary. And as the Lord told Joseph Smith, "If thou endure it well, God shall exalt thee on high" (D&C 121:8). But seeking celestial perspective reveals far more than a reward at the end of a difficult journey. Celestial spectacles have corrective lenses, allowing us sharper understanding of present experiences.

According to my mother, I have always been extremely independent, almost to a fault. My cancer crises have brought into focus how much I need help to journey successfully through this earth-life experience. For a number of years, I allowed the weakness of my right arm to keep me out of the temple. I pridefully chose not to go rather than ask for help. Finally, two persistent visiting teachers tackled my attitude and lovingly led me back to a place I had longed to be. It was not easy . . . for them or me! I felt embarrassed that I could not take care of my clothing myself. I wanted to be there, knew I had to be there. Yet at first, I cried every time I went. Sometimes my friends assisted me. Other times my helper was a temple worker. But help was always there, and inevitably, after the session, my helpers would thank me for allowing them to serve.

One day I was waiting in the Chicago Illinois Temple, thinking about my experiences, when I had one of those moments of "celestial sight." I realized that my inability to participate unaided in the temple has a corollary: I also cannot return to the presence of our Father without considerable assistance. I absolutely cannot do it alone. And that is the blessing of cancer for me. It has driven me to my knees, where I have begun to learn about the grace of the Lord Jesus Christ. He does for me what I cannot do for myself. He doesn't fix everything, but his presence in trial has given me strength to endure—with great joy. I have heard someone say that "joy is not the absence of pain but the presence of God." My experience tells me this is true.

As I put the finishing touches on this essay, I am sitting in familiar surroundings—the waiting room of my hospital's radiology department. A recent CT scan has revealed new and suspicious spots and shadows in my chest, so today I am having more tests. My oncologist will review the results and in a week or so tell me if it's cancer . . . again. As I consider the possibility, I am frustrated to think there may be another interruption in my life for treatment and recovery, more projects put on hold, more goals pushed aside. I am frustrated, but not afraid of the outcome, whatever it may be. My experiences have given me access to a celestial perspective to help me find my way over this rocky terrain. Again and again I have found peace, and I will once more. No matter what happens, everything will be all right.

NOTE

1. Russell M. Nelson, "With God Nothing Shall Be Impossible," *Ensign,* May 1988, 35.

FINDING HOLINESS IN EVERYDAY LIFE

MARY B. KIRK

I am a visual learner. If I can see something, I can remember it, and it's real to me. Christ always said, "Come unto me." But if I want to understand and know the Savior, I have to say to him, "Come unto me. Visit me in my house, in my space on earth." And if he would come and be right there close by me, I could say, "Lord, what wouldst thou have me do?" I have a good imagination, so I can see the Savior coming up the steps with the faulty rail, standing on my porch, and gently knocking on my door, wanting to come in and bring some peace and joy to my whirlwind. And I can see myself flinging that door open and saying, "Please, Savior, come in."

That is how I remember Christ and his atonement in my everyday life. I visualize him being here with me. Maybe you are a visual learner, too, so you can see this. "Jesus, see this clutter? It's evidence of something wonderful—it's proof of Thy blessings. See all these boxes in my workroom? I know, they take up a lot of space, but they are full of scraps of fabric my friends have given to me and old clothes and blue jeans and blankets and drapes. I weave them into rugs. Then I sell them

Mary B. Kirk is a homemaker and nutritional consultant. She and her husband, James S. Kirk, are the parents of five children. She served as a missionary in Canada and serves now as an early-morning seminary teacher and Gospel Doctrine teacher in Sunday School. She also directs the ward and Primary choirs.

to help pay the bills, and I give them away sometimes. And best of all, I love to make them. I can be creative and use these castoffs to make something of beauty. I really have a sense of satisfaction when I do that. Thank Thee for letting me have this gift.

"See this spilled dirt? My three-year-old, Logan, and I were planting some seeds the other day, trying to get a head start on the garden. We really enjoy the earth that Thou hast given to us, and we think dirt is fascinating. When we come home, wilt Thou teach us how this works—this dirt, these seeds, and this water? How does it work? How do they all become flowers and trees and vegetables and grass? We can't comprehend it!

"Now, come in the kitchen and see the dirty dishes. My firstborn son, with us fourteen years now, is on dishes this week. He's not at all sure that he should have to take a turn doing the dishes, but we're trying to teach him responsibility and self-sufficiency. We need him to be a contributing member of our family and of the community and the world around him. So he just gets to take part in it the same as the rest of us. I know, I could have done the work for him—that would be easier in a way—but how would he learn?

"Come see my laundry room. See all these clothes? I know that many people need these worse than we do, but we have them. In fact, most of them were given to us. And we use them all, but the laundry pile can be discouraging at times. I'm so grateful to have hot, running water. That is the thing that I am most grateful for . . . besides the Atonement. I know a lot of my brothers and sisters on earth don't have hot, running water—or even water. And see, the laundry is up here, not in the basement. I appreciate that! And today there are more clothes clean and folded than dirty and unsorted. When I work in here, I can see work clothes and school clothes and play clothes and church clothes. Looking at these clothes I can see Jim hard at work to provide for us. I see one of my sons sitting on the deacon's bench, getting ready to serve the sacrament. I see my other son running track in the rain and the mud. It's right there in the laundry room. I can see them. And I can see my girls playing dress-ups, pretending to be mommies and dancers and doctors and teachers and all those wonderful things. Imagining and dreaming . . . and who cares if they got lipstick on this shawl. I don't. And then I shake the sand out of one of these little socks, and I wonder how many trucks and tractors are buried in the sandbox.

"Listen. Canst Thou hear Logan sing 'I Am a Child of God' out there by the toy box? I can, even with the washer running. And he has clean socks on now, and I am so thankful to Thee who gave him to us.

"Remember when Matt was three years old and learning to dress himself? One day he came downstairs, and he had on his shirt and a pair of underwear—with the underwear on backwards. His father, after patting him on the back and praising him for his accomplishment, gently pointed out the problem. And do you remember that Matt said, 'It's not my fault, Dad. That's the way they were in the drawer'?"

I can find holiness in that. Can you? Children come here with a lot to learn, and that's one of the things we have to teach them. We may have to try lots of times to get them to put on their underwear the right way around. We need to try even harder to get them to study the scriptures and to feel like the Savior tours their life with them and cares about *all* that they do.

So then I ask the Savior to come sit on the porch for a minute, and we continue our conversation. "Remember when we were rewiring the house here before we moved in? Of course, Thou knowest. We never really thought it was necessary to put that extra kitchen light switch on the far end by the pantry. It's not handy there at all. But now that we've decided to build the garage on the west side instead of the east side, the door will come in *right there* and it's *exactly* in the right spot. I suppose it's no surprise to Thee, but we've wondered

115

in awe at Thy power to care for little details—unbeknownst to us—that prove Thine unending love."

Now you may think this is an odd way to feel the presence of the Savior and find holiness in your everyday life. But for me, any plan, any course, that can let me think of him more often, help me to acknowledge his hand in everything around me, feel gratitude for every aspect of my life, and serve him more readily is an okay road to take. And he teaches me as we go. I'm finally seeing that what I thought was mundane and bothersome is really meaningful and beautiful. And you can, too.

Your circumstances and work may be very different from mine, but you can find holiness in them. In Mosiah 18:12 Alma says, "O Lord, pour out thy Spirit upon thy servant, that he may do this work with holiness of heart." I want you to read it yourself, and you may find that it says something like this: "Oh Lord, pour out thy Spirit upon me, Mary, thy servant, that I may do this work with holiness of heart." Put your own name in Alma's prayer, and if your desire is pure, God will grant you holiness of heart—every day.

You know, it took my husband's great insight and a personal revelation to me to finally fix in my mind the fact that eternal life doesn't start at the Savior's second coming, that it's right now. Our relationship with God and Christ goes back all the way and it goes forward all the way and today is part of it. We need to think about each day as being an integral part of the great picture. In other words, the mere fact that we are *alive today* is holy in itself. We chose to participate in mortality. So let's "rejoice and be glad" in it, and acknowledge our stewardship over each day, and *feel* each day's potential for holiness.

In one Bill Keane "Family Circus" comic strip, Dolly and Jeffy are sitting high on a hill looking out over things. Dolly has her arm around Jeffy's shoulders, and he's looking teachable and very intent upon what she is saying. The wisdom of her words has helped me find holiness many times since I first read it. She explains, "Yesterday is the *past,* tomorrow is the *future,* and today is a *gift.* That's why they call it the *present.*" God is the author of the past and the future, and he's the giver of the present gift. He'll sprinkle holiness into today, and we will find it. He will pour out his holiness upon us at the rate that we open our eyes and perceive, open our ears and understand, and open our hearts and invite him in. And then we'll become like him.

NOTE

I appreciate the insight of Joan B. MacDonald in her book, *The Holiness of Everyday Life,* which helped me focus my presentation (Salt Lake City: Deseret Book, 1995).

THE ATONEMENT: A SEA OF PEACE

SALLY B. PALMER

When I was a little girl growing up in northern California, I loved going to the beach at Bodega Bay. There were long, smooth stretches of wet sand that no one had trampled. You could take a stick and make a furrow or write your name. Or you could take a shovel and throw up big, messy mounds and walls, make holes and tunnels and mountains and valleys. You could scoop up handfuls to throw at your sisters, or bury them in the sand. After a while the beach was all plowed up and looked like an excavation site.

But then a wave would come in farther than usual, curling and foaming across the sand. The cold water would run into and fill up every hole, every crevice, every tunnel and valley and indentation. It would cover the piles and hills and mounds, swirling over them all. Then it would recede, leaving the sand completely smooth and flat, cool and clean again.

Jesus said, "I, even I, am he that blotteth out thy transgressions . . . and will not remember thy sins" (Isaiah 43:25). He said, "In the barren deserts there shall come forth pools of living water; and the parched ground shall no longer be a thirsty land" (D&C 133:29). He said his voice shall be "as the voice of many waters, . . . which shall break down the mountains"

Sally Broadbent Palmer, the single mother of ten, is completing her Ph.D. at the University of California–Davis, where she teaches literature and represents graduate women on the Provost's Committee. She teaches in Relief Society and is a Cub Scout den mother and an adult-literacy tutor.

(D&C 133:22). Jesus said, "I will give unto him that is athirst . . . of the water of life" (Revelation 21:6).

The scriptures are full of images of Christ as water and of his atonement as the water of life. For me, the Atonement is that ocean wave at the seashore that makes everything smooth again. I like to carry that metaphor, that image, around with me in my pocket every day. It is an extremely useful item. Every once in a while I take it out and look at it—turn it over in my mind and notice things about it. I notice, for instance, that there's always plenty of water—always enough to fill the very deepest hole, cover the highest mound of sand, and make them level again. "Though your sins be as scarlet," says Isaiah, "they shall be as white as snow" (Isaiah 1:18). I also notice that the water is always there as the years go by, unchanging, constant, and endless as eternity. Amulek says nothing short of an infinite atonement will suffice for the sins of the world, the infinite and eternal sacrifice of the Son of God (see Alma 34:8–14). I notice, too, that the water leaves *everything* washed clean.

I don't know how others feel, but for me life is never a smooth beach. Every day, irritations will start piling up in my mind. It starts with the kids' complaints at breakfast. "Why do we always have to get up so early?" "Why is it still raining?" "How come we have to have oatmeal again?" Then, a bit later, in the car, somebody will cut me off in traffic or honk and make rude gestures because of something I did. Soon a disgruntled student calls to challenge a low grade, and my boss will send me a critical memo. Meanwhile the bank's giving me the runaround, and the car's making the same scary noise it did last week before I paid five hundred dollars to have it fixed.

There's no justice! Things become all plowed up in the gritty sand of my mind; I'm starting to feel annoyed and frustrated with myself and other people. Then I remember what's in my pocket. I take a breath. I close my eyes for just a second, and I can see the water coming. That wave quietly wells up and fills all the pits and cracks and holes in my mind. Then it

119

recedes, leaving them smooth and filled and even again. Through the Atonement, I can forgive and become whole and at peace.

To illustrate, not long ago my brother, who lives three thousand miles away, came to town on business, and we went to the temple together. It happened that we were seated next to each other in the session, which pleased me greatly. Not only is it rare that I can attend the temple with my brother but it is even more rare that a man and a woman are seated next to each other in the temple. Then another patron on our row stood up and asked my brother and me to move so that he and his wife could sit together. We moved, but I was inwardly steaming. "That man can sit by his wife twenty-four hours a day if he wants to," I fumed to myself, "but I'll never again be able to sit by my brother in the temple!" Just then the lights went out, and the film began. Up on the screen, there was the ocean, with its thundering, swirling waves. I thought of Christ's atonement, let it wash over the irritation in my heart, and immediately I was at peace. The incident dissolved away.

But let's up the ante a little bit and move beyond the small cracks in our surface contentment. Let's consider the huge cataclysms that split the terrain of our lives down to bedrock. I myself am an earthquake survivor. After a twenty-year temple marriage, my husband left me and our ten children for another woman. Only those who have experienced that kind of betrayal can understand the magnitude of the seismic tremors it brings to every area of life: physical, financial, social, emotional, and spiritual. Only they realize with immediacy that the aftershocks along the fault line continue for a lifetime. The injustices are profound and unending.

Every culture has its own concept of justice and rules for establishing it in their communities. But isn't it interesting that, much as they may try, human beings, even Latter-day Saints, are unable to bring justice about? We simply cannot do it. Think of examples in the media lately—are you impressed with what our own system of justice hands out? Often, in our attempts to flatten and smooth out the sand ourselves, we only make matters worse.

Maxine Hong Kingston writes of an aunt who lived in a village in China with her family. As a girl, this aunt had been raped and then was found to be pregnant, which brought great distress to her family. In China, rape is blamed on the victim. The girl's parents did not let her eat with the family after that, but she was permitted to eat at an "outcast table" by herself. Kingston's mother said, "On the night the baby was to be born the villagers raided our house. . . . Like a great saw, teeth strung with lights, files of people walked zigzag across our land, tearing the rice. . . . As the villagers closed in, we could see that some of them, probably men and women we knew well, wore white masks. The people with long hair hung it over their faces. . . . At first they threw mud and rocks at the house. Then they threw eggs and began slaughtering our stock. We could hear the animals scream their deaths. . . . Their knives dripped with the blood of our animals. They smeared blood on the doors and walls. . . . We stood together . . . [in the hall] and looked straight ahead. . . . They ripped up her clothes and shoes and broke her combs. . . . They tore her work from the loom. They scattered the cooking fire and rolled the new weaving in it. We could hear them in the kitchen breaking our bowls. When they left, they took sugar and oranges. . . . Some of them took bowls that were not broken and clothes that were not torn."[1]

This is a shocking story, but it is true. It illustrates how mortal attempts to bring about justice, to right wrongs, can just make things worse. In my own life and ward, and in yours, too, tragedies of sin and shame can begin and compound just as this one did. When one person begins to dig in the sand, others come along and kick the sand around, too. Perhaps they build a fire, or spill some toxic substance onto the sand, or leave rotting trash at the site to gather flies.

People in their ignorance and fear can misunderstand the source of sin. They gossip and condemn, they assign praise and blame, and they make things worse trying to straighten them out. They rationalize and lie to make the truth come out the way they want it to. Even when they mean well, they can aggravate both the heartache of injustice and the consequences.

When things get this messed up, how can they ever be straightened out again? How can wrecked lives be restored; how can broken families be healed; how can destroyed bodies regain wholeness; how can wasted years be brought back; how can crushed hopes and testimonies be regained?

"Restoring what you cannot restore, healing the wound you cannot heal, fixing that which you broke and you cannot fix is the very purpose of the atonement of Christ. . . . There is no habit, no addiction, no rebellion, no transgression, no apostasy, no crime exempted from the promise of complete forgiveness. That is the promise of the atonement of Christ."[2] That is a powerful statement from latter-day apostle Boyd K. Packer. Think of it when you lift that tiny paper cup to your lips Sunday morning and let those few drops slide across your tongue. This is just a symbolic portion of the mighty force of the living water. Not only can it heal the unhealable but its awesome power can change the landscape in other ways, too. It has the power to crash against the rocky cliffs, sending its spray high into the air; to crush huge boulders into sand, carve valleys out of mountains, and dash ships and cities into bits.

The Atonement is infinite. The ocean is endless; the waves, constant. Eventually, every hole, every gorge will disappear without a trace, no matter how ravaged the landscape, through the atonement of Jesus Christ. To qualify for that wave of cleansing water, we have to repent of the wrongs we have done. We must acknowledge the mess we've made, be sorry for its ugliness, and try to smooth it out ourselves. We may have to live with it for a time, while the tide's out, suffering perhaps by having to put up with the gritty sand blowing about in our eyes, or the salt, or the debris that's strewn around. But eventually the wave will come, and then, like Alma, we will exclaim, "Oh, what joy . . . yea, my soul was filled with joy as exceeding as was my pain!" (Alma 36:20).

Close your eyes; see the living water run into your soul and fill up your empty spaces with peace. Feel the cool spray on your cheeks, and hear the wavelet's whisper. "Every one that thirsteth, come ye to the waters" (Isaiah 55:1) and "with joy shall ye draw water out of the wells of salvation" (Isaiah 12:3).

NOTES

1. Maxine Hong Kingston, *The Woman Warrior: Memoirs of a Girlhood among Ghosts* (New York: Random House, 1989), 3–5.

2. Boyd K. Packer, "The Brilliant Morning of Forgiveness," *Ensign,* November 1995, 19–20.

"TEACH THEM CORRECT PRINCIPLES"

STEPHEN D. NADAULD

Many parents in the Church today worry about their teenagers. How can we save them from what lies around them in a difficult and dangerous world? I believe the key to success with our young men is no different from what it is with the young women, but because I am serving in the Young Men General Presidency, I have thought mostly about young men. Let me share with you three or four ideas.

First and foremost, we have to help them get a vision of who they are and what they can become. What do we hope will happen in the lives of young men? What is that vision? First of all, we want them to become converted to the gospel of Jesus Christ. Second, we want them to magnify their priesthood callings. Third, we want them to give meaningful service. Fourth, we want them to prepare to receive the Melchizedek Priesthood. Fifth, we want them committed to serve a mission. And sixth, we want them to live so that they can receive temple covenants and become righteous husbands and fathers. These six purposes of the Aaronic Priesthood have the power to provide a vision.

Stephen D. Nadauld has served as president of Weber State University and as a member of the Second Quorum of the Seventy. He also served as first counselor in the Young Men General Presidency until his release in October 1996. He and his wife, Margaret Dyreng Nadauld, are the parents of seven sons.

About four years ago, the Young Men General Presidency sat down to articulate this vision for young men in the Church. We hoped mightily that we could motivate the young men to move aside the Michael Jordan and Nirvana posters in their rooms and put there instead a poster with the purposes of the Aaronic Priesthood on it. I mentioned our thoughts in a priesthood commemoration fireside, and the most interesting and wonderful thing has happened. Priesthood leaders all over the Church have designed mission statements on posters, plaques, and wallet cards—in every size and shape. I have probably thirty or forty in a file that have been sent to me from around the Church. Wouldn't it be wonderful if every bishop could visit each twelve-year-old young man in his own home and say, "Here's the vision that I as your bishop have for you. Your father and I share this vision. Here's what you can become, my wonderful young priesthood holder." Together they could go over those six purposes of the Aaronic Priesthood. So this is the first point: there is enormous power in having a vision of what you can become, and we ought to share that vision with every young man in the Church.

The second point comes from studies we've made of young men. We've looked at and analyzed their behavior—their attendance at meetings, their participation in priesthood assignments. We have found that the single most important factor in determining whether or not a young man holds the Melchizedek Priesthood later in his life is his private religious observance. It's not his attendance at meetings; it's not his participation in sacrament meeting. Those things are important, but the number one predictor is private religious observance. Private religious observance is what goes on in the home—personal prayer, family prayer, scripture reading, tithe paying, Sabbath observance. The best predictor of whether or not a young man will really catch this vision we are trying to share is his private religious behavior.

That is why teaching doctrine is so important. In Alma

125

12:32 we read: "Therefore God gave unto them commandments, after having made known unto them the plan of redemption." This verse is not remarkable on the surface. I had read it many times, but one day someone pointed out something I had not noticed. The issue is the sequence of events: *before* God gave commandments—the dos and don'ts—to his children, he wanted to make sure that they understood the plan. "God gave unto them commandments, *after* having made known unto them the plan of redemption" (emphasis added). Instructions on what to do and what not to do—commandments, if you will—would be set in the context of a plan, a vision.

Visualize a flow chart. On the left-hand side is doctrine. On the right-hand side is application, or behavior. In the middle are principles.

DOCTRINE → PRINCIPLES → BEHAVIOR

Those of us who are parents or who teach from the pulpit or in any other setting, whether priesthood or Relief Society or family, may spend too much time harping on behavior, pointing out how somebody is not doing this right and how he needs to do better. Our challenge, I believe, is to redress the balance and spend equal time talking about the doctrine and the principles that flow from the doctrine. Doctrine is the foundation. From the doctrine flow certain principles, and from those principles flow certain behaviors, which are application of those principles.

Let me give you an example. Probably the most difficult challenge for young people today is morality. Never before have our young people been so bombarded with misinformation and temptation relative to standards of sexual behavior. As parents and youth leaders, we ought to provide clear, specific guidelines for conduct. We need to spend considerable time saying to them: Don't touch each other in inappropriate places; Don't lie beside or on top of each other on couches; Don't be out together late alone; Do double date with other couples; and so on. To counterbalance the media, our focus needs to be very much on behavior.

But in addition, I wonder how often we sit down with our young people and really talk to them about the doctrine and the principles. We may teach them the truth that immorality is next to murder in seriousness. But have we ever developed a logic that helps them understand why? The issue is one of authority. Can we explain the concept of authority and God's authority over life? Do we explain that only God has the authority to take and to give life? He reserves that to himself. That authority can be delegated; we can be authorized, as, for example, Nephi was authorized to slay Laban. Men and women are authorized to take life if they are protecting their homes, families, and children in times of war. By the same token, we have no right to start life unless we are given the authorization. The issue is not that sex is wrong or evil. The issue is authority. We don't have the right to start a life, and we don't have the right to take a life, unless and until we are given that authority. If we explain to our young people the doctrine, then we can lay out some logical principles regarding our commitment to chastity and the applications of those principles. Whenever we teach our young people, we would make more progress by first backing up a step or two to make sure that the doctrine is understood.

Often leaders want us to give specific and detailed prescriptions for every possible situation. For instance, one leader called to ask if the Church specified a policy about fourteen-year-old girls attending afternoon dances. We talked at length, and I tried to help this leader see that in a Church of approximately nine million members in nearly 150 countries, it is not practical or possible to provide a paragraph description of every possible application. It might be nice to be able to point to a rule from the prophet for every possible situation, but that's not the principle of agency.

We want to avoid what I call the IRS problem. The Church explains tithing with a ten-word description: give 10 percent of your increase on an annual basis. The IRS has shelves and shelves full of code books attempting to detail every specific kind of income and each exact kind of tax that ought to be paid, specifying all possible expenses and deductions, and so on and so forth.

As leaders and parents, instead of turning to a code book, let's talk with our youth about doctrine and help them identify principles that flow from doctrine. Then let's talk with them about reasonable applications. That is a process we should engage in ourselves as we solve problems at a local level. Should a fourteen-year-old girl attend a matinee dance? What makes sense? Local parents and leaders can discuss the issues and give counsel about how to apply principles to matinee dance behavior. Talking about the applications, helping young people understand the whys, becomes the basis for them to develop independence and the ability to cope with the tremendous number of influences from the world around them. Those influences become only more complex and complicated as they grow older. If we can ground our young people strongly in doctrines and principles, they can figure out the applications.

Consider a third idea: young men and women need to think of themselves as part of the engine and not as part of the baggage. The pioneers would never have made it across the plains if the teenagers had ridden in the wagons. They had to push, they had to pull, they had to carry—and as a result, the young men and women who crossed the plains had character, determination, and resilience that has carried through even to the present generation. Our ancestors' experiences have blessed us in ways we're not even aware of. Boys and girls need wood to chop. They need to think of themselves not as bystanders, not as spectators to be entertained, but as part of the engine. Only then will they be excited and enthusiastic about what's happening in their lives.

Let me relate a story that illustrates this point. A bishop in the Northwest was asked to provide the stake with some names of men and women in his ward who could do computer work in genealogy. They would be trained to extract names for temple work. The bishop compiled a list of fifteen names. His counselor said with a laugh, "You know, I believe every teenager in our ward knows more about computers than anybody on that list." The bishop replied, "You may be right." So he went to the Laurels and the priests and said, "I have a little computer project I'd like your help with." "We know about computers; we'd love to help," they replied. So he taught them how to do name extraction, and those young people began extracting away.

One day they asked, "What happens to these names?" The bishop then put on his hat as president of the Aaronic Priesthood and teacher of the plan of redemption and said, "You know when we do baptisms for the dead? These are the people you are baptized for." After a few minutes one of the young people noted, "Bishop, we've got a problem here." Others nodded. The bishop asked, "What's the problem?" The young man replied, "You know, we have only two temple trips scheduled this year." The bishop said, "Yes, what's the problem?" One of the Laurels joined in, "Well, we can't possibly be baptized for all these people in just two trips." The bishop invited more input: "How can we solve that problem?" And the young people responded, "We'll just have to go more often. You know, we've got to get this work done." So they scheduled four more trips to the Portland Oregon Temple that year.

On one of those trips, someone raised another question. "Bishop, what happens after the temple baptism is done?" The bishop again put on his special hat, ready now to teach doctrine. He taught about the temple endowment. They asked, "Bishop, who's in charge of making sure that work is done?" The bishop said, "Well, your parents are, I guess." When they asked, "Bishop, how are they doing?" the bishop hedged. "Well

. . . well . . ." So they said, "Now look, Bishop. We can't let these people sit in some dead letter file. We've got to figure out how to get this work done! What can we do to help you get our parents to the temple?"

Do you see the power of getting these young people involved in being part of the engine rather than being part of the baggage? When you do that, all of a sudden they begin to pull the whole load forward. That ward had the highest temple attendance in the stake, the most temple baptisms for the dead, and the highest sacrament meeting attendance, because young men and women were a working part of that wonderful engine.

Finally, and perhaps most important, our youth need caring parents who have made up their minds that this young man or this young woman is going to be nurtured, be taken care of, be blessed to achieve the objectives that they can set for themselves. Consider this: the scouting program is an extraordinary program for young men. Ninety-five percent of LDS Eagle Scouts end up being missionaries. Is that cause and effect? Does working on the Eagle award or learning all you need to know to advance in rank lead you to be a missionary? The answer is no, not at all. Though the two are highly correlated, one does not cause the other. What causes both to occur is an infrastructure of parents and caring adults in the ward.

To run a successful scouting program, you must find men who are willing to be committee chairmen, men who are willing to take boys on hikes, men who are willing to help with advancement, and men who are willing to teach boys skills. All of a sudden you have developed a tremendous infrastructure that includes the bishop, his counselors, advisors, and committeemen. When mothers are added to this equation, this powerful infrastructure can work wonders with young men. They become Eagle Scouts, missionaries, and Melchizedek Priesthood holders. A quarterly or bi-monthly bishopric-parent conference is an excellent way for parents and youth leaders to talk about what's happening, give feedback, and figure out how to provide that infrastructure.

Let me share an example of how important caring parents are in that infrastructure for their youth. About six months ago, I interviewed a young missionary in a southern state. The influence of the Spirit in the mission home plus good companions had convinced him that he had done wrong in his life that he had not repented of. He brought these mistakes to the attention of his mission president. After counseling with General Authorities and stake presidents, this young man had been sent home to continue the repentance process. I was interviewing him to see if he could go back into the mission field. After a rather lengthy interview, I said to him, "Elder, how were you able to keep your desire to serve a mission through a year's worth of difficult repentance?" He gave a very specific answer, "When I came home to our small town, to get off the plane I had to walk down a set of stairs to the tarmac. As I started down the stairs, there at the bottom stood my mother. Her eyes were brimming with tears. I said to myself right then, One day I am going to come down the steps of this airplane again and see not tears of sorrow but tears of joy in my mother's eyes. And that thought," he said, "kept me wanting to do it right."

Parents, please don't ever give up on these young men and young women. Help them catch a vision of who they are. Get the bishop to come by with that poster of the mission of the Aaronic Priesthood. Put it on the wall and talk about it often. Encourage their private, religious behaviors—reading, praying, pondering. Give them wood to chop; help them be part of the engine of the Church. And finally, provide them with the infrastructure of caring adults that just won't let them fail. You can bless their lives as nobody else can. Whatever they've done, whatever their present circumstances, please know that one day you may greet each other not with tears of sorrow but with tears of joy.

THE FAMILY: A PROCLAMATION TO THE WORLD

WE, THE FIRST PRESIDENCY and Council of the Twelve Apostles of The Church of Jesus Christ of Latter-day Saints, solemnly proclaim that marriage between a man and a woman is ordained of God and that the family is central to the Creator's plan for the eternal destiny of His children.

ALL HUMAN BEINGS—male and female—are created in the image of God. Each is a beloved spirit son or daughter of heavenly parents, and, as such, each has a divine nature and destiny. Gender is an essential characteristic of individual premortal, mortal, and eternal identity and purpose.

IN THE PREMORTAL REALM, spirit sons and daughters knew and worshiped God as their Eternal Father and accepted His plan by which His children could obtain a physical body and gain earthly experience to progress toward perfection and ultimately realize his or her divine destiny as an heir of eternal life. The divine plan of happiness enables family relationships to be perpetuated beyond the grave. Sacred ordinances and covenants available in holy temples make it possible for individuals to return to the presence of God and for families to be united eternally.

THE FIRST COMMANDMENT that God gave to Adam and Eve pertained to their potential for parenthood as husband and wife. We declare that God's commandment for His children to multiply and replenish the earth remains in force. We further declare that God has commanded that the sacred powers of procreation are to be employed only between man and woman, lawfully wedded as husband and wife.

WE DECLARE the means by which mortal life is created to be divinely appointed. We affirm the sanctity of life and of its importance in God's eternal plan.

HUSBAND AND WIFE have a solemn responsibility to love and care for each other and for their children. "Children are an heritage of the Lord" (Psalm 127:3). Parents have a sacred duty to rear their children in love and righteousness, to provide for their physical and spiritual needs, to teach them to love and serve one another, to observe the commandments of God and to be law-abiding citizens wherever they live. Husbands and wives—mothers and fathers—will be held accountable before God for the discharge of these obligations.

THE FAMILY is ordained of God. Marriage between man and woman is essential to His eternal plan. Children are entitled to birth within the bonds of matrimony, and to be reared by a father and a mother who honor marital vows with complete fidelity. Happiness in family life is most likely to be achieved when founded upon the teachings of the Lord Jesus Christ. Successful marriages and families are established and maintained on principles of faith, prayer, repentance, forgiveness, respect, love, compassion, work, and wholesome recreational activities. By divine design, fathers are to preside over their families in love and righteousness and are responsible to provide the necessities of life and protection for their families. Mothers are primarily responsible for the nurture of their children. In these sacred responsibilities, fathers and mothers are obligated to help one another as equal partners. Disability, death, or other circumstances may necessitate individual adaptation. Extended families should lend support when needed.

WE WARN that individuals who violate covenants of chastity, who abuse spouse or offspring, or who fail to fulfill family responsibilities will one day stand accountable before God. Further, we warn that the disintegration of the family will bring upon individuals, communities, and nations the calamities foretold by ancient and modern prophets.

WE CALL UPON responsible citizens and officers of government everywhere to promote those measures designed to maintain and strengthen the family as the fundamental unit of society.

"THE FAMILY: A PROCLAMATION TO THE WORLD"

ROBERT D. HALES

On 23 September 1995, the First Presidency and Quorum of the Twelve Apostles issued a proclamation to the world that marriage between a man and a woman is ordained of God and that the family is central to the Creator's plan for the eternal destiny of his children. When President Hinckley read the proclamation at the 1995 worldwide general Relief Society meeting, he gave it as a revelation for our time. The proclamation concludes with a call to government leaders and citizens of all nations "to maintain and strengthen the family as the fundamental unit of society."[1]

The family is not an accident of mortality. It existed as an organizational unit in the heavens before the world was formed; historically, it started on earth with Adam and Eve, as recorded in Genesis. Adam and Eve were married and sealed for time and all eternity by the Lord, and as a result their family will exist eternally.

The Bible records Adam and Eve's challenges in rearing children. We learn there of the influence of Satan on the first family on earth. Satan is clever, and he is also the father of all

Robert D. Hales was sustained a member of the Quorum of the Twelve Apostles on 2 April 1994. A graduate of the University of Utah, he holds a master of business administration degree from Harvard. He and his wife, Mary Crandall Hales, are the parents of two sons.

lies. Undermining the family as an institution furthers his goal to destroy the eternal nature and destiny of Heavenly Father's children.

Lehi's teaching of the plan of life and of Satan's opposition is important for us to understand. "For it must needs be, that there is an opposition in all things. . . . And to bring about his eternal purposes . . . the Lord God gave unto man that he should act for himself. Wherefore, man could not act for himself save it should be that he was enticed by the one or the other" (2 Nephi 2:11, 15–16). Of Satan's purposes, Lehi warns that "because he had fallen from heaven, and had become miserable forever, he sought also the misery of all mankind" (2 Nephi 2:18). Satan's opposition to our progress is very real, and disrupting our Heavenly Father's plan for the family is one of his goals.

Lehi, talking with his sons, warned that the devil "seeketh that all men might be miserable like unto himself" (2 Nephi 2:27). The only pleasure that Satan has is our transgressions. After we have transgressed, the light of Christ leaves us, and we are in darkness—just where Satan wants us—where we feel we have no hope. Note in 2 Nephi 31:20 that when Nephi speaks of hope, he refers to a "brightness" of hope.

After Christ's crucifixion, cities were destroyed because of the wickedness of the people. I can feel the anguish in the voice of the Lord as he cries out, "Wo, wo, wo unto this people . . . except they shall repent," and know that at the same time, "the devil laugheth, and his angels rejoice, because of the slain of the fair sons and daughters of my people" (3 Nephi 9:2). The laughter of the devil is something our children ought to be aware of—understanding that the only time the devil and his disciples rejoice is when we transgress and lose the light of Christ. To stand against Satan in this latter day, we must stand for the family. By sharing what we have learned and are still learning about the dynamics of our companionships and family life, we can answer the call to "strengthen the family as the fundamental unit of society."[2]

Found in the Book of Mormon is the account of Lehi and Sariah's challenges as they reared their children in love and righteousness. Their family lived among a people who did not follow the commandments of the Lord, even though Lehi tried tirelessly to warn them of the destruction that would come if they did not repent. Eventually, as prompted by the Spirit of the Lord, for their own safety Lehi had to gather his family and flee Jerusalem. He was given spiritual guidance for his family and had the faith to follow the Spirit. Mother Sariah also felt the Spirit and had faith to follow her husband's counsel.

Following counsel meant the family had to sacrifice. They had to leave their home and all their worldly possessions to dwell in tents in the wilderness. Married to daughters of Ishmael, the sons of Lehi started families of their own. Two sons, Nephi and Sam, were obedient, following the counsel of their father in the Spirit of the Lord. Two sons, Laman and Lemuel, were contentious. They murmured about having to give up their home, their inheritance, their gold, silver, and other precious belongings, and take nothing with them but the family when they departed. In the wilderness, Laman and Lemuel continued to yearn for the worldly possessions left behind.

Discord among the family tested the faith of each member, but *Lehi and Sariah did not let disobedient children affect their own faith and obedience.* Nor did they give up when their sons were beyond feeling. Father Lehi knew and taught that they would face opposition in all things, but it could serve to strengthen them. In 1 Nephi 5:8, Sariah bears testimony to her husband and sons: "Now I know of a surety that the Lord hath commanded my husband to flee into the wilderness; yea, and I also know of a surety that the Lord hath protected my sons. "

At the end of the vision of the tree of life in 1 Nephi 8, Lehi talks of the great multitude that entered a spacious building, meaning they went the ways of the world, and "after they did enter into that building they did point the finger of scorn at me and those that were partaking of the fruit [of the tree of life]. . . . And Laman and Lemuel partook not of the fruit [of the tree of life], said my father" (1 Nephi 8:33, 35). After telling them of his vision, Lehi confided to the family that "he exceedingly feared for Laman and Lemuel. . . . And he did exhort them then with *all the feeling of a tender parent,* that they would hearken to his words, that perhaps the Lord would be merciful to them, and not cast them off" (1 Nephi 8:36–37; emphasis added). Lehi never ceased caring about his sons. He "preached unto them, and also prophesied unto them of many things, [and] he bade them to keep the commandments of the Lord" (1 Nephi 8:38).

I hope that we will have the courage of Lehi to teach, preach, exhort, and even prophesy in a kind and loving way to our children of what we believe and that we will continue to encourage them to keep the commandments so that they may come to the tree of life. That is eternal life. There is nothing more poignant to me than Lehi looking down the "strait and narrow path" to see if Laman and Lemuel will perhaps come to the tree of life and partake of the fruit.

Nephi began the record of the Book of Mormon with a great tribute to his mother and father: "I, Nephi, having been born of goodly parents" (1 Nephi 1:1). Parents must make every effort to live so that children can honor them. Lehi and Sariah loved one another and were faithful to one another, although at times they had to work out problems or concerns.

President Elaine L. Jack has shared insights about how Lehi and Sariah built a relationship of trust with each other. She first explains what trust feels like: "When I trust someone, I feel I can put my soul in his or her hands and know it will be protected. I can speak my mind and heart without fear of being judged wrongly. I can be myself. I can do my best work—or my worst—and know I will be aided and appreciated."[3]

137

She then uses Lehi and Sariah as an example of marital interactions that build trust. She notes that Sariah was upset with Lehi because he had sent the sons off to get the records of the Lord. She feared that they would not return—that they would be slain by Laban. "In 1 Nephi 5, Nephi, one of the sons, tells the story as follows: 'She [Sariah] had supposed that we [her sons] had perished in the wilderness; and she also had complained against my father, [children do hear these arguments, don't they?] telling him that he was a visionary man; saying: Behold thou hast led us forth from the land of our inheritance, and my sons are no more, and we perish in the wilderness' (1 Nephi 5:2)."

Nephi let us know that he didn't record all that his mother said: "And after this manner of language had my mother complained against my father" (1 Nephi 5:3). Sister Jack continues: "Sariah was not only apprehensive about her sons' welfare, but concerned that the whole group would die in the wilderness, and didn't hesitate to express her feelings to Lehi. But after her complaints, here's the beginning of Lehi's response: 'I know that I am a visionary man.' Why do you think he responded that way? What effect might it have had on Sariah? In this response, Lehi acknowledged what she had said without recrimination. It seems to me that what she spoke *was* the truth and he verified it. He didn't defend himself by putting her down, or denying her observations, or complaining against her."[4]

There was marvelous communication when Lehi next said to his dear wife, "If I had not seen the things of God in a vision I should not have known the goodness of God, but had tarried at Jerusalem, and had perished with my brethren. But behold, I have obtained a land of promise, in the which things I do rejoice" (1 Nephi 5:4–5). Sister Jack comments, "He shared his testimony with her and explained why he had done what he had done and put her remarks in the broader context of their mission." By explaining that they were all on the Lord's mission he invited the Spirit into the discussion, and then he reassured her: "I know that the Lord will deliver my sons out of the hands of Laban, and bring them down again unto us in the wilderness" (1 Nephi 5:5). Sister Jack perceptively analyzes the whole interaction. Lehi had "clearly identified and acknowledged the source of her concern and responded to it. What was Sariah's reaction? Nephi explained, 'And after this manner of language did my father, Lehi, comfort my mother, Sariah, concerning us' (1 Nephi 5:6). Lehi reminded her of the source of comfort, bore his testimony concerning their sons and the Lord's goodness to them all. Sariah, being a woman of spiritual understanding, was comforted by the truth he spoke and by his explanation that all would be well with her sons. I imagine she felt the Spirit bear witness to her that he spoke the truth.

"In Nephi 5:7 we hear the end of this particular story. Nephi records, 'And when we had returned to the tent of my father, behold *their* joy was full, and my mother was comforted' [emphasis added]. I like the *their* in that sentence. Lehi was equally concerned about his sons. Sariah voiced fears, I am sure, that were also Lehi's fears. When he bore testimony and comforted her, he was also calming his own fears.

"As Lehi responded to his wife, he showed a profound respect for Sariah and a deep understanding of her character. He could have taken offense at her accusation that he was a 'visionary man,' but he did not. He seemed to understand that her comments were driven by her anxiety for her children, and he provided the comfort that she sought. Furthermore, he shared his most sacred feelings with her and finally rejoiced with her at their sons return."[5]

I am grateful to Sister Jack for her insights. Mothers and fathers have a companion relationship, which should include open communication with each other and the family members; we should be able to listen to suggestions for improvement from our best friends and critics, our brothers and sisters, our sons and daughters, our husband or wife, without taking offense.

Doctrine and Covenants 108 tells us to strengthen each other in *all* of our conversations, prayers, exhortations, and doings. It would be so much easier if it said *most*—in *most* of your conversations, *most* prayers, *most* exhortations, and *most* of your doings. But it says "in *all*." That process enables us to be one—of one mind, one heart, one purpose, one accord—knowing the desires of our companion and of each of our children. In this way we become one, as a family.

Of course we still have differences, but we just don't personalize them. We allow each family member a little space, a little private time. We encourage family members to have successful experiences and to be themselves.

As children learn to love and strengthen parents and brothers and sisters and to unite as a family, they are really preparing themselves to select their own companion and to parent in their own families. The family is a protective incubator for caring, testing, trials, and controlled growth. The family is where we can make mistakes and be loved, where we can trust. When I think of the prodigal son, I think of a father running to his son, throwing his arms around him and loving him. I would also hope that parents would remember to take time—not only with the children who are struggling with their testimonies or their obedience—but with those who are faithful, so that they, too, might know of their love and appreciation. Alma's words to his middle son, Shiblon, are an example: "I say unto you, my son, that I have had great joy in thee already, because of thy faithfulness and thy diligence" (Alma 38:3).

An article I read about communication estimated that about 70 percent of communication within the family is nonverbal: it's music, emotions, touching when we hug one another or when we express love for one another. Within the family structure we move beyond self-centered thoughts and develop concern for others. Much of our strength comes from passive and visual communication as we persuade one another through emotion and reason to do what is right. A family unit that works well gives its members a sense of security, making it easier to venture into the world and trust others. A smile, though nonverbal, expresses love and gives courage. It does not, however, take the place of telling our wives, husbands, and children, "I love you."

The things we do together bond us. I can remember as a young boy lying on the ground with my father and brother. We looked up into the clouds, and Father, who was an artist, asked us to pick out different animals or other shapes that we saw—kind of a nature's Rorschach test. I have long remembered those sweet moments.

In a 1993 general conference talk entitled "How Will Our Children Remember Us?" I pondered about how my children will remember me.[6] How will your children remember you? My warm memories of Mother's tiny slippered feet on top of Father's feet as they danced around the kitchen help me recall their expressions of love for each other. I remember sitting as a young boy on the floor by their bedside while they took turns reading aloud from the scriptures. We could join in whenever we desired. I have beautiful memories in later years of going to the Salt Lake Temple and watching Mother and Father participate in the presentation of a live endowment ceremony. These memories have been a guide for me.

One of the greatest privileges and responsibilities given to us is being a parent, helping to bring to earth children of God and having a sacred responsibility to love, care, and guide them back to our Heavenly Father. Children often look to their parents to learn the characteristics of their Heavenly Father. When they love, respect, and have confidence in their earthly parents, they often unknowingly develop the same feeling towards their Heavenly Father.

No parent on earth is perfect. Children can be understanding when they sense that parents truly care and are attempting to do their best. Faults will be overlooked and forgiven if children have been loved enough. Children need to see good parents having differing opinions and working out these differences without striking, yelling, or throwing things. Seeing calm communication that respects other's viewpoints and differences will teach children how to work out their differences in their own lives, both in their families and with those whom they meet in the world.

It is no secret that example is the best teacher. The Lord has said: "And they shall also teach their children to pray, and to walk uprightly before the Lord" (D&C 68:28). Children who are taught to pray and who pray with their parents when young are more likely to pray when they are older. Those who are taught at an early age to love God and believe in him will more often continue their spiritual development and increase their feelings of love as they mature. Yet even children reared with great love and care and carefully taught may as adults choose for a variety of reasons not to follow our teachings. How should we respond? What is our responsibility as parents? Basic to our faith is an understanding of and a respect for the principle of agency. Coercion is never part of God's plan. Rather, we pray that life's experiences will help those children regain their desire and ability to live in the gospel. They are still our children, and we love and care about them no matter what their beliefs and lifestyles. We do not lock the doors of our house against them, nor do we lock the doors of our heart.

If we think other families don't have difficulties, we just don't know them well enough. Some Church members feel they cannot accept or fulfill a church calling if one of their children is straying. They are filled with a sense of failure and unworthiness. Yet, accepting a calling and doing our best may have a profound spiritual effect on those we love the most.

If our parents' example has not been good, we can break the cycle. Humility, faith, prayer, and study can show us a better way, bless the lives of present family members, and teach

142

correct traditions for generations to follow. The Lord's promises are sure: "I will instruct thee and teach thee in the way which thou shalt go" (Psalm 32:8). And again, "And whatsoever ye shall ask the Father in my name, which is right, believing that ye shall receive, behold it shall be given unto you" (3 Nephi 18:20).

Let's review some practical advice about marriage. Temple marriage is of eternal significance. In the temple we are sealed by priesthood power in an eternal covenant, bound together for this life and for all eternity. Knowing of the importance of marriage from the time of Adam and Eve in the Garden of Eden until our day, what are some of the things that prevent our relationships from having joy and eternal happiness?

President Harold B. Lee helped me when Mary and I were sealed in the temple in 1953. After describing the eternal nature of marriage, he said, "What you do in all the eternities to come will depend on how you live this life. Court your wife in the same manner throughout your life as you did to have her choose to come to the temple with you." That is great advice. Then he said, "Bring flowers home often enough so that she doesn't say, 'What's the matter?'" Courtship and loving, then, are important parts of marriage. We should always keep our love alive by expressing it to one another any number of times during the day. Sometimes I will call my wife during the day just to talk to her and tell her I love her. Sometimes I call because I need the reassurance of her love.

We need to be quick to say, "I'm sorry." Try to get your pride out of the way and look at a situation from your spouse's point of view. When you say, "I'm sorry," try to have the humility to say, "I'm sorry, and I will do better."

Unhappy marriage partners are often struggling with the way they handle money. It's important to live within our means. Debt causes stress. When I counsel a couple before they go to the temple to be married, I give them one phrase to remember throughout their marriage to help them live within their means: "We can't afford it." And if mother and father are able to say, "We can't afford it," to each other, then it will be easier for them to say that to their children and in their family councils.

We need the courage to ask, How can I be a better husband and father? How can I be a better mother and wife? How can I be a better son or daughter? We should discuss our differences calmly when they are small, when they first happen. Unacknowledged, little problems become big problems.

At times I have been softly corrected by my wife. Let me tell of one instance. In 1975 on my first assignment as a General Authority, I spoke at Ricks College. My speech was informal and I enjoyed using humor. In answering the students' questions afterwards, I knew they were having a good time, and we laughed together as I gave all kinds of clever answers. I felt good about the meeting. As my wife, Mary, and I left Rexburg and were driving back to Salt Lake, Mary moved over next to me and put her head on my shoulder. "How do you think it went?" I asked, smiling. Her answer changed me: "They expect more of you than that." Her reply stung a bit, but that is why we have companions. That is why we go to the Lord in individual prayer and companion prayer and family prayer. If we will listen to our companions and to the Lord—and try to get our pride out of the way—we can accomplish what the Lord would have us do.

One of President Spencer W. Kimball's frequent topics was marriage. He taught that there is no such thing as soul mates; that is, marriages are not made in heaven—two people are not destined from the premortal existence to meet and marry. President Kimball felt that we had to work together and work through our differences, that we had to get over our selfishness and not be spoiled, that we had to sacrifice and to share with one another. I remember him telling us, "Don't just pray to marry the one you love; pray to love the one you marry." Praying together daily will help love grow. So will expressing love for one another daily—more than once. Doctrine and Covenants 42:22 says: "Thou shalt love thy wife with all thy heart, and shalt cleave unto her and none else."

The proclamation promises, "Happiness in family life is most likely to be achieved when founded upon the teachings of the Lord Jesus Christ." The Lord has given us agency to accept or reject this proclamation. It would be wonderful if every mother and father understood, as they held a newborn babe in their arms, that the child was sent from a loving Heavenly Father into their home to be nurtured, cared for, and loved. Our homes should be protected havens. Individuals who abuse their spouse and/or children violate the laws of both God and society. Both violence and words hurt, and Church leaders have counseled that more subtle forms of abuse are evil as well. James 1:19 gives us advice about communicating: "Wherefore, my beloved brethren, let every man be swift to hear, slow to speak, and slow to wrath."

Parents are responsible to teach their children to walk in the ways of truth and to love and serve one another—rejecting the devil's ways. In Mosiah 4:14–15 we read: "And ye will not suffer your children that they go hungry, or naked; neither will ye suffer that they transgress the laws of God, and fight and quarrel one with another. . . . But ye will teach them to walk in the ways of truth and soberness; ye will teach them to love one another, and to serve one another." If we will pray and ask for guidance and if we will covenant with our Heavenly Father to obey the commandments, we are assured that we will be given the strength to accomplish what he has asked us to do in our families.

I have been touched to hear fathers, knowing that death is imminent, bless their families, testifying of the Savior and encouraging them to obey the commandments of God—to be worthy of those blessings that come to the faithful. If we are wise, we will also teach daily and testify by the way we live our lives. We will let our sons and daughters know that our

145

Heavenly Father lives, that we lived with him as spirits in families in the premortal life, and we can return to his presence and live in families once again for all the eternities.

NOTES

1. This proclamation was read by President Gordon B. Hinckley as part of his message at the general Relief Society meeting, Salt Lake City, Utah, 23 September 1995. See this volume, 132–33.

2. Ibid., 133.

3. Elaine L. Jack, "Building Relationships of Trust," Relief Society Open House, Fall 1994, 1.

4. Ibid., 1–2.

5. Ibid., 2.

6. Robert D. Hales, "How Will Our Children Remember Us?" *Ensign,* November 1993, 8–10.

MEASURING UP TO EXPECTATION

HELEN B. STONE

My dad, J. Hobart Bartlett, was an active, energetic, healthy ninety-one-year-old who exercised daily, went to the Family History Library every day, worked hard, and one day fell as he was crossing the street in downtown Salt Lake City. Unconscious and covered with blood, he was rushed to LDS Hospital. Doctors there determined that he had suffered a traumatic head injury, which altered his swallowing, his speech, his hearing, and his general mobility. They put a gastrointestinal tube into his stomach, which provided liquid nourishment without his having to swallow. My dad had been single for thirty-five years (my mother died when we children were teenagers, and Dad never remarried), and his self-imposed diet left a lot to be desired. Every morning: oatmeal and orange juice; every lunch: cottage cheese and wholewheat toast; and every supper: tuna fish and apples. We actually thought his liquid nutrition would add a little spice to his diet after so many years of the other.

His hospital stay stretched on. The therapy he received—physical, speech, and occupational—seemed to have little effect in restoring normal function. After a month, the doctors told us he needed to be transferred to a care facility of some

Helen B. Stone has taught nutrition and food science at the University of Rhode Island and Cornell University. She and her husband, John R. Stone, who is president of the New York New York Stake, are the parents of five children. She is a homemaker and serves as her ward's Relief Society president.

kind or to someone's home. My brother, Jim, and sister, Janet, live in Salt Lake City; and they had been absolutely wonderful to our dad for the previous eleven years. They had done for him tasks he didn't have the inclination or the patience to do for himself, such as balancing his checkbook, shopping for groceries, tidying his home, or even at times finishing up some details of his genealogical research. He could have done those things; he just didn't want to. So now it was my turn. Because my brother and sister both worked outside the home, it seemed a natural choice to take Dad home with me to New York. We went straight from the hospital to the Salt Lake airport to New York—a very stressful trip but without incident.

Home was noisy and busy. At the time, my husband and I had three college-age children home for the summer, two high school students, and an adult nephew living with us. I thought the activity would be a wonderful stimulation for my dad. Still, we were all nervous about Grandpa coming to live with us; he had always expected a lot of himself, as well as of his children and grandchildren. We knew he loved us, but he had always wanted us to be working hard and accomplishing *all* of the time. Measuring up to expectation could be a challenge.

But Dad was in a weakened state now. It was hard for him to talk or walk. Though he could walk a bit with a walker and somebody by his side, he could do very little for himself. We brushed his teeth, bathed him, dressed him, and really did everything for him.

We converted the dining room of our old colonial house into a bedroom because the stairs were difficult for him, and we began our adventure. I slept on a mattress on the floor to be close to him through the night. That first night we made a bathroom trip every thirty minutes. Sometimes we made it to the bathroom, and sometimes we didn't. When morning came, I felt as though night had never been, but I kept thinking, Maybe he's just nervous and restless because he's in a new place. This pattern, however, turned out to be the norm for the rest of his life. So the first major problem we had to address was lack of sleep.

At first I enlisted everyone's help, but that wasn't fair to those who went to school or to work every day. I found that they became so tired they sometimes slept through Dad's needs for help. At this point my eldest daughter, Stephanie, who had just graduated from Brigham Young University and was looking for a teaching position, decided she would alter her life's agenda to help me. She set up a tutoring business—allowing her to set her own hours and take turns doing night duty with me. On her nights, she did not even try to sleep. Also, my husband, John, stepped in whenever he could (and sometimes even when it was very difficult for him) to spell me.

Dad was an avid walker before his accident. To keep his body and mind as nimble as possible, we wanted to continue his walking however we were able. It gave Dad hope that life could continue as before his accident. So every hour, just about, we would laboriously walk down the street and back. These were very tender times for me because every single time we walked together, Dad, in his very limited speech, would express to me his gratitude for my care and his joy at being in our home. I felt a new softness and sweetness in him that I believe was a gift of the Spirit given to him at a time when it would make caring for him an easier task.

At the outset of our experience together, I was reminded of my favorite scripture in Job 29:13, in which Job is defending himself against his friends' unsympathetic comments. Job, among other things, says: "I caused the widow's heart to sing for joy." This was a major trial in my father's life, and I determined from the start that we as a family would do all that we could to make Dad's heart sing for joy. It didn't take a lot: little walks, little talks, gentle kisses, little touches, a listening ear, and mostly just a quiet presence. The children all visited his bedside each morning when they left for the day to explain their upcoming activities. Then at the end of the day they

149

would report back to him. This made him see that he was still the patriarch of this family and very much part of the activities of our home. My kids were fabulous.

One month into his stay with us, I left his bedside at 10 o'clock at night to make a short phone call. I didn't intend to be away very long, but in the middle of the call, my nephew rushed in to say, "Aunt Helen, Grandpa has fallen." He had been in bed. He must have tried to get up by himself, I thought. I ran into the room and found blood all over. He had fallen on the arm of the chair that I sat in most of the time right beside his bed. His eye was gouged, and blood was everywhere. I didn't know what to do, but I got a cloth and covered his eye. My daughter drove us to the nearest hospital emergency room. After six hours of surgery, we returned home, sobered about the responsibility that we had committed ourselves to. We realized now that someone (that quiet presence) had to be by Dad's side all of the time. He still wanted to be independent, so if anybody left his room, he tried to get out of bed. Thereafter that first year, we had to stay beside him day and night to prevent him hurting himself by trying to get up.

The second year, Dad was bedridden and began to choke a lot. He couldn't swallow, and phlegm collected in his throat. We rented a suction machine and eventually had to suction him regularly. He was peaceful and calm if someone was sitting by him. He was anxious and scared if no one was there. Arranging for someone always to be with Dad presented another major problem for me as the caretaker. I eliminated everything else from my life. Three of my children had gone back to school, my nephew had left, and I had two children at home—my daughter Stephanie, who was still doing night duty, and my high-school-age son, Greg. I was the only one left to be by his side during the day. I had a choice. I could either make this a happy experience for me and my dad, or I could begrudge every minute that I sat there thinking of other things that I needed to do.

For a long time I had wanted to make a serious study of the Old Testament. This seemed the perfect time. I brought in my scriptures and study books and put them around my chair in Dad's room. It tickled him that I was studying the scriptures like that. I often shared with him the things that I was learning. I also decided to attempt a "Families Are Forever" cross-stitch to put up for Dad to look at. I had never had the patience to cross-stitch in my life, although I had admired other people's needlework. So I learned to cross-stitch while I sat beside my dad. After the first one, I did several others. There was something very soul enriching about creating miniature works of art (though only I would call them art). These two projects helped me through a difficult period. My husband, my daughter, and my fifteen-year-old son, who were the only ones around after that first summer, spelled me in our constant vigil.

The physical demands of caring for Dad were enormous. Before he was bedridden, the lifting on and off the toilet and the daily bathing exacted effort from our legs and backs and feet that we really didn't know we had in us. After he was bedridden, it was position changing, suctioning, and totally sleepless nights. The toll was beginning to mount. I can't offer a solution for that, because I didn't cope well with the problem. I will probably always pay the price for not taking care of myself during this period. I was an avid walker before my dad came, but as his stay lengthened, I became less and less physically able to walk. Occasionally, when I could get someone to cover for me, I went swimming. That was my exercise. If I were to do it again, I would consult a physical therapist or specialists to learn both how to preserve my body and how to care better for a bedridden individual.

Even as my dad's expectations of me lessened, my expectations of myself increased. My bishop and close friends always said, "Oh, Helen, you're so strong. You are so wonderful to do this." And I thought, How can I ask for help when they think I'm so wonderful and so strong? So I forged ahead, too proud to get help, though people offered. I allowed overly high expectations of myself to drive me on past good sense.

Let me give you an example of how I felt. I wrote in my journal just six months before my dad died: "I have come to a point where I really and truly feel that I will not live long enough to finish taking care of Dad. There is not a single part of my body that is not in pain. I have headaches the likes of which I've never had before (and I've had some pretty grue-some migraines in my day). A few days ago I thought my head would blow up, and I called Dr. Cardillo. I told him I needed some help fast. He sent me right to the hospital for a CAT scan of my head. There were no tumors . . . nothing showed on the scan. What to do now?

"I took my problem to the Lord and begged for help. I told him that I was willing to care for Dad for as long as was nec-essary, but I just plain could not go on with my headaches (it was getting so I could not sleep for more than an hour at a time without being awakened with intense pain). I needed to know what to do for my pain, or I needed Dad to be taken to his heavenly home. It was the *next* day that Dad became so ill he had to be taken to the hospital. I felt this was absolutely a direct and forceful answer to my pleadings. I needed help, and I needed it fast. I was on the Lord's errand and he blessed me . . . as he always does. I felt so bad for Dad, but I honestly did not know how I could keep going. The headaches have eased, the pain in my legs, feet, and back has diminished, and now I feel like I can go on."

Because Dad was being fed via a G-tube, he sometimes aspirated his food, resulting in pneumonia. His fever would spike, and he would become very ill. The first time that hap-pened, the doctor gave me the option of sending him to the hospital for a quick IV antibiotic treatment or letting him stay home and possibly die. We discovered considerable opposition to the "rush" for help. It became apparent that the attitude of many people was that because his care was so difficult and I refused to put him in a home, we really ought to let him die at home with one of his bouts of pneumonia.

I'd spoken to the Lord about it many times, and I had felt a great peace about doing all we could to help him live. I felt the Lord was in control and that He would take him when the time was right. So every time he got really ill, I felt at peace helping him live.

Towards the end of Dad's life, we had little contact with people outside our immediate family. That troubled me, especially at Christmas time. As Dad got older and sicker, he could no longer talk, and people felt uncomfortable visiting him. I understood and forgave that, yet I still longed to have friends come. Christmas was nearing, and I thought how wonderful it would be to have someone besides our family carol to Dad for a little while. I didn't want to ask anybody because the holidays are family times and I knew how busy everyone is. So instead I talked to the Lord and specifically asked him to send somebody to carol to Dad. Surely it's a righteous desire to make this request of the Lord, I thought. He wants us to comfort the sick, he wants us to serve and uplift and bless the lives of others. So I prayed several times for that specific blessing. On Christmas Eve, a group came to our home, walked past the rest of us, and headed for Dad's room, asking, "Can we sing to your dad?" I know the Spirit led that family to sing to my dad and also to comfort me that Christmas Eve.

The day Dad passed away, 6 July 1994, I wrote in my journal: "The night was horrendous for Dad. His fever spiked, and he started horrible vomiting. He finally went to sleep at 6 o'clock this morning. I didn't want to turn him at all because he seemed to be so peaceful. It didn't really occur to me that he was probably in a coma. I thought he was just sleeping peacefully. By noon I was feeling pretty guilty that I hadn't changed his position . . . and when I tried to turn him I realized that he was not conscious. I called the nurse . . . she stopped by abt. 2 at which point Dad was struggling to continue breathing. The nurse told me that I would have to tell him it was okay to leave. I had a very hard time doing that, as I really did not want him to go. Finally, about 3 P.M. I hugged Dad and kissed him and told him that we had had a great time together and I considered him such a good pal, but now maybe it would be okay to go to Mom . . . she had waited a long time for him to come home. 50 minutes later he died. Oh—I'm so sad! Dad has been such a champion of me and my causes—all my life. What to do now? I feel so lonely."

Among the many things I have learned from this experience, one of the most important is that unrealistic expectations of others or self needlessly complicate life. Shakespeare described me when he said, "Expectation whirls me around."[1] Rather I would hearken to the counsel of the Lord: "Let your hearts be comforted . . . ; be still and know that I am God" (D&C 101:16). And when I think of Dad, I feel the joy that Jacob talks about when the Lord of the vineyard says: "If ye labor with your might *with me* ye shall have joy" (Jacob 5:71; emphasis added).

NOTE

1. Shakespeare, *Troilus and Cressida,* act III, scene ii, line 17.

DANCING TO DIFFERENT TUNES

SANDRA PETREE

I am married to a kind, loving, supportive husband who is, as far as he knows how to be, an excellent father. He is not a member of the Church. He goes to church every Sunday with us; we have regular family home evenings, family prayer, and scripture study. He drives to youth events and helps me with lesson preparation and anything else I have to do. No doubt some of you are wondering what I have to worry about.

But there are some problems, the most significant of which are hidden, with having such a supportive nonmember husband. One problem is that some people at church tend to think that it must be my fault, or the children's, that he hasn't joined yet. Another problem is that every new set of missionaries feels that all my husband needs is a direct challenge. He's had hundreds! Still another problem is that home teachers tend to concentrate more on trying to convert my husband than on trying to provide priesthood leadership for my family.

But the most serious problem is that when my children look at this good, kind, loving man, see his sacrifices for his family, and feel his warmth and his love, it's very hard for them to recognize the distinct benefits of membership in the Church. When they see our fairly solid, twenty-six-year marriage, it's

Sandra Ailey Petree is a candidate for the doctoral degree in English at the University of Arkansas. She serves as an institute of religion teacher, ward in-service leader, teacher development teacher, and Relief Society teacher. Sandra and her husband, James H. Petree, are the parents of five children.

hard for them to believe that marriage in the temple is worth waiting for. And, in a subtle and deadly way, my husband's decision year after year not to join the Church, even though he reads the scriptures and hears the lessons, has sometimes influenced my children to believe that commitment is unnecessary and even to wonder if the Church can really be what we say it is. Sometimes it seems that the result of my husband's terrific support is actually a removal of the underpinnings of testimony.

Some years ago as I crossed the living room where my children had left the television on, something caught my ear or eye, and I paused to watch two dancers, a male and a female, in a beautifully choreographed, synchronous ballet. I know very little about music or dance, but the grace and power and control of their movements were fascinating, and I sat down on the floor, leaning against my couch with my dust cloth and can of Pledge in hand, to watch.

It was breathtaking. The stage was dark, with no props or stage-setting, only the lights playing on the leaping and gliding figures of the dancers. They moved together, matching each other's steps and leaps and turns, touching occasionally, perfectly complementing each other, and their bodies seemed to be at once energized by and expressive of the music itself. I had the sense, sitting there in my sweats on housecleaning day, that I was watching something terribly important, a threefold meld of dancers and music so absolutely interdependent that none could have meaning without the others.

At one point, the female dancer stepped gracefully back into the shadows, and her partner had the spotlight alone. His dance was riveting. He leaped high, his powerful muscles demonstrating the vibrant tones of the music. I found myself moved to tears at the majesty of his movements. When his solo was finished, his partner moved back onto the stage, and again together they soared and bowed and swayed. The music seemed to engulf them—and me. Soon the male dancer, in his turn, dropped into the background, and the woman, alone, performed exquisite, intricate, delicate movements, truly inspiring to watch. Towards the end of her own lovely piece, she seemed to pause a moment and then stretched herself, arms together, high above her head, as though she were reaching for something beyond human sight. She reached from the points of her ballet shoes upward in one unbroken, graceful, elongated line. I was struck with admiration. Then, just as she stretched her own body to its utmost height, her partner stepped in and with his powerful arms lifted her off the floor, higher and higher, until the two of them seemed to form a straight conduit to the heavens.

When the dance ended, I turned off the television and sat with my dust cloth in my hand, weeping. I had received a revelation. The dance symbolized our Father's plan for marriage, a plan whereby a man and a woman, joined through the powers of the holy priesthood, might dance together and reach heights neither of them could achieve alone. Oh, what a melancholy revelation that seemed for me. Usually when the Holy Spirit teaches me, it is gentle, kind, encouraging, and uplifting. I wondered, Why would the Lord want to point out to me what I am, frankly, missing?

Since then I have learned more fully the meaning of that day's revelation. I cannot detail everything, but I would like to share with you the high points of how this revelation changed my life. The first thing I learned is that partners in an exquisite and eternal dance must develop their own powers and strength individually. The quality of our dance does not depend, and indeed *cannot* depend, upon our partner. We must develop spiritually and physically so that when (and I say *when,* not *if*) opportunity comes to dance a duet, we will be strong and skilled. How can we do that?

First of all, *we can readily do hard things.*

As you know, this is not a dispensation for wimps. At general conference, I have been struck by the number of times speakers refer to powerful and dynamically spiritual women. This is a dispensation that calls for powerful women. The greater our challenges, the more powerful the results can be.

In 1979, President Spencer W. Kimball addressed the women of the Church in the worldwide Women's Fireside Address, a remarkable event. Because he was in the hospital at the time, he asked his wife, Camilla, to read his remarks. President Kimball said: "I stress again the deep need each woman has to study the scriptures. We want our homes to be blessed with sister scriptorians—whether you are single or married, young or old, widowed or living in a family. . . . Become scholars of the scriptures—not to put others down, but to lift them up!"[1]

Easy things do not build power. We must study the scriptures. We must accept challenging callings. We must strive diligently and powerfully to teach our children (and our partners) the gospel of Jesus Christ. And we must develop ourselves to our fullest and finest potential. President Kimball went on to say: "Seek excellence in all your righteous endeavors, and in all aspects of your lives. . . . Much of the major growth that is coming to the Church in the last days will come because many of the good women of the world (in whom there is often such an inner sense of spirituality) will be drawn to the Church in large numbers. This will happen to the degree that the women of the Church reflect righteousness and articulateness in their lives and to the degree that the women of the Church are seen as distinct and different—in happy ways—from the women of the world. . . . Thus it will be that female exemplars of the Church will be a significant force in both the numerical and spiritual growth of the Church in the last days."[2]

In short, we must fill the measure of our creation. To me, that is the essence of President Kimball's message. No matter who I am married to, or what my parents or my children may choose to do, I must never lose sight of who I am. I am a daughter of Zion, a mother in Israel. Oh, sisters, the *power* in those names! Eleanor Roosevelt said to the women of America at a hard time, "You must do the thing you think you cannot do."[3]

What might that be? It differs for each of us and comes at different times in our lives. Perhaps you know within yourself that what you need to be working on right now is becoming a scriptorian, developing a talent, continuing your education, beginning an exercise program, learning to sew, bridling your tongue, disciplining yourself in one or a thousand ways. To make your own dance a thing of beauty, you must *do hard things*—and do them cheerfully and well.

Second, *we must hear, know, and feel the music, which is the gospel of Jesus Christ.* Our goal is for the music to become so intricately a part of our mental and physical landscapes that we develop perfection in the rhythm of the dance. This means, of course, that we must practice living the gospel seriously every day, every hour of the day, until the music springs up within us, until we are prompted to our exquisite dances by the pulsation of the music of the gospel of Jesus Christ within our own souls.

Third, *we must not become resigned to feeling that we are alone, that we dance entirely alone.* Remember that our partners are dancing, too—only they are hearing different music. Now, that sounds ridiculous—how can we dance with a partner whose beat differs, sometimes wildly, from our own? This surely is not a dance but cacophony and confusion! "Besides," we may complain to ourselves, "it's impossibly hard! Trying to match such a partner makes it harder for me than for anyone else!" Perhaps it does; but, if so, *what might our own dances be if we learn to do this hard thing?*

Stephen Robinson taught an important lesson from an experience he had at a diving competition when he was young. "While the rest of us did our crisp little swan dives, back dives, and jackknives, being ever so careful to arch our backs and point our toes, [one young man from the less

159

affluent part of town] attempted back flips, one-and-a-halfs, doubles, and so on. But, oh, he was sloppy. He seldom kept his feet together, he never pointed his toes, and he usually missed his vertical entry. The rest of us noted with smug satisfaction as the judges held up their scorecards that he consistently got lower marks than we did with our safe and simple dives, and we congratulated ourselves that we were actually the better divers. . . . The announcement of the winners was a great shock to us, for the brave young lad with the flips had apparently beat us all." Full of outraged justice, a disgruntled Stephen stomped over to the scorers' table to demand an explanation. "'Degree of difficulty,' the scorer replied matter-of-factly as he looked [Stephen] in the eye. 'Sure, you had better form, but he did harder dives. When you factor in the degree of difficulty, he beat you hands down, kid.'"[4] Think about that.

Henry David Thoreau said, "However mean your life is, meet it and live it; do not shun it and call it hard names."[5] This is not only good advice but is inescapable advice! We each must live the lives we have. President Brigham Young said, "Every trial and experience you have passed through is necessary for your salvation."[6] No one doubts that it is hard to dance when the partners hear different music. But if that's the stage we're performing on, that's what we have to do. Can we do it? Yes, we can. James 4:6 says, "But he giveth more grace." More grace than what, we may ask? More grace than life can give trials. We *can* do it.

As to the cacophony, the truth is that if we listen for them, there are many times when the two strands of music, the one your partner hears and the one you hear, actually correspond. When that happens we can dance wonderfully and joyfully together. It may be through discovering the places where we can dance together that our greatest learning and joy and most significant mutual growth will occur. In my marriage, my husband and I have very similar desires for our children and hopes for their future. In that measure of our music, we dance perfectly together.

There are cautions, of course. We can never compromise our own forms, we can never dance to music we do not hear, and we can never permit other tunes to drown out our own music. Remember that in doing hard things, we must always do them to the tune of the gospel of Jesus Christ. In this we are not without companionship and support. The most important part of what I learned from my revelation of the dance is this: *There are never only two partners on the stage.* The third and most powerful partner stays out of the spotlight, but his strength and his presence are always available. The Lord Jesus Christ hears *both* strains of music. He responds to both, and he loves both dancers. He is the choreographer who enables the dance to go on.

When we stretch ourselves to the utmost limits of our reach, when every muscle from our toes inside our ballet shoes to the tips of our fingers is extended to its farthest point, when we feel our hearts might burst with our efforts and we agonizingly call for a partner to lift us those last few inches that we simply cannot reach on our own, then the third partner *will always* step in from the sidelines. I testify to you that *we never dance alone.* The Lord himself, our third partner, will lift us, raise us, extend our reaches until we, too, soar in power and joy.

Meanwhile, the Lord continues to reveal to us how to dance out our lives on the stage of this earth, which is of course only a dress rehearsal for eternity. One day by inspiration, counsel from Isaiah came to me in a time of serious reaching, when I needed help stretching far enough. Reading Isaiah, especially chapter 30, almost always comforts and encourages me. This particular day, as I knelt weeping and pleading for the soul of one of my children, I felt inspired to read this chapter again. After I had read verse 15, "In quietness and in confidence shall be your strength," I exclaimed, "But,

161

Lord! Look at me! I don't feel quiet, and I certainly don't feel confident! I need help!" And then he answered, as he always does, quietly and gently, "No, dear. The quietness must be in *you*, but the confidence must be in *me*." And so it is.

NOTES

1. Spencer W. Kimball, "The Role of Righteous Women," *Ensign*, November 1979, 102.

2. Ibid., 102, 103–4.

3. Anna Eleanor Roosevelt, *You Learn by Living* (1990), quoted in *Bartlett's Familiar Quotations*, 16th ed. (Boston: Little, Brown and Company, 1992), 654.

4. Stephen E. Robinson, *Following Christ: The Parable of the Divers and More Good News* (Salt Lake City: Deseret Book, 1995), 34–35.

5. Henry David Thoreau, *Walden; Or, Life in the Woods* (New York City: Macmillan, 1992), 231.

6. Brigham Young, in *Journal of Discourses*, 26 vols. (London: Latter-day Saints' Book Depot, 1854–86), 8:150.

LESSONS FROM THE PRODIGAL SON

WENDY L. WATSON, ELOUISE TROTTER, AND WENDY EVANS RUPPEL

The following is a panel conversation among three women: Wendy L. Watson, the moderator, and two Latter-day Saint women, Elouise Trotter and Wendy Evans Ruppel, who have had intimate personal experience with prodigals in their families.

WENDY W. (MODERATOR): We cannot cover everything related to the complex, heart-wrenching, and soul-stirring topic of prodigals, but we invite you to reflect on some key issues and lessons from the prodigal son. A *prodigal* is defined as a reckless, wasteful person; the term *prodigal son* designates a returned wanderer, from the account of a family told in Luke 15. We hope to uncover here some ideas about what helps and

Wendy L. Watson is an associate professor, teaching marriage and family therapy graduate classes in the Department of Family Sciences at Brigham Young University. She serves as stake Relief Society president in a BYU stake.

Elouise Trotter is the mother of six and grandmother of nineteen. She and her husband, Eugene W. Trotter, also reared three foster sons and participated in the Indian Placement program. She worked as a secretary for the United States Army and served a mission in Texas. She has served as Gospel Doctrine teacher in Sunday School.

Wendy Evans Ruppel holds a master's degree in counseling from Hawthorne University and a CAC (certified addiction counselor) certificate from the University of Utah. She is the clinical coordinator for Lifeline, a rehabilitation center, counseling adolescents with addictions, behavior problems, and sexual abuse issues. She is the mother of six and grandmother of seven and teaches the Laurels in her ward.

what hinders our relationships with the prodigal sons in our lives, whether our prodigal son is a son or a daughter, a husband, a mother, or a sister. Elouise Trotter and Wendy Evans Ruppel bring rich and diverse personal and professional experience to the topic of prodigals. These are women of depth, great understanding, and wisdom. I wonder if loving the prodigals in our lives draws forth these qualities in women, or if these women were always this way. Many of us have increased depth, understanding, wisdom, and charity because of our experiences as prodigals or with prodigals. Let me begin by asking Elouise and Wendy to sketch their own "prodigal son" experience or experiences.

ELOUISE: My son left home at fourteen. During the next few years, I came to know a number of sheriffs and police chiefs in the surrounding communities, as well as in outlying states. He was away for fifteen years. One day I received a call from Australia (he had lived all over the world). He said he was going to walk across China, possibly wouldn't see me again, and wanted me to know where a few of his things were. I told him I thought I could find a six-foot-four inch, long-haired redhead in China. Two days later the phone rang, and my son said, "Mom, I'll be in Salt Lake in an hour. I haven't time to talk. Meet me."

I met him, but he was neither redheaded nor fair-skinned. He was deeply tanned and had long blond hair. He had lived, virtually alone, on an island in the South Pacific. I didn't know what had happened, but here he was, at home. "Mom," he said, "you promised that if I'd ever live like I was supposed to and follow your rules, you would educate me. I'm ready to be educated." In three years, he graduated from the University of Utah with honors and received a twenty-thousand-dollar scholarship to the University of Miami law school. I finally felt there was hope. He went to law school and then decided that wasn't what he wanted to do. He came back home and worked as a radio announcer for a while. He's now with one of the airlines.

In the middle of all this, he married a wonderful Latter-day Saint girl. She has a master's degree and is a nurse practitioner. She's been in Russia on medical teams and she's run a 26K, so you can see she's up to him. It's going to work. He's not the boy I dreamed of, but he's so much better than I imagined possible in my most despairing moments.

WENDY R.: I offer not only the experiences of my own family but my experiences as a counselor who works with young people. I see more potential prodigal sons in a day than people see in a lifetime. I am no stranger to the heartache of watching a child make poor choices. As the wife of a former stake president and bishop, I have found it really interesting to sit on the lawn of the jail and wait for my own son to walk up the ramp so I can take him home. I've done that. I've been there with more than one of my own children who had difficult times.

WENDY W. (MODERATOR): Within the Church, we sometimes find women and men who are blaming of families with problems, including themselves if they are the ones experiencing the problems. Some even believe that families have prodigals because they don't live the gospel correctly. Such a belief may actually exacerbate the situation. Some families won't admit they have a problem because of what they believe that says about them. They will ignore what is happening, keep secrets about their problems, or wait inordinately long to seek help. "If I don't look at a problem, it doesn't exist." What other beliefs worked against your being able to deal with problems?

WENDY R.: I think every home has its prodigal in one way or another. All of us struggle in various ways. Believing that if we are obedient and obey the commandments, everything in life will turn out okay is a fantasy. How many times have your kids said to you, "Mom, it isn't fair" and you have said, "Honey, life isn't fair." But we also need to teach them that eternal life *is* fair, that in the long haul there is justice in all things. One of

165

our sons was told in his patriarchal blessing that the Savior would embrace him, call him by name, and tell him, "Well done, my good and faithful servant." This son didn't cut his hair for nine years after his mission, he has twenty-seven tattoos on his body, and he's a very interesting person. But that doesn't mean his blessing isn't valid, because Heavenly Father truly knows his soul and his spirit and what he deals with. I'm grateful I don't have to judge him—or anyone else's child, either.

ELOUISE: Judging from outside appearances was a disaster for us when we first moved to Utah from California. My thirteen-year-old son and I were able to carry on conversations 80 percent of the time, I'd say, on a level where we didn't blast out each other's ears. (The rest of the time we did argue rather pointlessly.) My son was reading when he was four, and he came home from kindergarten at age five to tell me he was no longer going to school because he knew everything the teacher was teaching. In California at age twelve, he audited high school classes. Then we moved to Utah, and we found that he was neither fish nor fowl in this new environment. Number one, he didn't know anything about Utah history and, worst of all, he had long hair. In the 1970s, long hair was a dirty word. I'll never forget talking to the school counselor that summer. He said, "When he gets his hair cut, he'll be welcome here, Mrs. Trotter." My son's hair was touching his collar. So he had it cut. On registration day I dropped him off at school, and as I was driving out of the school yard, my son came running after me and jumped into the car. He related that as he entered the school, the school counselor had grabbed him by the neck, pushed him down to the floor in front of the other students, and said, "You've got to get your hair cut, Trotter. The minute it touches your collar you are out of here." We calmed down and left, but that night my son ran away.

WENDY W. (MODERATOR): While we're talking about

cultural beliefs that can be arbitrary and hurtful, let's look at the beliefs, even about yourselves, that the prodigals in your lives have helped you to give up. Some women, for example, believe "I am right and they are wrong." Emotional violence occurs when we hold an idea to be true and insist that another's idea is wrong and *must* change. It's the "and must change" part that causes the violence. Can you think of any beliefs about yourself that you had to shift, that you found initially constraining?

ELOUISE: You have hit a nerve with me. My number one problem with my runaway son was that I figured I was right and he was wrong. And I wanted him to be all that he could be. He once sent me a card in which he had written, "I am who I am." That helped me give up trying to reinvent my son. I finally eased back. His overachieving father was also part of the problem. My husband had sold his soul to the company store, as even he now admits. He was known as Mr. Perfect at his company. His hours were unbelievable. I raised the children alone. I remember once when our son was four or five, his father came striding through the door looking like a million bucks, and my little boy said, "Daddy, can I touch you? I washed my hands." Does that give you an idea of what my husband and I were doing wrong at this point? That's probably another reason our son ran away at age thirteen.

WENDY R.: There's a hideous, damaging myth of the perfect parent that some of us invent inside our heads when we are told that we must bring our children back to Heavenly Father. Doing that doesn't mean we bring them back kicking and screaming and saying, "Mommy, I don't want to go." But sometimes we try to do that anyway, only more subtly. We make ourselves incredibly helpful. (You know that old joke, "Behind every Eagle Scout there's a pushy mother.") We've probably all been there. We "suggest" to our child. We wake him up every morning; we go back and wake him up again. In fact, it's a pattern. He doesn't get up the first time because he knows we'll come back a second time. Getting him up becomes our responsibility. When we suggest, when we schedule for them, when we help them with everything under the sun, when we're there, there, there—what's the message? At a family counseling session in my office a son looked at his mother and said, "Mom, when you do so much for me, that makes me believe that I'm incompetent and can't do things for myself." Latter-day Saint women may easily fall into this trap. We may convince our children they are incompetent by being too helpful and full of suggestions.

WENDY W. (MODERATOR): That's similar to what one woman told me: "Things started to change when I realized that my husband still believed in the gospel; he just didn't believe in himself."

WENDY R.: For years Mother's Days were particularly painful for me. They were a reminder of all that hadn't gone right with my children. One Mother's Day I stayed home from church meetings because I was in so much pain. When I was thirty, I went through a windshield, had 250 stitches in my face, broke my ribs, my shoulders, and burned my hair off. It was a painful, horrendous two years, but I would go back and do that again before I would live through the kind of pain I went through as I watched my children, by their own choices, leave. I felt they were abandoning me and my value system. That particular Sunday I cried so hard that if my neighbors hadn't all been in church, I'm sure they would have called the paramedics. I cried and cried and cried. As I walked around the corner in my bedroom, I caught a glimpse of a small statue of the Savior in the Garden of Gethsemane that had been a gift to me. Reflected in several mirrors, it was like a vision repeated over and over again of the Savior at Gethsemane.

A message, a feeling, a knowledge came into my head: this is what the Garden of Gethsemane was about. The Savior bled at every pore because of his sorrows and sadnesses for us. I was struggling with only three prodigals, and he struggles with millions. I promised myself and the Savior that day that I would never let my children's choices ruin the quality of my own life. Suddenly I understood more about Christ's crucifixion and atonement than I ever had before.

WENDY W. (MODERATOR): What other beliefs helped the two of you through your experiences with prodigals? What beliefs gave you hope? What beliefs provided perspective and facilitated patience?

ELOUISE: Foremost in my life is knowing that I'm not on an island, white-knuckling through my children's problems alone. I've always felt that Heavenly Father was there, that he knows what's going on. We've been a family of miracles, and I've had my share. Often when we were having problems, we would talk about the nice things that had happened to us as a family. I kept my son in touch with his sisters, even when he was into drugs and living a life I did not approve of. He called and asked one summer, "Can the girls come over and spend some time?" It was hard, but I let them go. Being with his sisters, I think, kept him in touch. (Today he is very close to them.) I felt my Heavenly Father guided me to do that. How do you get that guidance? By living the gospel and doing the best you can, keeping their names on the temple prayer roll, having daily prayer, reading scriptures, doing all that you can, supporting everyone in what they're doing, and trying to love their father unconditionally.

That last part was the hardest for me, because my husband was excommunicated in the midst of all this. Somehow I kept my marriage together. I had a great bishop and a great stake president who helped me through. I used to say that I was holding on by my toenails and looking for the toenail clipper. Once I went to my stake president and said, "I can't do this any more. I've got too much on my plate." He told me to stay with it. For years, my mother had been telling me, "Get out, get out, get out!" I called her up and said, "Mother, I'm getting out." And my mother said, "What's the matter with you? You get hold of your bishop right this minute and get a blessing." So I called my bishop, and he said, "I'll be right up." He gave me a blessing and told me that this wasn't a trial of my husband and of my son—this was a test for me.

WENDY R.: The teacher of an Old Testament class I once took told the story of a very dear friend of his who was faithful and true. The friend had a son who had taken his parents down the road and back, and they were weary. Finally the son had killed someone and was at the state prison. His parents were distraught. The father prayed and fasted, read the scriptures and studied and pondered, trying to understand what he had done wrong and what he could do now to rectify the situation.

As he sat in the temple one day, he had a strong impression that his home had been picked specifically for this soul, a young man who had been present in the premortal existence, to be taught the principles of the gospel, to understand right from wrong. When the time came that he chose to commit murder, he needed to be fully accountable for his choice. Now, if anything doesn't seem fair, that doesn't. Look what these parents went through.

But if we aspire for eternal increase, we can't make a choice on either side of the veil to refuse assignments and avoid hard experiences. Our Father's plan was not the plan whereby none of his spirit children would be lost, and he weeps for his children when they suffer and make poor choices. When Abraham was asked to sacrifice his son, he must have had a glimpse of how difficult it may be to have eternal increase. We cannot choose eternal life unless we've had the painful as well as joyful experiences upon which to base our choices.

WENDY W. (MODERATOR): When a friend loses a family member to death, it seems natural to join her in grieving and offer support in a variety of ways. But when a friend's daughter is immoral or a husband turns to drugs, support seems more difficult. We are often tempted in such situations to offer advice. What is the best and the worst advice you received during your experiences?

ELOUISE: The worst advice I ever received was from a well-meaning soul who said, "This is just a phase. He will grow out of it." You do wait for the prodigal to grow out of it, and, therefore, you miss opportunities. My son came to me once, trying to tell me about his father. He was the first one to pick up on the trouble brewing in our marriage. I said, "You're all wrong. That's not right. I don't know where you got that. I've observed and that's not happening." I refused to communicate. Families with problems need to take time to talk and communicate, not wait for one another to "grow out of it." I try to avoid judging children on little things, like hair or clothes or food choices, so I can be open to every possibility within them, to talk about beliefs.

My best advice is to refuse to get hung up on things that aren't important. My children grew up in California, and I saw long hair. Once I walked into my family room to find asleep on the floor eight long-haired people I had never before seen in my life. When they started to leave, I discovered that one of them was my son.

WENDY R.: The worst advice I ever heard was from someone who said, "Parents cannot be happier than their saddest child." That is simply untrue. The Savior does not stop *his* eternal progression when things aren't going well for *us*. He continues in his work. He may cry for us, but he doesn't discontinue his work.

The best advice I ever had came from a definition related to my specialty, which is drug- and alcohol-abuse counseling.

171

A colleague of mine said an addict is a person who answers a spiritual call by going to the wrong address. That didn't make sense at first, but then I thought about it. All of us, when we're not doing well, have an empty place inside us that we want to fill. Some of us go shopping; some of us eat; some of us get See's chocolates; some of us go to Vegas to gamble; some get involved sexually. Whatever our addiction is, what we really want deep down is to be happy and feel close to our Heavenly Father again. That longing is okay. But we go to the wrong place and try the wrong remedy, and it doesn't work. That's what makes addicts. The *only* way we can fill that empty hole inside is by having faith in Heavenly Father. That is the only thing that works.

WENDY W. (MODERATOR): When we're in the midst of problems, we often ask ourselves agonizing questions—questions that may have no answer and that may actually increase our suffering. For example, when Alma the Younger did his prodigal wondering and wandering, Alma the Elder, if he was a typical parent, probably asked himself, "How can I remain president of the Church when I have family problems? How can I, who am so ineffective with my own son, counsel others?" So, Wendy and Elouise, what questions have you agonized over?

ELOUISE: Number one was, Did I really agree to this? And number two, when I looked in the mirror and saw my mother, I asked myself, "Why are you repeating her mistakes?" Do you find your mother showing up in your life in the way you deal with your own children? Do you remember having said, "I'm never going to do that to my children." I used to say I'm never going to have kids with runny noses. I had six of them.

I came really late to the gospel party. I didn't show up until I was in my twenties. And when I did, I was so excited. Since then, the gospel has been my life, my sailing ship in the stormy sea. I turn to the gospel for everything. In fact, when they were growing, my kids tired of hearing their mother quote the scriptures. But I have a scripture that's my own. I made it up, with the help of the scriptures. It goes, "Be still my mouth. Trust God and lean not to your own understanding."

WENDY R.: Perhaps the biggest question when you're in agony is just *Why?* The answer is different for every occasion. I take comfort from what Elder Orson F. Whitney, interpreting a statement of Joseph Smith, taught in a 1929 general conference: "The Prophet Joseph Smith declared—and he never taught more comforting doctrine—that the eternal sealings of faithful parents and the divine promises made to them for valiant service in the Cause of Truth, would save not only themselves, but likewise their posterity. Though some of the sheep may wander, the eye of the Shepherd is upon them and sooner or later they will feel the tentacles of Divine Providence reaching out after them and drawing them back to the fold. Either in this life or in the life to come, they will return." I waited all my life—all my life—to hear that. So what can we do now? Elder Whitney says simply, "Pray for your careless and disobedient children; hold onto them with your faith. Hope on, trust on, till you see the salvation of God."[1]

Unusual trials are upon us in the latter days. In my profession, the comment I hear most often on what is happening is, "We must be reaching the bottom of the gene pool." But it's more than just biology. It's spiritual. Every day the battle becomes more severe and more serious, and a lot of our "why" questions don't have answers that we can understand in this life. So for me it's a matter of faith, of truly knowing the Savior well enough to know that there is a reason and that there is justice in all things. More important, there is mercy in all things. Sometimes all I can have faith in is that Heavenly Father and Jesus Christ know what they're doing. In the end it will all turn out.

WENDY W. (MODERATOR): The moral agency of the

prodigal family member influences much of what tran-
spires; however, some women find that their responses to the
choices of a prodigal often only make the situation worse. For
example, some women find that in their effort to set a good
example and to get their loved one back on the road again,
they're really sending the message, "Do you see how far you
are from my standard?" So, although we may have very little to
do with the initial wandering of loved ones, our best-intended
efforts may actually exacerbate the prodigalness in those we
love. As we prod our prodigals with our version of the iron
rod, we may actually add to their suffering and to ours. Can
you share an example of well-intended efforts that only drove
your prodigal even further away from where you hoped he or
she would be?

ELOUISE: Several of our children were teenagers when we
moved here from California. Doctors thought the drier air here
would be better for my lungs, which had been damaged by
polio. My children did not like Utah. Our backyard in
California had been thirty thousand acres of virgin redwood.
My kids had lots of room, lots of animals. We came up here
with cats, dogs, and horses. We found a cement pond to live
by and a yard the size of a postage stamp, comparatively
speaking. We didn't include the children in our decision to
move—we just said that the doctors had given me only four or
five years to live if we didn't move to a drier climate.

That mistake hit Mark the hardest. What happened at
school with the counselor was a repeat of what had already
happened the first Sunday we attended our new ward. The
bishop walked over and put his arm around my boy and said,
"Son, when you get your hair cut, you'll be welcome here." I'm
not saying that the bishop was wrong. I am saying that my son
was ready for that. He wanted to hear it. It justified his being
who he was and how he was. I tried to talk him out of his feelings instead of letting him have them. I think that was my

biggest mistake, not letting my children have their feelings and express them freely in front of me.

WENDY R.: Imagine this scenario: Your daughter has fallen down a mine shaft and you stand at the top and holler down to her, "You get up here right now." It's probably an impossibility for that child to climb out by herself. But if we climb down, put our arms around her, and climb out of the mine shaft together, things work a lot better.

When we take our perfection yardstick and measure our children every day, they notice that they keep coming up short. Our constant reminders drive them away. Parenthood is about going through life *with* our children; it's not about criticizing them or constantly reminding them of their inadequacies. Share your own inadequacies with them; they've probably already noticed. Take a few minutes and share with your children how hard it is: "I know this is hard for you. It is for me, too. What can I do to help?" You'll work together a lot better.

ELOUISE: Don't be afraid to fall off your pedestal. It really doesn't hurt.

WENDY W. (MODERATOR): Robert Millet, dean of Religious Education at Brigham Young University, said: "It is a sin against charity and a crime against human decency to ignore or belittle or speak unkindly—to judge—those whose children [or other loved ones] stray. I believe God will hold us accountable if we do so."[2] Elouise and Wendy, how did the bond of charity affect you in your relationship with yourself, with the prodigal, and other family members?

ELOUISE: A stream of unkempt young people flowed through our house for several years. My son said he sent them to test my Christianity. They came from all walks of life, from beggars to sons of college professors. Those young people taught me to listen, something I didn't do before. I learned to cut hair. I learned to clean out fingernails—ones that hadn't been cleaned forever—of kids who couldn't believe that anybody cared that much about them.

We found a counselor through LDS Social Services who saw us those first few years of working with Mark. Mark liked him and confided in him. He was from Chicago and had been one of these kids—he'd been where they had been—before he joined the Church and eventually became a bishop. One day, after we had had an especially rousing session with Mark, the counselor said, "Let him go. Let him go. He will be okay. He can take care of himself. If you keep holding him like you're doing, you're going to destroy your family." And he also said, "It's better that one should perish than that a whole family go down." That's why we let him go.

As I said, out of all of this, I became humbled. I prayed to my Heavenly Father. I had moments when I knew the Holy Ghost was guiding and directing me, not only for my son but for other people. I remember when we took in our Korean son, Yong-in Shin. There was a marvelous moment when I knew that was what my Heavenly Father wanted me to do. I couldn't handle my own son, but I could handle other people's. Yong-in Shin went on to receive his doctorate. Another boy we worked with called us from a prison in California, and I said to him, "Read your scriptures and get your head together." He came back to Utah, and we baptized him a member of the Church. I couldn't do it with my own son, but I could do it with a stranger's. Isn't that something? But the Holy Ghost was a constant, wonderful presence during those times. I knew wisdom was being distilled from heaven into my mind, telling me how to deal with those boys whose mothers were worrying and weeping as I had.

WENDY R.: I think Elouise's advice about letting go is absolutely perfect when you've done everything you should do—not everything you *could* do but everything you *should* do. Then you need to let go and turn the whole situation over to God, because he knows better than we.

God knew there would be only one perfect person on this earth, and it wasn't you or me.

WENDY W. (MODERATOR): What words do you have for a woman who fears she is losing a loved one to the influences of the world?

ELOUISE: First of all, recognize that in all of us the gospel operates at different levels of obedience, belief, comprehension, and testimony. Stick with the truth, whether it makes you look good or bad. Don't lie to your children. If you have made a mistake, say so. Ask for forgiveness. Lies are wandering ghosts—they show up when you least expect them, and they can make more trouble in your life. You may think, "Oh, this is something the children shouldn't know. This is something we shouldn't tell them." But don't lie to them, and don't play with their minds. They sense what is going on, and they need you to clarify things for them.

Help your children remember that God is in their lives. Talk about him daily. Thank God for what he has done for you and for your children. Start early to help your children see God in their lives. You never know what will influence them. For instance, my son legally changed his name from Mark to Nick. When I asked why, he explained, "Mom, there were many times when I thought I was dead. In fact," he said, "I've had guns this far from my face. And somehow I would find myself out of the situation, so my friends nicknamed me 'Nick,' because I was always out in the nick of time." And he said, "You know what? I told them the reason I'm out is because my mom keeps my name in the temple and my mom prays for me."

Keep their names—and yours—on the temple rolls. Who's to say who needs the most help, you or your child? When you go to the temple, be worthy of the blessings you seek. Don't go seeking something you can't handle. You've got to be able to handle the blessings God gives you. You've got to live so they're viable in your life.

That marvelous Social Services counselor told us to speak love every day of our lives. When my children were little, we put a small message box by each of their beds. No matter how much trouble we'd had during the day or how much had gone wrong, I would go into my room, write out little messages, and put one in each of the boxes each night. They read them before they went to bed. It made a difference for them. My son said to me of his years away, "I had some nights when I would look for the little box."

Remember that no matter what you're going through, it will not last. The Book of Mormon has a phrase that you read over and over again: "And it came to pass." Remember that whatever comes into your life, it came to pass—it didn't come to stay. Heavenly Father wants what we want—an eternal family. His goals are constant. He is committed. We must be also. Center our lives in Christ. I don't care what else goes on around us. We will never fail if we center our lives in Christ.

WENDY R.: One of my prodigals came back home for a short spell. We did not want to scare him off with three thousand rules about behavior and deportment, so we established four or five most-important, bottom-line rules of our home. Because I have sons who are addicted to drugs and alcohol, I know that one of the rules is that you can't drink alcohol or use drugs anywhere on the planet and live in this house. That may sound a little heavy, but that's the way it is. When your child is an addict in the process of using, he or she can take your home right down the drain and all the younger siblings with it. It's a very difficult thing. So, you have to set up that rule: You drink or use anywhere, you can't live at home.

Other rules are, Don't smoke anywhere around here—if you want to smoke, do it someplace else; You need to go to sacrament meeting with us; On occasion, participate in some family events. Only a few rules, but you need to set a bottom line about the things you absolutely cannot tolerate. It's your home; you have a right to refuse to allow a behavior to be there.

Heavenly Father never ever takes away our agency. We always have choices in our lives, and our children do, too. We do not have to compromise our family value system to have our children be at home, but we also need to resist constantly measuring them by our own yardstick. We need to listen to them. We need to realize that life is not a destination but a journey; it's our job to go through the journey side by side with them. We need to refrain from being judgmental. Those of you who've been there know the pain of going to your son's friends' farewells and the pain as you sit in your bench and say to yourself, "Well, at least my son's alive." Sometimes that's all you get.

Don't be judgmental. Don't set your expectations too high. Be accepting. Love them. Always follow the example of the Savior.

WENDY W. (MODERATOR): I'd like to offer some final thoughts about the prodigals in our lives who are listening to a different drum, a drum that's deafening their ears to the sweet sounds of the gospel. As we clothe ourselves with the bond of charity, we can seek gifts of the Spirit. One gift, the gift of discernment, allows us not only to detect evil in one that appears righteous but to detect goodness in those who appear unrighteous.

We commenced this discussion by defining the terms *prodigal* and *prodigal son*. Synonyms for *prodigal* as an adjective include "profuse, lavish, extravagant, excessive, abundant." How differently would we approach the prodigals in our life if we remember the synonym *abundant* when we think of them? Do the prodigals in our lives show us the abundant love of the Savior for ourselves and for our wandering loved ones?

I'm also interested in words related to *prodigal*—words such as *prodigious,* which means "marvelous, amazing," and *prodigy,* meaning "marvelous thing, or person endowed with surprising qualities or abilities." A colleague of mine says that problem children in LDS families are her most interesting cases. So my question is, How is the prodigal in your life a wonderful example of some quality? When we prod our prodigals and try to turn out a product, we miss the prodigious aspects, the marvelous, amazing aspects of our currently wandering loved ones. So another question is, What amazing aspect of your prodigal have you been overlooking?

The causes of prodigalness are many and varied. Some women may find it helpful to ask themselves, How differently would we approach our wandering loved ones if we saw the defiant behavior as something arising from their moral agency, not as arising from a deficiency in us or in our relationship with them? Robert Millet wrote: "As a parent I can bear testimony, live my religion, encourage my children to search and ponder and pray, but in the end the depth of their testimony and the level of their commitment will be largely a product of their own choosing. The exercise of agency can be painful."[3]

Women often seem to prefer to feel guilty rather than out of control. When we feel guilty, it means we did something or failed to do something. So although we feel guilt, we also feel we can do something differently next time. We might ask ourselves, How differently would I approach my loved one if I didn't feel responsible for everything he is or is not doing? Other women find it useful to consider, How might my responses be exacerbating the situation? When those we love choose to turn away from gospel truths, do we turn away from them? As long as we keep distance between us and the wanderer (or as long as the wanderer experiences distance, despite what we believe we are doing to express acceptance), things do not get better. So we might ask, How might the distance that my loved ones are feeling from me increase how distant they feel from the Lord?

Another set of questions: Do we allow the prodigal to come home or do we show through our relentless questions on the same theme that we really don't believe that they will ever change or that change is even possible? If you were to believe that the prodigal in your life is closer to home than you think, perhaps even just around the corner, what would you give up thinking, asking, and doing? Do we show that we believe Christ when he says, "Though your sins be as scarlet, they shall be as white as snow"? (Isaiah 1:18). Are we seeking to understand and access the power of the Atonement in our own lives?

In our efforts to fix the situation, we may unwittingly find ourselves in the arena of unrighteous dominion. In the July 1989 *Ensign,* Elder H. Burke Peterson points out that all of us can drift into unrighteous dominion.[4] A colleague, Jim Harper, and I adapted Elder Peterson's marvelous questions to family situations:

- As a Church member, believing in the doctrine of agency, how do I guard and protect the agency of others in relationships?
- Do I insist that others obey me and do most things my way?
- Do family members seem reluctant to talk to me about particular feelings and concerns?
- Do I dislike sharing the power and responsibility for decision making in family matters?
- Do I feel I will lose respect and authority if I admit to being in the wrong?
- Do I ask for and appreciate feedback?
- Do I expect to be the main source of inspiration for my family rather than expecting others to listen to the Spirit?
- Do I criticize family members more often than I compliment them?
- Are my best intentions to live the gospel as fully as I can felt by others as oppressive or loving, as constraining or freeing?
- What would I look for in others that would tell me that, despite the sincere intentions of my heart, others feel that I exercise unrighteous dominion?

Let's get on with the business of building our relationships with our prodigals and loving them as the Savior loves. And how does the Savior love? According to President Howard W. Hunter: "God's chief way of acting is by persuasion and patience and long-suffering, not by coercion and stark confrontation. He acts by gentle solicitation and by sweet enticement. He always acts with unfailing respect for the freedom and independence that we possess. He wants to help us and pleads for the chance to assist us, but he will not do so in violation of our agency. He loves us too much to do that, and doing so would run counter to his divine character."[5]

May we clothe ourselves with the bond of charity and love our prodigals and ourselves as the Savior loves.

NOTES

1. Orson F. Whitney, in Conference Report, April 1929, 110. Elder Whitney also notes: "They will have to pay their debt to justice; they will suffer for their sins; and may tread a thorny path; but if it leads them at last, like the penitent Prodigal, to a loving and forgiving father's heart and home, the painful experience will not have been in vain."

2. Robert L. Millet, *When A Child Wanders* (Salt Lake City: Deseret Book, 1996), 46.

3. Ibid., 39.

4. H. Burke Peterson, "Unrighteous Dominion," *Ensign,* July 1989, 6–11.

5. Howard W. Hunter, "The Golden Thread of Choice," *Ensign,* November 1989, 18.

FINDING A FAMILY

MARLENE B. HILLESHIEM

I was born in Manila, the Philippines, in December 1972. Three months after escaping from a physically abusive marriage, my mother, who was in her early twenties, discovered that she was already four months pregnant with me. In that condition, earning barely minimum wages, she did the hard physical labor of a housekeeper. She worked right up to my birth. I was born at home, and my mother almost died from excessive bleeding and malnourishment. Yet as soon as she could, she was up working again so the two of us could have food, clothing, and shelter. She begged for work and took me with her to each house. What she earned was not enough, however. By the time I was seventeen months old, I was very ill. My stomach bulged with severe malnourishment. My skin, rough like a lizard's, draped loosely over my bones. My ribs showed clearly, and I had very little hair. Mother knew she could lose me at any minute.

Word reached her of an American military couple stationed in Angeles City, the Philippines, who could not have children and were trying desperately to adopt. Fearing for my very life, my mother went to this couple and begged them to take me. The American woman was very touched and took me to the

Marlene B. Hilleshiem managed a local insurance agency in Suisun City, California, after receiving her license in health and property/casualty insurance. Now a homemaker, she and her husband, Foster Brian Hilleshiem, are expecting their second child in March 1997. She serves on the homemaking board in the Orem Cherry Hill Second Ward.

military hospital immediately, where I was hospitalized for three months. When I was released, I had creamy olive skin, big, brown eyes, and I was full of life. I even had little rolls of baby fat, and my hair flowed freely past my ears. My birth mother barely recognized me when she held me for the first time in several months. While my adoptive parents were stationed at Clark Air Force Base, my birth mother visited me daily. Six months later my adoptive parents also adopted a newborn baby boy. Soon after, they were reassigned to the United States, to Sacramento, California. I can only imagine the pain my mother must have felt in having to let me go.

I have lived in the United States since that time and have never returned to the Philippines. Unfortunately, my adoptive parents were not what they had appeared to be. Life with them was a nightmare. My earliest memories of sexual and physical abuse are at the age of five. My adoptive mother became a severe alcoholic. My adoptive father was deeply troubled by earlier wartime experiences. The abuse I suffered was ongoing.

At age fifteen, I could not bear my situation anymore. For many years I had kept silent, partly because I did not think anyone would believe me and partly because I did not want to be separated from my adoptive brother. We had been through a lot together. I cared for him as if he were my own child. From the time I was five and he was two-and-a-half, I had changed his diapers, fed him, and cared for him in every way. As we grew older, however, especially after he entered his teenage years, he began to replace me with friends, drugs, and alcohol. My grades in school were dropping, and without my brother's support, I felt my life was falling apart. I could not bear to see him self-destruct anymore, and I could not bear the abuse.

I went to my brother's probation officer and told everything. I was removed from my home and placed in a halfway house with kids who had broken probation or committed misdemeanors. As one who had never even skipped school, let alone ever committed a crime, I felt frightened and out of place. The children I shared the house with were rough, physical, and used foul language. For three months I felt I was in prison. The other children taunted me because they knew that I had never been in trouble, that I wasn't tough.

After a few months, the halfway house sponsored a writing contest. I had often written poems to help ease my pain. My therapist suggested I enter the contest. It took a lot of courage for me to get up in front of those "tough kids" and express my deepest feelings, but I did. I will never forget the silence in the room. The air seemed to echo my pain. As I looked up from my paper, I saw many eyes filled with tears. I then realized these children were not as tough as I thought they were. They were much tougher. They were survivors. Sharing my hidden experiences and feelings somehow helped them accept me. We realized together we had shared similar abuse situations but had responded to them differently. I became a friend, and during my remaining six months there, I helped others express their pain. It was a learning and strengthening experience for me. We gave each other hope, and our spirits were lifted.

In spite of the trauma I suffered at the hands of my adoptive parents, I had always felt Heavenly Father close to me. I felt his protection, his comfort and love. My adoptive parents never taught any religion in their home, but I investigated many churches on my own.

At sixteen I was released from the halfway house on a pilot program. The state of California gave me six hundred dollars a month for six months to help me get started on my own. Before they would release me, I had to prove that I would continue my counseling, attend school, hold a job for at least six months, and attend "On My Own" workshops, which taught budgeting and homemaking skills. I was assigned a mentor, who checked on me weekly. I did very well with the program. I went to school on independent study, worked three part-time jobs, and attended counseling until I was eighteen. One part-time job was working as a telemarketer for a local insurance agency. As soon as I was released from the halfway house, I began working directly for the childless couple who owned the agency. For the next two years, they encouraged me to go with them to their church, The Church of Jesus Christ of Latter-day Saints. Each time I refused. I worked every day, and if I wasn't working, I was studying. They never gave up inviting, however.

Finally one Sunday, I gave in. We attended not a regular Sunday meeting but a stake conference. I heard several people bear their testimonies and heard a talk given by a General Authority. My heart swelled with peace and joy. I cried throughout the rest of the meeting. This felt so right. I knew it was something I had been searching for. My prayers had been answered, and a week and a half later I was baptized.

In May 1990, right before I was to graduate from high school, my LDS employers invited me to move in with them. They could see I was overburdened with school and three jobs. They wanted me to get licensed as a state insurance agent as soon as I graduated from high school. By living with them, I could concentrate more on school and prepare for the licensing exam. I quit my two part-time jobs and worked only at the insurance office. I was very grateful for the compassion and love and genuine concern this couple had for me.

The next six months were the beginning of a new life for me. I graduated from high school and passed the state insurance exam. My employers, Mike and Julie Schoonover, had become like family to me. We had holidays together, celebrated birthdays, and built many cherished memories. Our temporary situation became permanent. They gave me a lot of love, increased my standard of living, and raised my expectations of life. They taught by example and expressed deep feelings for me—the child they never had but had tried so hard for. We found joy and peace with each other.

I met my future husband in February 1993 at a dinner party

held by the ward missionary leader in Suisun City, California. My future husband was a full-time missionary, and he took mission rules seriously. I knew the standards of the Church regarding missionaries talking to young women, and I was proud that he did not bend the rules. Though we did not speak then, he flew out to see me after he was released in June 1993, and we were engaged four days later. We were married that September.

A year later in September 1994, I wrote a letter to the First Presidency. I wanted to be sealed to the wonderful couple I had grown so close to since I was sixteen. We had been a family in every sense except through the sealing power of the holy priesthood. My request was granted, and on 24 September 1994, we were sealed as a family in the Oakland Temple. At last my birth mother's hopes that I would find a better home than she could provide me were fulfilled.

Despite its hardships, I am thankful for the long, difficult journey that has brought me an eternal family. I am thankful for the sacrifice and support my sealed parents have given me. They have helped me to understand my adoptive parents' pasts and childhoods. I am able to have compassion for the abuse they suffered. I can forgive them and am thankful that I have not continued the vicious cycle of child abuse. My sealed parents also helped me to understand my adoption and my birth mother's great sacrifice in seeking a better life for me. Both of them have enabled me to enjoy the wonderful blessings of my eternal family. My son, who is nineteen months old, reminds me daily of love and purity and Christ's perfect love for me. I am now filled with love, gratitude, and the desire to share my story that others will see that through Jesus Christ, the love of others, hope, and faith, we can have true happiness.

CHARITY IN CHILDBIRTH

WENDY C. TIDWELL

I spent my first seventeen years on an Idaho dairy farm being conditioned by wonderful role models to be a wife and mother. It never occurred to me that my life would not follow the same familiar pattern: graduate from high school, attend college for a year or two, find Mr. Right, settle down (probably back at home), and rear a family. I don't remember having any strong feelings one way or the other about being a mother—it just seemed the natural thing to do.

I spent the second seventeen years of my life being conditioned away from that pattern. I was the first woman in my family to graduate from college. I lived in Washington, D.C., and worked on Capitol Hill. I served a mission to Spain. While remaining politically active, I worked in the travel business and eventually was the vice president of a tour company, escorting performing groups internationally. Then, in case I didn't have enough variety in my life, I returned to school and got my law degree.

Those first seventeen years were only dim memories by the time, as a recent thirty-five-year-old law school graduate, I met my husband. In the intervening years, I had developed a mortal dread of labor pains and delivery, and I met the prospect of pregnancy with ambivalence. I had faith that I would find

Wendy C. Tidwell is an attorney who has served on the staff of Utah Congressman Bill Orton and does consulting. She served as a missionary to Spain and is the Mia Maid advisor in her ward. She and her husband, Lyle J. Archibald, are the parents of a daughter.

mothering rewarding, but I admit a substantial skepticism about the process whereby I would *arrive* at mothering. From the outset, I dealt with issues of control.

Married at thirty-five, I felt immediate pressure to start a family, even though I would have liked to enjoy the "honeymoon" with my husband a little longer. At my age I felt I could not postpone pregnancy, yet I did not welcome the urgency I felt to change my life irretrievably. Once pregnant, I lost control over seemingly all aspects of my life. My otherwise very healthy body turned on me immediately and didn't stop until weeks after my child's birth. I was sick for five and a half months and dealt with complication after complication throughout the pregnancy, culminating in a forty-hour delivery.

I also lost control of people's perceptions and treatment of me as a professional woman. It was a little hard to maintain a polished demeanor as I waddled into a committee hearing carrying thirty extra pounds of weight and then had to excuse myself to "use the bathroom." I had worked hard to establish myself as a professional Mormon woman, and now people made all sorts of assumptions about who I was. Those assumptions had very little to do with my hard-won identity. All that happened before I even got to labor and delivery!

Unlike many women who view childbirth as a spiritual opportunity, I saw labor and delivery as a compulsory, traumatic, life-threatening episode filled with unspeakable indignities of which I wanted no part and had no right of first refusal. To those who asked *if* I would have an epidural, I replied, "Are you kidding? There are reasons we don't stab ourselves with knives or walk out in front of moving vehicles. Why would anyone ask to experience pain if it's avoidable? Like pregnancy has been such a pleasant experience?" I reveal all this to give you some insight into the two principal lessons—cultural and spiritual—that I learned from my childbirth experience.

Birth is a universal human experience. Giving birth, however, is an experience unique to each woman, and from this I learned an important cultural lesson. Just because giving birth is a common experience does not mean that we hold in common all the details of that experience. We often set up for each other unrealistic expectations of what pregnancy and childbirth will be like. For example, many women made pronouncements to me about what I would feel, physically and emotionally, at different stages of the pregnancy. They would say, "You will be so excited when you find out you are pregnant . . . start to show . . . hear the heartbeat . . . feel movement." But the *ultimate* pronouncement for me was, "When they put that baby into your arms, you will forget it all." I could not imagine what kind of brain lapse I would have to experience to forget two skin conditions that caused unbearable itching for the last six weeks of pregnancy, not to mention several other unpleasant and unhealthy complications I was dealing with. But, I thought, if it was possible for those other women to forget, maybe it will be for me, too.

When my daughter was born, they didn't put her "into my arms" for hours. She was not breathing well after such a long and difficult delivery, and they whisked her away to the nursery oxygen tent. When it was all over, I was left with the "clean-up crew" for extensive repair work. When I finally held her for the first time, I had been awake for almost forty-eight grueling hours. I was so medicated and exhausted that I could not possibly appreciate the significance of her being there. I felt cheated and disappointed at the loss of that oft-promised "moment," and I am sorry to say the trauma of childbirth still haunts me almost a year later.

I don't deny many women have the "forget-it-all experience," but some of us don't, and I hope that we will be sensitive to the diversity of each other's experiences and value our sisters' experiences that are different from our own.

Childbirth did, however, give me a glimpse of tremendous compassion and charity, a spiritual lesson of great value to me. In the care I received from the nurses during and after delivery, I saw firsthand what it is to be "willing to bear one another's burdens that they may be light . . . and comfort those that stand in need of comfort" (Mosiah 18:8–9). I was treated with respect, dignity, and kindness by women who were and still are strangers to me. I never once felt that I was just another pregnant woman on an assembly line. I was not just a job for them to do and collect a paycheck.

Instead, they spoke to me of their own children and experiences in childbirth. The first postpartum nurse to care for me bathed me, and I will never forget how good it felt to be clean, despite my immodesty. As important as the bathing were her touch and kind words of encouragement. She told me of her own six-week-old baby and how worth it that child was. I was hooked up to tubes and IVs, so showering was difficult. Sensitive to my situation, another nurse offered to shave my legs. Under any other circumstances, I would have been mortified, but I appreciated immensely that small act of consideration.

Those women cared for me in a Christlike way that demonstrated they knew my pain but also knew the joy I would ultimately feel. How I pray all women might see each other as the sisters we truly are and show that depth of compassion, care, and understanding in whatever circumstances we find ourselves and others in.

While I still struggle to be reconciled to my difficult childbirth experiences, I am deeply grateful for the blessings of being a wife and a mother. My husband was the consummate partner to me throughout the birth of our child, as he is in whatever other challenges we face together. At eleven months old, MacKenzie daily brings joy and wonder into our home. She is worth every moment of discomfort, pain, and fear I experienced. I am infinitely thankful for the ways motherhood is teaching me more about the perfect love the Savior demonstrated in his holy atonement.

We truly are sisters and uniquely share the childbirth experience as well as many others. As we interact with each other in all aspects of our lives, both in those that we share in common and in those that set us apart, may we "above all things, clothe [our]selves with the bond of charity, as with a mantle, which is the bond of perfectness and peace" (D&C 88:125).

ONE BLESSED THING

NEIDY MESSER

Years ago, along the beach where waves
touched our bare feet, I walked
beside my father collecting
sand dollars, those delicate
offerings of the sea. Later
he said what rattled inside
were angels or bearded old men,
according to how you turned
the inner shells. So I broke one open,
spilled the tiny, wraith-like rattles
into my palm—the angels, the old men.

Now my father sleeps more than wakes,
nodding in his chair
nearly the whole day, sweater buttoned-up
even in summer. At first
I keep music low, but soon see
no need for quiet rooms or hushed voices.
Nothing disturbs him, he says, nothing
but dreams, the same one recurring
like day after day in his chair.

Neidy Messer lives in Boise, Idaho, with her husband, Bill Messer, and their two sons. She teaches English at Boise State University. She was Writer-in-Residence for 1990–91 for the state of Idaho. A book of her poems was published in 1991, and she is completing her second book.

Lost inside a tall building,
he wanders room to room
looking for a door.

He says he feels confused,
angry someone would build this place
with no doors, no way out. What does it mean,
he asks, and I hedge his question
remembering angels and white beards.
On the beach that day, sunset turned the sea
brilliant amber, our own long shadows
haloed on the sand, and finally,
darkness falling fast, we made our way
to the car without speaking,
without the need to say
one thing, not one blessed thing.

WITH YOUR ARMS UNFAILING 'ROUND THEM

SHARON LEE STAPLES

A story by Mohammed Diarra is told in Mali, Africa, of a hyena who has treed another wild animal. The hyena is trying to convince the animal to come down from the tree so that he might eat him. He begins:

"You may come down from the tree, for I have eaten your friends and I am not hungry."

"No," says the animal.

"I have eaten your brothers and sisters, and you may come down because I am full."

"No," repeats the animal.

"But I have eaten your mother and father, and I am very full and you can come down."

"No," is the answer once more.

"Well, I have eaten your hope," the hyena finally says.

"If you have eaten my hope," says the animal, "then there is no need for living, and I will come down."

Hope, whether in a child or an adult, is the beginning of faith and trust. To have a sense of community, a sense of neighborhood, one needs to be able to trust and to have faith

---

Sharon L. Staples is a professor and chair of the Department of Humanities and Philosophy at Utah Valley State College. She has served on the Young Women General Board and the Adult Correlation Committee of the Church. She teaches the seven- and eight-year-old CTR class in Primary.

195

in others in a variety of situations. I served in our ward nursery for almost two years and loved it. I loved the children and had a delightful time, enjoying many rewarding experiences. One of my favorite memories is of helping the children offer prayers. I would put my arm around them, my mouth next to an ear to whisper words. Think of the many parents who trust that their teachings about prayer will be confirmed and sustained by someone else, such as a nursery leader. Initially, nursery leaders may be strangers to the parents of many of the children with whom they have been entrusted. Yet, trust is extended.

Not long after my nursery experience, I was doing much the same thing for a woman in her late thirties at the Utah State Prison. Attending church services is an earned privilege there. I was assigned from a group of four volunteers to visit the women who had not earned the privilege to attend Sunday School and Relief Society in the main gathering area, usually the cafeteria. I passed through three steel doors on my way into their tier of cells to sit on the cement floor with them and give a Sunday School lesson. The women were bundled up in blankets and in their pajamas. There was no music, and I'm a monotone, so that part was always basically just dreadful.

One morning the lesson was on prayer. At the end I asked a sister, "Would you offer the prayer for us?" When she shook her head no, I said, "Well, can we help?"

"I never prayed in front of people before," she blurted.

"Would you like to try?" I offered.

"Will you help me?"

"Yes, I can help," I replied.

She was on the other side of the room from us, and because of prison rules I could not simply go over to stand with an arm around her as I did the nursery children. But we began, and I taught her the same way that I taught the three-year-olds.

"Dear Heavenly Father," I said.

"Dear Heavenly Father," she repeated.

In nursery, I was putting my "arms unfailing round [them]," as the hymn says, to teach them the basic steps of prayer.[1] I was doing the same with this incarcerated sister. Such intimacy required a great deal of trust on her part, for this woman at a very young age had probably had two things taken away from her that are essential to human development: hope and trust.

Sissela Bok, a modern philosopher, tells us that "*whatever* matters to human beings, trust is the atmosphere in which it thrives."[2] We know from developmental studies that children learn to trust during their first year of life. They have a scant twelve months to learn to trust this new world around them. The second year they learn autonomy; the third year, hope. This sister had to trust that I would not make fun of her and that the other women and sisters in the tier would not make fun of her.

Another modern ethicist, Annette Baier, notes that "to entrust is intentionally and usually formally to hand over the care of something to someone."[3] We really are vulnerable when we acknowledge our ignorance to a group of peers, as this woman did in acknowledging in front of other inmates that she did not know how to pray publicly. We turn over our self-esteem, hoping and trusting it will be honored and not denigrated. How difficult it must be to trust at this level.

I am not married, and I have no children. But I am part of the citizenry of a community of Saints with many other single, divorced, and widowed brothers and sisters who can and do instill hope, faith, and trust in children, young people, and sometimes adults. We are often influential in a child's formative years. Unfortunately, many of the women I meet at the prison did not have a good first twelve months of life. During this formative period, many of them were alternately neglected and abused. An excerpt from one inmate's letter illustrates for me how not being nourished in a trusting home can cause some young women to isolate themselves from others and suffer throughout their lives: "Dear Sharon, . . . I lied to you. . . . I told that [lie] to push you away from me. . . . When I had realized how close I had allowed you and others to get, I got scared and was determined to push you all away before I got hurt. In the past, I would either deliberately hurt people or just leave before I was hurt. My trust level is still nil when it comes to anyone who shows care and concern toward me." More caring individuals in this young woman's life will help to give her hope and trust. Already with this letter she is opening the door a crack.

I am fortunate to be a homeowner with a dear friend who holds a similar philosophy of the importance of community. In attempting to contribute to those around us, she and I hold an annual Easter egg hunt for all the neighbor children. We color Easter eggs and buy balloons, bubble blowers, jacks and other little toys, and plenty of candy. We hide them all over our end of the block. It is such a treat for us to watch the fascination of these little ones (and one chocolate-freak father) as they delight in discovering each little treasure. These parents trust us with their children, knowing that our intent is to help their children have a concept of neighborhood—their neighborhood.

Last year another effort was to allow one eager four-year-old neighbor to help us plant our garden. Our plants came up already sorted into a mixed green salad! We also keep Disney movies on hand to entice the children to visit us. For us it's a delight to have two six-year-olds knock on the door. "Hi. Can we borrow a video?"

"Sure." They come in, go upstairs, look through all of the videos, and choose one to borrow. The next day they bring it back.

"Hi. Can we borrow another video?"

"Sure." Seeing their precious little faces at our doorstep often makes my day better. We are their neighbors, not just their parents' neighbors. They can have a relationship with us apart from mom and dad, in addition to *with* mom and dad.

We are a part of their community—one in which they can experience hope and acceptance.

My encouragement to parents is to get to know their neighbors, especially single sisters. Let us help instill hope and trust in your children. My favorite Shel Silverstein poem from *Where the Sidewalk Ends* describes from a child's perspective what hope feels like. He marches out all the MUSTN'TS, SHOULDN'TS, and DON'TS—words that a child hears daily—but ends with this whispered secret:

> Anything can happen, child,
> ANYTHING can be.[4]

A sense of hope and possibilities is essential for adults as well. I taught an ethics course to several women at the prison. One of their assignments was to write their philosophy of life at the conclusion of the course. The following excerpt from one of those philosophies gives me hope that "anything can be."

"My philosophy on life has changed so much over the past seven months. It used to be 'live and let live' and do what you can get away with. I don't think like that anymore. My philosophy on life is to be with the people that I love the most—my husband and my children, to enjoy life by being happy with them, enjoying their company, watching my children grow; have a happy house. . . . I believe that there is good in all people. . . . I believe in myself as a mother, wife, and human being."

To me, putting our arms around Heavenly Father's children means encouraging them to believe in themselves, to trust and hope. And as we are able to help create trust and instill hope in children or adults, we advance their ability to contribute to others. They may perceive that they are part of a community of Saints in their own right—that they are capable of giving trust, faith, and hope to us.

NOTES

1. "God Be with You Till We Meet Again," *Hymns of The Church of Jesus Christ of Latter-day Saints* (Salt Lake City: The Church of Jesus Christ of Latter-day Saints, 1985), no. 152.

2. Sissela Bok, *Lying: Moral Choices in Public and Private Life* (New York: Quartet Books, 1978), 31.

3. Annette Baier, quoted in *Great Traditions in Ethics,* ed. Theodore C. Denise, Sheldon P. Peterfreund, and Nicolas P. White, 8th ed. (Belmont, Calif.: Wadsworth Publishing, 1996), 441.

4. Shel Silverstein, *Where the Sidewalk Ends* (New York: Harper and Row, 1974), 27.

THAT THE WORKS OF GOD MAY BE MADE MANIFEST

SANDRA TANNER

My eighteen-year-old son, Richard, is developmentally delayed. He functions mentally at about a six-year-old level, and some of his behavior is unusual (such as flapping his hands or repeatedly opening and closing a door). People who have never seen him or others with similar disabilities frequently stop and notice. As challenging as it is to parent a child with a disability, other problems in my life have been equally heartbreaking and difficult. Some of what I experienced with Richard has, in fact, helped me with my other problems. So, what have I learned?

QUESTIONS

I am learning not to ask "why" questions, or when I do ask them, at least to do so for a shorter time. "Why" questions are often confrontive and unanswerable: Why did this have to happen? Why me? I encourage myself to move on to better questions. Questions that begin with "what" are better because they are answerable, they engage the brain in active problem solving, and they lead to a possible course of action. For example, asking, "Why was Richard born with this problem?" evokes

Sandra Crandall Tanner and her husband, Mike Tanner, are the parents of three sons and two daughters. She has a master's degree in early childhood education and serves in her ward Relief Society presidency.

201

feelings of grief and loss and doesn't provide me with a direction for action. I just feel sad and helpless. Asking, "What can I learn from Richard's disability?" changes my thought process. My answers may include, "I can learn about this disability. I can learn not to be so worried about what other people are thinking. I can learn faith and patience, and I have an opportunity to practice what I say I believe."

Even these questions and answers, though better, are not specific. Answering "what" questions about a *specific* problem gives me specific actions I can take. For example, "What can be done about Richard?" is vague. A better question would be, "What can I do to help Richard learn to dress himself?"

HONESTY

Honesty in answering questions is critical. I have found that God can do more for me and with me when I am honest about my feelings. Sometimes that takes me a little while, especially if I have judged whatever emotion I am having at the moment as "bad." Deciding it is wrong to feel a certain way gets me into a cycle of trying to deny what I am really feeling. For example, thinking, "I have no right to feel thirsty; I had a drink of water just an hour ago" is foolish. I have learned when I am experiencing a strong feeling just to say, "I feel angry," or "I feel anxious," or even "I'm tired and hungry." Identifying my feelings is usually all it takes to diffuse them. I can move from emotional reactivity to self-clarity. If I don't stop to recognize my feelings, I may get off on tangents, such as having an argument with a family member instead of getting something to eat or taking a nap. Of course, some feelings are not as easily and quickly resolved as getting a drink of water. Sometimes I just have to be sad or frustrated for a while before I can move on.

PRAYER

Questioning is frequently an important part of my prayers. But I have learned that how I ask questions influences the answers I get. When I have prayed, "Why this? Why now?" I usually don't feel answers, partly because I am blaming and just feeling mad. In time I am able to pray and ask different, better questions, such as, "What can I do about this?" or "What is a purpose for this, now?" (Again, "what" works better than "why" for me.) In prayer I also find I need to be honest about my emotions. When I pray, "Father, I am afraid of what my future with Richard holds," I am expressing honest emotions.

I believe the scripture in Isaiah 55:8–9 which reads, "For my thoughts are not your thoughts, neither are your ways my ways, saith the Lord. For as the heavens are higher than the earth, so are my ways higher than your ways, and my thoughts than your thoughts." So frequently my prayers include requests such as, "You know how I feel about this; please help me to change how I am feeling, if that is what I need to do," or "Please help me have a more accurate understanding of this situation." I also ask for strength to endure what I cannot change and wisdom to know and accept those things. Of course, I also repent for the times I have failed to seek or accept help and have been unteachable, impatient, or unwise.

FAITH

I believe God hears and answers our prayers: he has answered mine. Because of what I have been through, I no longer walk solely by faith. I know. God says, "If thou art called to pass through tribulation . . . know thou . . . that all these things shall give thee experience, and shall be for thy good. The Son of Man hath descended below them all. Art thou greater than he?" (D&C 122:5, 7–8). Those words, spoken to the Prophet Joseph Smith in Liberty Jail, comfort and instruct me. They teach me that in this life we are to learn from our experiences. Yet we are also counseled to have faith: "Faith is not to have a perfect knowledge of things; therefore if ye have faith ye hope for things which are not seen, which are true" (Alma 32:21). Like our experiences, our faith varies.

I don't see faith as something all wrapped up in a tidy package to be given or received in one moment. I see faith at any given moment as a rainbow of shades. For me different areas of faith correspond to different hues of varying intensity, depending on the amount of faith I have in that particular area. Perhaps in my rainbow of faith, for instance, the band of red is faith in God. This color may be brilliant, but at the same moment in the blue shades is my faith in my own abilities to endure whatever happens to me. There the color may be pale and faint. I think faith may also be mixed with doubt. I see this mix in the father who brought his son to be healed (Mark 9:17–27). The father asked, "If thou canst do any thing, have compassion on us, and help us." Jesus told him, "If thou canst believe, all things are possible to him that believeth." The father replied truthfully, admitting to both faith and doubt. He "cried out, and said with tears, Lord, I believe; help thou mine unbelief." The child was healed.

At various stages of Richard's development, I have become depressed over the loss of the child I had hoped he would be. That was not a constant feeling, but it was recurrent. When Richard moved into junior high school, I almost decided that I would never get over my depressed feelings about his condition and just be able to accept him and his disability. Add it to the list, I thought sarcastically. Here's one more thing I am not doing well. Then I read an article by a mother of another child with a disability. She wrote of going through minidepressions whenever her child went through a life transition. That gave me hope: I was normal, what I was experiencing was normal, and maybe I am coping better than I thought.

Anne Morrow Lindbergh has written: "I do not believe that sheer suffering teaches. If suffering alone taught, all the world would be wise, since everyone suffers. To suffering must be added mourning, understanding, patience, love, openness, and the willingness to remain vulnerable."[1] Suffering and life's trials offer ways for us to develop faith. An important step in this development is to recognize that we can choose to stay teachable, vulnerable, and thus keep learning. The cost of the lesson is to risk pain and suffering. Faith in the Savior can help us choose to pay this price, especially as we remember the price he has paid for each of us.

ENDURING

Part of what I am learning is to endure and wait for change, because conditions—my abilities, me, my son, medications, treatments, everything—are always changing. Not all miracles result in healing. Sometimes the miracle is strength to "hold on thy way" (D&C 122:9). I love an organized, everything-in-its-place home. Richard is tall and skinny; he snacks constantly. At the table I offer him peanut butter and jelly sandwiches, a bowl of Cheerios, and other favorite foods, but he likes to put snacks in his pocket and walk around the house munching. He pockets uncooked macaroni, a handful of spaghetti, dry cereal, even uncooked rice, to mention only a few foods. I often ask him to sit at the counter to eat; sometimes he does, and sometimes he doesn't. Sometimes I insist, and sometimes I don't. Up very early to work one morning, I found a line of verse drifting through my mind.

> At 4 A.M.
> On the laundry room stair,
> I see Rich's rice trail.
> It's leading . . . where?

The rhyme made me smile. So I sweep and vacuum and try to accept the pasta trails and trials, because that's just the way it is right now.

One key to enduring is humor. Sister Chieko Okazaki has said, "I'd like to share with you my favorite Japanese proverb, which gives advice you might find helpful when life gets difficult. It's a short saying, and it comes from the ancient book of Okazaki, chapter one, verse one: Lighten up! If you're doing the best you can, that's good enough. . . . If you make a mistake, give yourself credit for trying. . . . If you do only half of what you wanted to do, or do it only half as well as you would have liked, pat yourself on half your back. But lighten up!"[2]

TEMPLE BLESSINGS

Temple blessings offer hope for the future, but I believe the power we are endowed with in the temple is also to be used now to overcome the tests of this life. I see the temple ordinances as expressions of our Father in Heaven's love and his faith in us. He wants us back with him. He knows the opposition we face, so he gives us these gifts to help us. I pray frequently for the realization of these blessings.

APPROPRIATE EXPECTATIONS

What do you expect your life should be like? If we imagine that the problems we face will be fixed quickly and permanently, we will not be satisfied with what life really gives us to learn from nor will we become more like God. God's power is grounded in knowledge of eternal law. He knows that if you plant carrot seeds, you get carrots. The same principle holds true in all spheres of being. Eternal laws govern outcomes. Life will inevitably test what my Uncle Bill calls our "firm, fixed ideas, some of which are false" so that we can learn what eternal law is and then function from a position of increased knowledge and truth. I believe this learning often requires the breaking of our hearts. It is a lifelong, never-finished process. In fact, we will not learn it all in this life, so we need to expect that the process of trial and error, struggle and learning is just the way life is. My goal is to do my best with what I've got.

One false idea I sometimes run into is that a person with a disability is guilty of some kind of sin. Even the Savior was asked by his disciples, "Master, who did sin, this man, or his parents, that he was born blind? Jesus answered, Neither hath this man sinned nor his parents: but that the works of God should be made manifest in him" (John 9:2–3). At a recent women's conference, a woman asked, "I found out eleven months ago that my three-year-old son has autism. What have I done to have this happen to me? Or is it not really anything I've done wrong?" One of the panelists answered, "Maybe you did something right, and the Lord knew you could be trusted to raise this child." I like that answer a lot. Elder Boyd K. Packer has said, "It is natural for parents with handicapped children to ask themselves, 'What did we do wrong?' The idea that *all* suffering is somehow the direct result of sin has been taught since ancient times. It is false doctrine. . . . There is little room for feelings of guilt in connection with handicaps. . . . Afflictions come to the innocent."[3]

It is reported that Mother Teresa was once asked why she kept trying to help the poor and the sick in India when the task was so impossible. Her answer was, "God does not require that I succeed, only that I do what I can."[4]

HELP

I have always been taught that it is better to give than to receive, and I guess I believe it because asking for help is not easy for me. I have a stubborn streak, and sometimes I don't want help. I want to do things myself. As I look back over my eighteen years with Richard, I am sure I have not used all the resources available, because I was too busy wanting to do everything myself. I didn't realize or admit I needed help. I wanted to be just like everyone else, not a special case.

Let me give you an example. A few years ago, my mother told me she wanted to do something for Richard. My mother loves me. It has been hard for her to see me struggle with Richard, and she has helped me a lot. Mom had found a class about clowning taught at the local community school. She had signed up to learn how to be a clown because she knew Richard loved clowns and she thought they could develop a clown act of their own. I was not very enthusiastic about her idea. I wasn't sure what Richard would do. I wasn't sure I wanted people to laugh at him. Because the class was for adults, Richard attended only a couple of times, but my mom went every week. She learned how to tie balloons in animal shapes. She learned jokes. She found a tape with just the right song for their act: "Me and My Shadow." Mom made matching costumes for herself and Richard, and they decided how to wear their clown make-up. When all was ready, Richard and my mom went to his school class and performed. The children loved it, and everyone had fun! I was embarrassed for failing to appreciate this great woman and her gift of love to me and my son.

HOPE

The hymns and the scriptures are like water to my sometimes parched soul. It helps to immerse myself in them frequently. Some of my favorite quotations include the following:

"Loud may the sound of hope ring till all doubt departs."[5]

"Fear not, I am with thee; oh, be not dismayed."[6]

"As thy days shall demand, so thy succor shall be."[7]

"Know ye not that ye are in the hands of God?" (Mormon 5:23).

"Yet will I not forget thee. . . . Behold, I have graven thee upon the palms of my hands" (1 Nephi 21:15–16).

When I remember what is on the palms of our Savior's hands, I feel like weeping with gratitude. I know he will always help me, and with his help I will go on.

The "works of God" have been "made manifest" in my life through my son Richard. I have learned and stretched because of him. I am moved and motivated by the examples of many other parents of individuals with disabilities. Richard and I have been the recipient of Christlike service from teachers, friends, and family. Isn't this the work of God being made manifest? I believe it is.

NOTES

1. Anne Morrow Lindbergh, quoted in Bruce C. Hafen and Marie K. Hafen, *The Belonging Heart* (Salt Lake City: Deseret Book, 1994), 178.

2. Chieko N. Okazaki, *Lighten Up!* (Salt Lake City: Deseret Book, 1993), 5–6.

3. Boyd. K. Packer, "The Moving of the Water," *Ensign,* May 1991, 7–8.

4. Mother Teresa, quoted in Stephen E. Robinson, *Believing Christ: The Parable of the Bicycle and Other Good News* (Salt Lake City: Deseret Book, 1992), 99.

5. "Our Savior's Love," *Hymns of The Church of Jesus Christ of Latter-day Saints* (Salt Lake City: The Church of Jesus Christ of Latter-day Saints, 1985), no. 113.

6. "How Firm a Foundation," *Hymns,* no. 85.

7. Ibid.

"THAT'S HOW THE LIGHT GETS IN"

NANCY BAIRD

It is snowing. Late February, the idea of spring so real you can smell the steaming dirt, feel the south wind curving around your throat. But it is snowing, a blizzard really, the heavens emptying themselves of months of winter. And so we wait for the sky to finish, for the earth to dry and break open again. We wait for the crack.

There is a line from Leonard Cohen that I love. It reads: "There is a crack, a crack in everything, that's how the light gets in."[1] If I have found any peace in this life, it is from understanding two truths: that in the adventure of life, the journey itself—the "finding"—is everything; that there are reasons for the trouble that follows us, for the "cracks" that occur in our lives to let in God's light. I find great comfort and hope in the apostle Paul's belief that "my strength is made perfect in weakness" (2 Corinthians 12:9).

Anyone who has, as I have, spent a lifetime stuttering, would flinch to read these words of Malcolm Muggeridge: "Everything I have learned in my seventy-five years in this world, everything that has truly enhanced and enlightened my existence, has been through affliction and not through happiness."[2] Must that be so?

Nancy Hanks Baird was named Utah Poet of the Year in 1996. She received her bachelor's degree in English from Brigham Young University and has worked as a freelance writer and editor. She and her husband, John K. Baird, are the parents of five children. She is the Gospel Doctrine teacher in her ward Sunday School in Salt Lake City.

To stutter is to experience a series of feelings every time you open your mouth: amazement, confusion, embarrassment, betrayal, grief, disillusionment, rage. Why the amazement after forty-four years? Because stuttering is not an integral part of who I am. It is a foreign beast that lives within, a thief sleeping on my tongue, and I am always, always, amazed, if not surprised, when it flaps into view.

> [The word] is caught in her mouth
> like a frantic bird in a cage.
> Her tongue beats the word,
> Her mouth fills with feathers. . . .
>
> She feels the words rising;
> music in her throat,
> quicksilver between her teeth.
> The devil in her wounded tongue
> licks them in.[3]

Where—I stamp my foot, as do all human beings who have had pieces of their life stolen—where is there comfort and peace for me? Has not my heart been broken enough?

I believe the balm of Gilead, that resin of regeneration, must come from within, from achieving a perfect inner harmony with oneself and the Spirit of God. I have found this place a few precious times, and so I know what it feels like, to be so grounded in God's Spirit that nothing, no pain in this world, can shake you. It is a place where "your whole bodies shall be filled with light," where "that body . . . comprehended all things" (D&C 88:67). Oh, to be there always!

There are paths to that place.

God says that every human soul is precious to him, and I believe him. "One [sparrow] shall not fall on the ground without your Father [knowing]" (Matthew 10:29). Someone must have loved Deborah, Rebekah's nurse, very much to have stopped the narrative of the prophets in Genesis to include the four lines of her death and burial: "But Deborah Rebekah's

211

nurse died, and she was buried beneath Beth-el under an oak" (Genesis 35:8). Deborah, an unknown, beloved woman, remembered forever.

I believe that every life has purpose, and that every soul can make a difference.

One summer years ago, while living in Honolulu, I went on a morning run, ending at the Diamond Head lookout, an outcrop of road high above the ocean by a lighthouse, a favorite stopping spot for residents and tourists. I rested on a stone wall and watched the sun lift, lucent as a pearl, over the Pacific, while my feet dangled above piles of garbage—the detritus of many human visitors. And I watched, stunned, as a local man finished his morning coffee and then spent five minutes picking up other people's garbage and putting it in the trash before getting into his car and driving away.

My son's Eagle Scout project was to gather used books for a school in our city where there are many underprivileged and transient children, most of whom have never owned a book. He gratefully received piles of donated used books—some in good shape, some not—and one small stack of brand-new books from our neighbor, a single mother, who wanted a few children to have their very own, new books. Joseph Smith said, "A man filled with the love of God, is not content with blessing his family alone, but ranges through the whole world anxious to bless the whole human race."[4]

In our "finding" we cannot be detached from others' pain. "For the hurt of . . . my people am I hurt," cried Jeremiah (Jeremiah 8:21). Jesus was not detached. How could he be with what he saw—hypocrisy, pride, rapacity, materialism, treachery, debauchery? But he taught us to love extravagantly.

To love extravagantly. What beautiful words. Think of the Samaritan, reviled by all nations, yet stopping to help one of the very people who rejected him. And think of Christ himself. With whom did he spend his time? Adulterers and thieves, the ill and the lost. Where would we find him eating today? No doubt with drug addicts, homosexuals, gang members, the homeless, and the excommunicated. He never held back his love. He spent everything.

Indeed, one of his disappointments was that he was not sought for what he came to give. People were eager for physical cures and material benefits—"Ye seek me . . . because ye did eat of the loaves, and were filled," he said (John 6:26)—but often had no interest in the spiritual gifts he wanted to give them. Yet some did. As recorded in John 4, the Savior offered the Samaritan woman at the well "living water" (v. 10), that water which Ezekiel described as "issu[ing] out from under the threshold" of the temple and healing every living thing "whither the river cometh" (Ezekiel 47:1, 9). The woman went into the city and bore testimony of the Redeemer: "Is not this the Christ?" What an amazing offer Christ makes—to permanently satisfy and heal a soul.

This is the path of comfort, the balm of Gilead—to truly live by his word. The hard part, of course, is accepting his love and "casting all your care upon him; for he careth for you" (1 Peter 5:7). It is hard to take that step into the unknown void of faith and believe what he says.

Moses couldn't do it at first. "I am slow of speech, and of a slow tongue," he said when God called him to lead Israel. And God answered patiently, "Who hath made man's mouth? . . . I will be with thy mouth, and teach thee what thou shalt say." But Moses could not fly into the chasm, and the window that God opened for turning his weakness to strength was closed. He asked for Aaron to be his mouthpiece, and "the anger of the Lord was kindled against Moses" (Exodus 4:10–14).

Compare his experience to Enoch's, that fiery soul. Enoch, too, was "slow of speech." "All the people hate me," he said. He, too, was told to "open thy mouth, and it shall be filled, and I will give thee utterance." Enoch, though, "went forth." So simple! And they said of him: "There is a strange thing in the

213

land; a wild man hath come among us" (Moses 6:31–32, 37, 38).

We all have wounds, cracks in the perfect surfaces of our lives. That is how our hearts are broken and through which may be filled with light. That is how we know our strength. Indeed, the Greek word for *trial* means "the tried or proven part," or, in other words, the part of us that is genuine. The web of cracks and fissures in every life is the grid through which, every day, we are poured, and the blueprint by which we learn, as did the apostle Paul, to "be content" (Philippians 4:11).

And of course, God, who loves us so completely he has "graven [us] upon the palms of [his] hands" (Isaiah 49:16), expects us, having received comfort, to comfort others: "Who comforteth us in all our tribulation, that we may be able to comfort them which are in any trouble, by the comfort wherewith we ourselves are comforted of God" (2 Corinthians 1:4). Surely we are expected to leave in our wake the fragrance, the footprints of grace.

I seek the finding. I want to leap under the thundering sky, be struck by lightning, be splintered and cracked open and so filled with light that Jeremiah's "burning fire" transforms the dark places of my spirit (Jeremiah 20:9). Only then will I become a "wild man" in the land (Moses 6:31) and find the peace that "passeth all understanding" (Philippians 4:7).

NOTES

1. Leonard Cohen, "Anthem," *The Future,* compact disk, Sony Music Entertainment, Columbia Records, New York City, 1992.

2. Malcolm Muggeridge, *A Twentieth Century Testimony* (Nashville, Tenn.: Thomas Nelson, 1978), 17.

3. Nancy Baird, "Saying Scissors," *The Shell in Silk* (Salt Lake City: Publishers Press, 1996), 53.

4. B. H. Roberts, *A Comprehensive History of The Church of Jesus Christ of Latter-day Saints, Century One,* 6 vols. (Salt Lake City: The Church of Jesus Christ of Latter-day Saints, 1930), 4:227.

RIGHT PERSON,
RIGHT PLACE, RIGHT TIME

MARTI HOLLOMAN AND MARCIE HOLLOMAN

In our home we have a very old and beautiful Chinese porcelain jar purchased when my husband and I served in the United States Embassy in Beijing, China. Adorned with two happiness characters, this "double happiness" jar, once a fixture in every Chinese home, is a symbol of happiness and blessings overflowing.

If this old jar could talk, it could tell quite a story. It has lived through several dynasties and through wars and revolutions. It has seen the rhythm of generations in a Chinese family, and witnessed births, deaths, celebrations, and New Year's festivals. Then it was packed in a box for a dark and bumpy ride across the ocean. Now it knows the rhythm of my family. I'm sure that after the initial culture shock wore off, this old jar probably realized, "Why, they're a lot like the family in my home village. They've got challenges and hopes. The same sun

Marti Shaffer Holloman has lived in Asia for ten years and worked at the United States Embassy in Beijing, China. She received her bachelor's degree from Brigham Young University and is a cross-cultural trainer for business and government agencies. She and her husband, Richard C. Holloman Jr., are the parents of four children. She serves as compassionate service leader in her ward's Relief Society.

Martha Ann (Marcie) Holloman, a daughter of Marti and Richard Holloman, attended high school in Beijing and Hong Kong. She has worked as an intern at the Library of Congress and at the American Institute of Taiwan while studying at Taiwan Normal University. She has served as Gospel Doctrine teacher in her BYU ward Sunday School.

rises on their land, and they too light firecrackers for their festivals and sing lullabies to their babies—in a different tongue, but all under the same moon." I hope that this old jar has truly found a double measure of happiness: one in China and one here.

To be the right person, in the right place, at the right time—surely that must bring us a *triple* measure of happiness and a true sense of personal peace. Have you had a time of closeness to the Spirit—feeling the pure love of Christ in your relationships, the peace of knowing that you're right where you're supposed to be, just at the right time? Times like that last for a glorious season, and then the clouds roll in, and a crisis hits with a fury. Strong winds of change disturb once-peaceful and well-ordered lives, shaking us loose from our moorings and shattering our jar of happiness and some of our hopes. On both diplomatic and military assignments, our family has been moved from place to place at unpredictable intervals; our sense of self, timing, and place has often been challenged.

"But everything was going so beautifully!" we would chorus in protest. "Why *now,* Lord?" And each of us had our own individual concerns: "How can I be the *right person* for this calling, Lord—I feel so inadequate. There are others so much more capable!" "But I love this *place! Do we have to move in my senior year? Can't we stay in Beijing just one more year?" "It's not *time* yet! I've just had a baby, and I'm not ready for another international move with four kids! Just tell those people to wait!"

The scriptures abound with examples of Heavenly Father's children struggling with these same basic issues. Enoch questioned, "Why is it that I have found favor in thy sight, and am but a lad, and all the people hate me; for I am slow of speech; wherefore am I thy servant?" (Moses 6:31). Can you feel his discouragement? His message was loud and clear: "Lord, I'm not the right person! You've got the wrong guy!" But Enoch went forth and did as the Lord commanded and established Zion, the ultimate Right Place, where everyone was of one heart and mind.

Esther was the right person and the *only* person who could orchestrate a very complicated and dangerous mission to save her people. Only by being at the right place with her impeccable sense of timing and great courage could she accomplish her crucial task "for such a time as this" (Esther 4:14).

We all seek to be that right person in the right place at the right time—the perfectly whole, unbroken jar—but it is unrealistic to expect to maintain the equilibrium. To have our yin and yang completely balanced is rare—we should enjoy it while it lasts. Most of the time we struggle, perhaps feeling less than whole, questioning who we are, why we find ourselves in a certain place, or why certain experiences come so unexpectedly and with such force. These normal challenges, however, are one of the main purposes of our earthly existence. Struggle can mean growth.

RIGHT PERSON

Sometimes we can be the one crucial link for someone, the right person at a time of need, or another individual can be that for us. Eleven years ago we lived in a town in southern China on the dusty corner of Liberation Street and Patriotism Road. On average we had power and water only half the week and shared our house with a parade of local fauna—rats, bats, snakes, poisonous spiders, and lizards—even in our computer files. Just down the road were beautiful pastoral scenes unchanged for centuries—terraced rice paddies, water buffalo, and walled villages.

We were the anachronism here—a Western family with three very exotic red-headed children. Marcie was the first foreign student to attend the nearby school. She marched to martial music and recited her characters in unison with the class under the tutelage of her teacher, Miss Plum Blossom.

217

Whenever Miss Plum Blossom left the room, Marcie was surrounded by her very curious classmates. Our children opened many doors for us and dissolved international barriers. Border guards would break into smiles and speed our crossing at the sight of the children; female uniformed police in pigtails would run from their posts to hold and kiss the baby. Once when we were stranded far from home in a crowded train station, railway officials announced there were no tickets available to return home. A man seeing our plight took our baby boy in his arms and held him high above the crowd, which then parted like the Red Sea. Tickets suddenly materialized for us.

A-ngaan, a bright young woman from the countryside who lived with us, had never met foreigners before she came to help us. She became a treasured part of our family—Marcie called her JieJie (older sister). She loved our baby as if he were her own. She would sing Chinese opera every night while embroidering with silk on a handmade loom. Marcie and her sister April would sit under that loom, listen to the operas, and watch the silken threads become brilliant peonies and cranes. Together A-gnaan and I killed chickens, bailed flood waters, washed laundry with our feet by her "stomp" method, and talked in Cantonese about life.

A-ngaan's only problem was that she didn't like our Laap Saap (garbage) lady. That was very unfortunate, because Mrs. Yip, the Laap Saap lady, had become a self-appointed permanent fixture around our house and made the whole neighborhood's affairs her business. Both women were rather territorial when it came to the baby. At dawn Mrs. Yip would come with her wheelbarrow and shout through the gate; the baby would go running in his pajamas to her open arms. At lunch she would come and carry him on her back to go "eat rice," and again in the evenings she would sweep the street with her bundle of branches and visit once more. She had gold teeth, leathery hands, a high-pitched accent, and a very big heart. She was from an ethnic minority group called Haaka, literally "guest people," who are generally looked down upon and assigned menial jobs. The Haaka women were known for their distinctive, black-fringed hats, although, curiously, I had never seen her wear one.

She good-naturedly fended off a daily barrage of very unkind remarks from neighbors and schoolchildren about her heritage, her accent, and her appearance. She would just smile patiently and go about her business, but I suspected that at some level, the unkindness must have hurt her.

I couldn't convince A-ngaan of her prejudice against Mrs. Yip. "Haaka people are not beautiful, not good people," she said matter-of-factly. She thought Mrs. Yip was superstitious and was particularly critical of her medical skills. Mrs. Yip was trained as a "barefoot doctor" in the Cultural Revolution and knew the medicinal value of every plant and growing thing. When the baby had a bad fall, she rushed over with a home-made folk remedy—marigold whiskey. Just the smell of it could knock you across a room. Thankfully, her intent was to apply the brew topically, and it worked wonders. (She certainly made Doctrine and Covenants 89:7 come alive: "Strong drinks are not for the belly, but for the washing of your bodies.") When the baby had a fever, she rushed over to give him a bath in noodles, which A-ngaan thought was ridiculous but which seemed to help.

The neighbors all made fun of her when she tried to tie a string around the borders of our yard and shake water in the corners to bring a good harvest to our newly planted garden. But Mrs. Yip was steadfast; she believed in what she did. She had certainly internalized the principles of communal property: one Saturday afternoon, after returning from a trip, our exhausted family took a nap. We were deep in slumber when the bedroom door swung open and in marched Mrs. Yip. My husband and I sat straight up, startled. Without missing a beat, she started a cheerful update on the local news and inquired about our trip. She showed not the least embarrassment or reticence. She just came in the gate, in the front door, up the stairs, and into the bedroom to talk to us. Perfectly natural in a Communist system—our home belonged to the people, and therefore she was entitled to enter. We learned she was a devout Buddhist when she invited us to her home for a New Year's celebration. She used nearly her whole month's food ration to prepare her feast, part of which she offered at a small shrine in the corner of her room. For many years she had not been allowed to worship, and we could see that performing her rituals for her ancestors meant a great deal to her. She sang a melancholy chant, walked in circles, and blew off firecrackers in the doorways to frighten evil spirits. She succeeded in frightening us, too, when one nearly blew up in her face.

Later in the year, she invited us to visit her home village. We rented a van, piled everyone in (including some of her relatives, whom we picked up in the foothills), and then proceeded on a steep and treacherous journey to visit her ancestors' temple, nestled high in the mountaintops. Usually a three-day climb on foot, this was a sacred pilgrimage for her, the third visit in her life. She and her sister poured themselves into their ceremony, chanting, singing, and presenting offerings of food and gifts. This temple experience for her seemed to be as sacred as our own. At the end of the day, she and her sister came singing down the mountainside, arm in arm, replete with joy. On the way home she stopped by the marketplace and there bought two black-fringed Haaka hats, one for me and one for herself. Though we commonly saw people in these hats every day, no one had ever seen her wear her native hat before. But from then on, she wore it daily. Evidently, word had traveled quickly in the neighborhood of our visit to her village. The next day we noticed she was treated quite differently by the neighbors—respectfully and even kindly. Our journey with her somehow validated her as a person in our little community.

In the process, A-ngaan was compelled to see Mrs. Yip in a

different light, looking past ages-old borders of prejudice and enlarging the borders of her own heart to include her new Haaka friend. She proclaimed with a smile, "Haaka people are very good!" That brought us double happiness, because we loved them both.

Years later another treasured friend, Lao Yang, came into our lives. We called him Lao (meaning "old") Yang as a form of respect and endearment, though he was only six months older than I. The Chinese also use family titles as loving forms of address with one another. In an extended family of more than a billion people, they are truly brothers and sisters: the middle-aged woman at the vegetable stand is "aunt," the elderly man on the bench is "grandfather," the friend younger than you are might be "meimei" or "little sister," and so on. It is a heartwarming tradition that makes you feel related as all God's children.

Lao Yang, an extremely intelligent and capable man, was our cook in Beijing. Assigned by the government's Diplomatic Service Bureau to that Communist work unit, he had no control over his career or education. He could have been a lawyer, a brain surgeon, a professor, but he was assigned to be a cook. Our cook. He was excellent and took great pride in his work, and we showered him with heartfelt praise—something rather new to him. After school the children loved to visit with Lao Yang—he taught them Chinese, juggled knives in the kitchen for my awestruck son, and demonstrated *tai chi* and martial arts after supper. His tiny home could have fit into our child's bedroom. He had one small coal stove to keep his family warm in winter and rode his bicycle ten miles to work, in rain or snow. We were his livelihood.

When we entertained guests for a diplomatic function, I would sometimes enter the kitchen and feel a pang of sadness to see this man of such great personal dignity waiting patiently to serve us our next course. I wished that he could be our guest and that *we* could serve *him*. Once, during one of our talks in the kitchen, I said, "You know, if you had been born in America and I had been born in China, I might have been your *ayi* (maid)." He laughed, but he understood my message. He brought a whole new meaning to the scripture: "But he that is greatest among you shall be your servant" (Matthew 23:11).

Every interaction with one of Heavenly Father's children is an opportunity to give something and to receive something. We were the right people to help A-ngaan experience a change of heart. Lao Yang was the right person to teach us the meaning of service. With each person we encounter, we should ask ourselves: What can I learn from this person? What wisdom can he give to me that I lack? What can I give him that will make his load easier to bear?

RIGHT PLACE

"I'll go where you want me to go, dear Lord," but please don't take me out of my comfort zone! Every transition moves us into uncharted territories. Twenty-three moves have taught me that the only constant in life is change; and though each move brought me a calm assurance that we were in the right place at the right time, my own struggle was whether or not I was the right person for each new adventure. I learned that by the time the Lord accomplishes his purposes, we have *become* the right person in the process.

The Lord sometimes chooses as his workplace uncomfortable places and situations. We love the periods of happiness and peace and often are caught off guard by storms and crises. The Chinese word for crisis—*wei ji*—is rich in meaning. It is created by combining the two characters for danger (*wei*) and opportunity (*ji*). We may perceive a crisis to be dangerous—"dark clouds of trouble hang[ing] o'er us, [that] threaten our peace to destroy,"[1] perhaps putting our jars of happiness in peril. In reality, winds of opportunity are blowing in our direction, bringing the possibility for growth and change. The Lord stretches us and proves us with every danger/opportunity. The issue is one of perception.

An old friend from Hong Kong asked us to take her back to her home village in China after the government sent word that the family home was being returned to her. A-ha had left China thirty-five years before and had not been able to return to see her family. She longed to return, yet she was fearful, and so, at this first opportunity (a true 'danger/opportunity' in her mind), she took our family along as an "insurance policy" that she would return safely. We took several trains and an eternal bus trip and then rode in the back of a bread truck to get to her *Lao Jia* ("ancestral home"). She was laden with gifts for her brothers and sisters and for a host of new family members she had never met. I was concerned: How would they recognize her after all these years? She had left a young woman in her thirties and now she was nearly seventy!

Without modern systems of communication, she had been able to send them a letter stating only the day we hoped to arrive and she hadn't heard back. What if they weren't there? We arrived in the late afternoon, at dusk. As we helped her out of the truck, she looked around expectantly and then spotted the family delegation coming down the dusty road ahead. Chinese reserve would allow them only to grasp hands, but it was a glorious moment. A-ha's relatives then greeted our family as though they hadn't seen *us* in thirty-five years—and linked arms with each of us and paraded us all triumphantly through the village to her sister's home.

The home had earthen floors, no plumbing or electricity, and a communal kitchen shared with four other families. Waiting for her there was "Number 3 Mother," a tiny grandmother in black pajamas and a black silk cap who had been A-ha's father's third wife. She continually gave us a thumbs-up sign and a big grin to show approval of our baby. The reunion was bittersweet. A-ha learned of the terrible hardships her family had endured: her mother, father, and brother had been killed, their treasures and beautiful porcelain jars smashed by the Red Guards, their genealogies burned. The family home, it turned out, had been used as a grain silo by the army and was overgrown, filthy, and home to wild animals. But her heart had found its home, and it wasn't that crumbling structure she had come to reclaim; her home was the love of her family.

The right place doesn't have to be physical but, as illustrated by A-ha's experience, can occupy instead a place in the heart. During Marcie's senior year, she and her classmates volunteered in a Chinese orphanage. The dire conditions were sobering. The children were bedridden, despondent, handicapped, sick, and attended by a well-meaning but overburdened staff. The initial unresponsiveness of the children was daunting: how could this possibly be the right place for anyone? The volunteers wondered how they could hope to impact children in such dismal circumstances. They didn't have the medical or technical training needed to change conditions. All they could offer the children, besides the toys, music, and "things" they brought, was their time and their touch.

Marcie was drawn to the lonely children in the back room. Some lay motionless, others perpetually moaned. One particularly emotionless, unresponsive child was three years old, but her body was that of an infant, her limbs rubbery and useless, and her senses seemed to tune out stimulation. Because she was a hermaphrodite, she was given minimal care. But Marcie felt the child deserved the same love and enthusiastic attention she would have given her own baby sister—though her hopes of enlivening this unresponsive little girl weren't high. One day, however, as they began to dance to the beat of "Penny Lane," some Beatles music she had brought in, a particularly energetic movement of Marcie's caused the girl to giggle infectiously, earning her the nickname thereafter of "Penny." To the great interest of the staff caretakers, day by day Penny's giggles grew more frequent and her face more animated—she was loved, noticed, and alive. Marcie's heart was overflowing when by the end of the week Penny uttered her first "word"—perhaps no monumental miracle, but the joy of that moment helped them forget the dirt, stench, and dreariness of their surroundings, drinking in the comfort of this new place of the heart. Any place where love can temporarily shove pain and loneliness away is a "right place."

So, when the Lord calls, drop your nets as Peter did and follow. Don't look back. Go forward and prayerfully ask, What am I to learn from this place, from these people, from this particular situation? What gifts can I give that are needed here? It is sad to see those who view change as a threat to their peace and happiness, who refuse to embrace new opportunities because they might be dangerous.

RIGHT TIME

Our Chinese friends have a great deal of patience, part of which is a cultural endowment. They think in terms of thousands of years, whereas we, impatient Westerners, want everything yesterday. Their sense of time is culturally different from ours. So is the Lord's from the world's. We want immediate fixes for cracks and breaks and immediate answers to our prayers, but we forget that our time is not his time. We pray for peace and happiness but forget that the peace he gives is "not as the world giveth" (John 14:27).

Perhaps one of the greatest lessons of patience and grace we learned was from our dear friend and a gifted artist, Wang. We met Wang at an art exhibit one December. He inquired where my husband learned his Chinese. "You were a missionary?" he said with whispered excitement. Quietly he told us he had learned his English from American Protestant missionaries some forty years earlier. Because his family members were Christians and wealthy landowners, they suffered at the hands of the Communist revolutionaries. His father died, the family lost their home and their money, buried their Bibles, and kept their faith safe in their hearts. His dream of attending a

225

university to study art was short-lived. During the Cultural Revolution, he was expelled and eventually imprisoned for being both religious and an intellectual. Yet throughout this ordeal, his faith never wavered.

Hearing his story, my husband felt impressed to invite him to a caroling party we were hosting. It was part of a cultural exchange with the Chinese university at which my husband studied and we both taught. This exchange occurred only because we were there during a rare window of time when there was far greater openness to Western ideas than in the past.

The previous year our lecture on Western Christmas traditions at the university drew standing-room-only crowds—with our middle-aged students dancing afterwards with wreaths around their necks and garlands on their heads, declaring that the next week they would have a university Christmas party in the lecture hall. They felt the infectious joy of the season. The school cook made two cakes that said "Christmas Happy," we had an obligatory power failure, and by candlelight Santa Holloman came "ni hao-hao-hao-ing" into pandemonium. So, by this, the second year, we were inundated with requests to produce multiple university celebrations to accommodate all the new Christmas enthusiasts.

With that precedent and the administration's blessing, we welcomed Wang and a huge crowd of students into our home on Christmas Eve to have cookies and cider, see their first Christmas tree and stockings, and to sing carols in the neighborhood (rehearsed as part of our English lesson). Santa Holloman led the band of carolers through the streets on that starry Christmas Eve. They sang by candlelight and delivered plates of cookies to Mrs. Yip and other bewildered but delighted neighbors, workmen, and soldiers.

In the midst of all the faces struggling to read the unfamiliar songs, we saw our new friend, Wang, his head held high, singing the carols from memory and with such exuberance that he captured the hearts of all the carolers. When the party was over, he lingered. He had brought gifts for each one of us—the finest treasures from his art exhibit. These were true gifts from the heart. He felt such joy in giving them, yet they surely represented many month's wages for him. What made us feel worse was that in the midst of all the preparations we had forgotten he was coming and had no gift for him! But the Lord, in his perfect timing, had seen to it that my brother's gift to us arrived that very day: a Metropolitan Museum of Art book entitled, *Christmas by the Great Masters*. It was the perfect gift for an artist, and as we presented it to him, Wang explained that he hadn't seen such paintings since his childhood. "Da-vinsky!" "Oh, Michelangelo!" "Oh, so beautiful!" he exclaimed as he looked at the paintings of the Nativity that had once been banned.

With great enthusiasm, he asked, "Could we please sing more carols?" So we gathered by the tree and sang. Then he turned to my husband and said, "Mr. Holloman, would you please tell the Christmas story?" That request presented us with a dilemma: we were allowed to worship in the privacy of our own home but were strictly forbidden to proselyte (a law we steadfastly honored). We were allowed to share Christmas traditions with our students, but we were not to talk about their religious implications, other than a cursory mention that the season did commemorate the birth of Jesus Christ.

Now it was, after all, Christmas Eve, and every year of our lives we had read the Christmas story on Christmas Eve—it was part of our culture. And here was this earnest request before us. It was nearly midnight, and our children were waiting. My husband drew a breath and began reading the familiar words from Luke. We looked at our friend and realized that he was silently mouthing the words he had committed to memory as a child so many years before. "Please, more carols!" he said, and we sang and sang, ending with "Silent Night." The lights of the Christmas tree reflected tears in our friend's eyes, and as he stood to leave, he said, "Oh, thank you! Thank you! This is the first Christmas I've had in thirty-six years."

Wang became our dear friend, a favorite "uncle," and a most devoted art teacher for our children. He prepared page after page of handwritten notes to teach them about the lives of the great masters and painstakingly taught them to sketch, to use charcoal, oils, and watercolors. I have never seen anyone match his enthusiasm in teaching.

Wang's willingness to wait on the Lord's time for a chance to renew his Christian faith was a humbling lesson to us to wait with faith for the "Lord's time" whenever "our time" doesn't hold the desired outcome. Wang's faith was always active and strong—hidden safe in his heart.

We consider another miracle in our lives to be our *ayi* ("maid"), Xiao Wai. Our paths crossed at a time when we both had needs only the other could fill. We had known other families to whom she had been assigned previously, and she was beloved by all. From the first day I met her, we were a team. We got down on the eternally dirty tile floor together and laughed and scrubbed till our knuckles were raw. The floor still looked terrible, but it was the start of a wonderful friendship. I was struck by her intelligence and wit, her steady endurance and gift of discernment. Like Lao Yang, she too had the capability to do anything, but she was assigned to be a maid. She was a marvelous mother, possessing wisdom and calm perfectly suited to a mother of many. Yet Chinese law strictly forbids couples having more than one child, and her one child was a lovely daughter. We often discussed our children and theories on child-rearing, and she knew the children loved and respected her. For us she was a role model, a treasured "aunt," a mentor and friend. Given her circumstances, I felt almost embarrassed to confide in her that (after several losses) I still longed to have another child—Why, I had three beautiful children, a truly bounteous posterity!—and I knew the intensity of this longing must have been far greater for her than for me.

When I told her I was expecting and then shortly thereafter had another miscarriage, she reacted with deep compassion. She was someone who knew the loss of what might have been. I cannot think of anyone who could have offered me more solace during that difficult time than she did in her quiet way.

Heavenly Father did bless us with a successful pregnancy not long after, and Xiao Wai and Lao Yang went into warp speed with advice, strange soups, and herbal preparations "to make me strong." Both were extremely protective of the precious cargo I carried.

When I came home with a little red-headed bundle and laid her in this dear sister's arms, I will never forget the look of joy and wonder and tenderness on her face. This was a second child—one she would never be allowed to have—and somehow the baby sensed this. They formed a mother-child bond on the spot. Surely Heavenly Father ordained this! When I would try in vain to quiet the baby's crying, she would instantly relax in Xiao Wai's arms, transfixed in a loving gaze at her Chinese mother—to Xiao Wai's sheer delight. She would talk to her, sing to her, recite poetry, and dance with this little baby, showering upon her all her maternal love. I knew that for us, this was something holy, facilitated at a special time by a loving Father in Heaven. I called Xiao Wai "Number 1 Mother," and myself "Number 2 Mother"—an honor she deserved and a token of the sacred bond of motherhood we share.

In the thick of our struggles, we sometimes wondered if the Lord's timing was off. We yearned for Xiao Wai and questioned why she had to be denied family blessings because her time for motherhood and a government policy arrived at the same time in her life. Yet her spirit was resilient, and she found other channels for her love. This was the time when her needs and ours coincided. While Wang was denied the freedom to worship his God openly, his time of silent suffering was well spent building solid reserves of faith. He gave depth and texture to the admonition, "wait patiently on the Lord," and his strength was renewed as promised. He taught us to look past our finite understanding and ask, "Is this a time when the Lord needs me to wait patiently on his timing?" Because of Xiao Wai, we now think to ask, "What can I do to bring about the right time for someone else?"

In closing, I'd like to tell you a modern parable—the parable of the shard boxes. Sometime in the mid-1980s, after the Cultural Revolution was over, small porcelain boxes in myriads of jagged and unusual shapes began appearing in Beijing. They were made of broken pottery shards from lovely blue and white porcelains, Ming and Qing vases, and jars of double happiness that had probably been smashed by Red Guards. The shards were given new life by Lao Han, the shard box man, who collects these old broken pieces of pottery and crafts them into "shard boxes." He sees potential in the discards of others and turns them into treasure. No two shards are alike; each one's irregular shape is uniquely created by the force that broke it. Lao Han, a gentle, honest soul, labors in a small workshop. First, he takes a jagged piece of porcelain and carefully molds a silver shell around its edges to fashion a top, and then he creates a matching silver bottom. He knows pure silver alone is too soft to withstand everyday use, so he adds a little copper and a tiny bit of nickel to give it strength. By heating these elements together in a refiner's fire, he creates the alloy known as sterling silver, which gets its sheen and innate beauty from the silver and its strength to stand up and be firm from the nickel and copper. Finally, Lao Han embosses the silver sides of the boxes with beautiful designs while the metal is still hot and malleable from the refiner's fire.

The silver that emerges from that refiner's fire glows—just as the pure love of Christ makes someone's countenance glow. In our trials of fire, the Lord sends others into our lives to give us strength, people of sterling character, people who glow with that same love of Christ. They are the nickel and copper that give us the strength to stand up and be firm.

Shard boxes reflect the effort to make something beautiful and useful out of destruction. Beautiful, because each shard, like a piece of a puzzle, reveals part of the lovely pattern of the original unbroken jar. And useful, because the once-useless pieces are remade into practical containers that can once again store things, hold treasures, have a purpose.

I have found some shard boxes with part of the double happiness pattern on them, part of some ancestral jar that was passed down through the generations of a family before it met its fate. I wonder if it would give happiness to some of those long-departed owners to know that their family treasures, once thought to be destroyed, are now bringing beauty into the world again in new and useful forms? Why, think of it—one shattered vase can create many shard boxes! Where one vase served one purpose, the many shard boxes created from that same vase can have many useful purposes. Whatever crisis breaks the vase also brings opportunities to create beauty in its aftermath.

If in the storms of crisis, your double happiness jar is broken and you feel you can never be whole again, or be the right person again, look at your experience from an enlarged perspective. Out of one shattering experience, you have the opportunity to take each piece of your broken heart, bind it with the pure love of Christ, and come out of your trial of fire with many beautiful and useful shard boxes born of your pain. The Lord, like the shard box man, molds you and leaves his mark upon you after you have gone through the refiner's fire— while you are hot and glowing and humble. In the end, there are more parts to you than there were before: more practical experience, more wisdom, more compassion, and even more happiness. You are different but in a new and infinitely better configuration.

I keep a shard box made from part of a double happiness

jar right next to the matching whole jar as a testament to the resilience and endurance of the Chinese people. Wang and A-ha lost their homes and possessions, yet each took the fragments of their past and created beauty out of the pain. The right place was in their hearts. Xiao Wai took the precious parts of a mother's love and gave that love to those around her, at just the right time. She was there for me. After we left China, we got a letter from A-ngaan. It was uncharacteristically emotional—she used the words literally translating to "shatter spirit" to convey her feelings that she missed us and she missed the baby. I, too, felt as if my heart had shattered when I left those dear friends. But I see that I now possess many wonderful shard boxes created from each experience and each person that touched my life in a special way.

These experiences are beautiful and eternally useful. The lessons we learned from our Chinese friends—that only they could teach us—are forever embossed upon our souls. They were the right people for us, China was the right place, and we were there at a remarkable time in history. The greatest miracle of the shard boxes is that the sum of the parts is more than the whole. We came back from our journey with so much more than we took—carrying treasures that we surely can carry home to heaven, from whence they came.

NOTE

1. "We Thank Thee, O God, for a Prophet," *Hymns of The Church of Jesus Christ of Latter-day Saints* (Salt Lake City: The Church of Jesus Christ of Latter-day Saints, 1985), no. 19.

MY ALTERNATIVE DOZEN

MARILYNN THORPE BROCKBANK

In 1952, when I was a tender thirteen-year-old, I went to a Myrna Loy–Clifton Webb movie called *Cheaper by the Dozen,* a heartwarming story of the trials and joys of a family with twelve children. The hopes and dreams of my preadolescent heart had, for some time, been focusing on my future as a wife and mother. I sat in the dark grandeur of the old Egyptian Theater, and a powerful conviction filled my soul that this was *my* greatest goal in mortal life. It has never once even wavered in the ensuing forty-three years. In fact, the inability to give up that dream has caused me nearly all of my life's pain.

Within a year of marriage, my husband, Virgil, and I had found that we would never have children by the usual method. My cherished dreams and goals, my carefully thought-out plans—marry a good man, build a big house with a big porch, plant flowers and trees, and placidly consume the moments and the years of my life bearing and rearing twelve beautiful children—shattered when reality backed me up against the wall of faith.[1]

We turned to adoption. Many times, upon learning that my children were adopted, a miserably pregnant friend would

---

Marilynn Thorpe Brockbank has made a lifelong career of homemaking. She feels privileged to have been able to choose a vocation on the basis of passion rather than remuneration. A business administration graduate, Marilynn is a substitute teacher in seminary and a writer. She serves as music chairman in her ward. She and her husband, Dr. Virgil W. Brockbank, have four children and nine grandchildren.

glibly inform me that I had "done it the easy way." There was nothing easy about it. Our first roadblock was that we were too young; our second, that we had not been married long enough to prove stability. Once we had to move to be in "acceptable" housing. When it was time to finalize the adoption of our second child, we were temporarily denied because my husband had gone back to school full time to finish his education. That, we were informed, was "proof" that we had adopted children before we were sufficiently mature. We endured very personal questionnaires, soul-searching life histories, and intense scrutiny of every financial aspect of our lives. Home visits displayed us like cattle at the country fair hoping for a blue ribbon. It was not an easy way to "give birth."

So, while waiting for roadblocks to be removed, I embarked upon a lifelong service project of foster care. Our very first child, a thirteen-month-old named Randy, took a huge section of our hearts when he went back home. I wonder how we managed to try again. Before we were allowed to adopt our own first child, we had four foster children plus many of our friends' children come and go. Our friends looked to us as a temporary mom and dad for their children while they vacationed or went to the hospital for a new sibling. During that period, I fostered my first older child when we took in a terrified fourteen-year-old unmarried mother during her confinement and the emotional upheaval of surrendering her baby.

When we were finally able to adopt Paul, I gave myself completely over to the fulfillment of my teenage dreams. The reality was better than the fantasy, made sweeter still by five and a half years of bitter craving. It was, indeed, like playing house. I drifted through those first two years in my rose-colored haze like the ultimate mother with her perfect child living the happily-ever-after storybook life. When we were blessed with our second child, Karin, a stunningly beautiful but high-strung daughter, Heavenly Father abruptly set me back down on the real terra firma. After six months of our baby's constant colic, however, once more I became a contented, normal, happy young mother enjoying that especially precious season of life.

To keep us afloat during my husband's schooling, I began to babysit and take in foster children again. One day in early May, Social Services asked if I could immediately take in a baby that had been abandoned the previous evening in a bar. I could but unexpectedly added that I would do so only if I could adopt the child if parental rights were terminated. In their haste and need, the social worker immediately said yes, with the caveat that I shouldn't get my hopes up. Within half an hour, a social worker appeared at my door with a dirty, pale, sickly, and unresponsive baby girl dressed only in a wet diaper and filthy undershirt. Her eyes were fixed and glazed. I trembled as I took her in my arms, thinking that this child was going to die in my care.

She was four and a half months old and weighed an ounce over nine pounds. The back of her head was flat from lying in one position. She was somewhat jaundiced and nearly into the stage of marasmus that precedes death in a child who fails to thrive. She did not turn her head or focus her eyes when I spoke to her. The agency gave me their doctor's number to call for an appointment the next day and left.

I changed her cloth diaper, using one from the box I had on hand from my children's diaper days, wrapped her in a blanket, and headed with my little ones in tow for the Grand Central two blocks away. There I purchased several one-piece stretch-terry playsuits, undershirts, plastic pants, diaper liners, pins, powder, lotion, shampoo, and receiving blankets. Next I picked up canned formula and plastic liners for the baby bottles I had used with my children. Finally we headed home for a bath, rubdown, clean, soft clothes, and lunch. I don't know if she was hungry during any of these tasks because she never made a peep. No whimpering or lusty crying for food.

She seemed entirely resigned, as if she simply did not care any-more.

After putting Paul and Karin down for naps, I fed and rocked the tiny waif, singing to her and caressing her while she slept peacefully in my arms. I pleaded with the Lord not to take her while she was in my care. I came to believe firmly during the course of that afternoon that had she been aban-doned a day later, she would have died.

During the succeeding days and weeks, Catherin—the name we gave her—slowly began to respond. We discovered immediately that she was allergic to formula. After trying soy and other substitutes, I contacted the La Leche League and found nursing mothers willing to provide me with breast milk. Soon Catherin began to gain weight, focus her eyes on me, and communicate with coos and smiles. She was bonding and thriving.

During this four-month period, her mother was found and ordered to appear in court. On the first two court dates, she was in jail. When she appeared on the third date, the judge ter-minated her parental rights. That happens only very rarely, which is why the social worker had so quickly, and unfortu-nately, made her rash promise to me. In this case, however, the mother had two older children who had been in foster care for some time because of her alcoholism and neglect. The judge was through giving her chances and took all three children away.

The morning after the court hearing, I got a call from the Division of Family Services. "I have good news and bad news," were the case worker's first words. The good news was that, to her surprise, Catherin was available for adoption now. The bad news was we could not have her. She apologized pro-fusely for her unauthorized promise and begged for forgive-ness. Her superiors were adamant that because we were not on the waiting list for adoption and were approved only for foster care, this child could not be placed with us. She belonged to the next family on the list. I felt stunned, ill used, deeply wounded, and finally enraged. In the first few hours after receiving the news, I planned ways to abscond with Catherin and my family to the edge of the earth and hide until they were all grown up. Then I vowed to get a lawyer and fight this treacherous injustice. Then I fell to my knees and pleaded with the Lord to give me this child for my own, something I had not done before, nor have I done since, with someone else's child. Finally I realized, and admitted to God, that he was in charge of his world and knew what he was doing. I told him of my love for Catherin and my desire to keep her, but I knew that she was, first of all, his child, and he would send her where he willed.

Because the justice system allows for appeal when defendants believe they have been unfairly treated, Catherin could not be legally placed for thirty days. The couple who were to get her did not want to chance having her taken back in a month, so Catherin would stay in foster care for another four weeks. Out of respect for my anguish and need for healing, our case worker asked if I wanted her placed in another foster home during that time. I declined. Catherin was doing so well and had come so far. I feared that one move would be hard on her, let alone two. Thus it was that the Lord answered my prayer in a small way—I still had her in my home to care for and cherish a little longer.

During this time the agency, the adoptive parents, and I decided to smooth the way for Catherin's eventual move by getting her familiar with her new mom gradually. For their first meeting, I dressed her in a new, blue ruffled dress, with lace-trimmed panties and socks, and took her first to the photographer and then to her new parents. It was awkward at first, but they held her and looked her over. We made an appointment for the mom to come to my home three days later to spend the morning, give Catherin a bath, and feed and play with her for a few hours. Later she would take her for a short outing and, finally, keep her overnight a time or two.

The morning the adoptive mom was to arrive, the case worker called. "You are not going to believe what I have to tell you," she said. The future parents had decided they did not want Catherin for reasons that were hard to believe: she had blue eyes instead of brown, she was eight months old instead of six, she did not appear healthy enough, and she was not pretty enough. "Do you still want her?" The case worker had prevailed upon her superiors for a change of heart.

Father Abraham was called upon to demonstrate his faith in a way I had never been able to comprehend. How could someone sacrifice a son? While I could not imagine passing that test of obedience, I now understood the magnificent lesson the Lord taught him—and me: When we put aside our self-interest to say—and *mean*—thy will be done, then we receive the "peace of God, which passeth all understanding" (Philippians 4:7).

If this were a fairy tale, I could tell you that I now know how to wrestle with the Lord to get whatever I want. But my life is not a fairy tale. I never got my cheaper-by-the-dozen family. *This* time, like Abraham and Isaac, we lived happily ever after. Catherin became our beautiful, healthy daughter, who at twenty-nine is an expectant mother herself. But the magnificent lesson the Lord taught me was how to find peace, not how to get my prayers answered in the way I want. Although I have cared for many dozen foster children from twelve hours to twenty-one years old, the Lord has given no other ones to me when I expressed my desire to keep them. He has, however, given me Christlike love for them. He taught me how to take joy in them, influence their lives, and then let them go peacefully.

Once having discovered the key to finding peace, it would have been be nice if I had been able to make universal application of it in my life. Alas, I have found myself kicking against the pricks quite persistently along my journey. Whenever the answer is no and the assignment hard to live with, I have to exert much effort to remember and apply the principle I learned half a lifetime ago.

Take comfort, then, in Christ's words in Gethsemane: "O my Father, if it be possible, let this cup pass from me: nevertheless not as I will, but as thou wilt" (Matthew 26:39). Jesus surrendered himself to the Father's will in Gethsemane and thereafter, regardless of whatever else he went through until he said "It is finished," he was at peace. After his trial in the Garden, Jesus went to Calvary in pain, in humiliation, and in agony. Notwithstanding, Jesus went to Calvary in peace.

NOTE

1. President Ezra Taft Benson said that "every man eventually is backed up to the wall of faith." *The Teachings of Ezra Taft Benson* (Salt Lake City: Bookcraft, 1988), 206.

WHEN ONE DOOR CLOSES, ANOTHER OPENS

TERI H. TAYLOR

In November 1993 on Thanksgiving day, my family's life changed forever. Spencer was twenty months old and normally developed. He could say more than sixty words and loved playing with his older brother and sister, Carlton and Candice. My husband, Matt, and I were very pleased with his development, and I had even written in his journal how well he was doing. He was starting to put two words together, like "good morning" and "hop down." He loved the horses behind our house and would point and say "horsie."

On that Thanksgiving day, all three of our children became ill with a virus. The two older children recovered within a few days, but Spencer continued to seem lethargic and stopped talking and responding to his name. We consulted our physician and other specialists over the next few months, trying desperately to find out what was wrong. We ourselves detected changes in Spencer's language, social skills, and behavior.

At first we thought Spencer must have a hearing problem because he no longer looked at us when we called his name or talked to him. We had his hearing tested; it was fine. Over

Teri Hansen Taylor serves as a member of the Autism Society of Utah Board of Directors. She has served as a missionary in the Tennessee Nashville Mission. She and her husband, Matt Taylor, are the parents of three children, the youngest of whom has autism. She serves as a Webelos leader in the Scouting program.

the next six months, Spencer's language regressed until he could say only five words, but even getting him to do that was a struggle. Eventually he lost all of his language.

Though he had once enjoyed others, he now became afraid of people. If I was holding him and talking with friends, he would cry and try to push them away. He stopped playing with Carlton and Candice and avoided eye contact with everyone. Other unusual behaviors soon became apparent. Spencer ran around the sofa for long periods of time. He stared at his hands a lot and walked around the perimeter of our yard repeatedly. He became fixated on videos and would watch them continually if we allowed him. We felt confused and panicked. What was happening to our son?

In May 1994, we met with a pediatric neurologist, who diagnosed Spencer as autistic. Though we had heard the word, we didn't really know what it meant. Over the next few weeks we did a lot of reading. What we learned was not very hopeful or helpful. Autism is a lifelong neurological disability that appears in a child before age three. In many children, the symptoms are apparent from birth. Others, like Spencer, may have a period of normal development before symptoms appear. There is no known cause of autism, and no cure. Special-education programs and speech therapy offer the only treatment available.

Matt and I were stunned. For the first few days and weeks after the diagnosis, we sat at the kitchen table, cried, and wondered what was ahead for our son and family. I couldn't face my daily responsibilities of cleaning, cooking, and laundry. I couldn't eat. Every morning I awoke with a heavy feeling. I was grieving the loss of my healthy son. It was hard for me to accept that Spencer, who had been totally normal six months ago, now had a lifelong disability.

I searched everywhere I could think of for help. I found treatment services, but frustrating waiting lists denied us access to many of the programs. I also read everything I could about

241

autism. Finally Matt told me to stop reading the medical information because most of it made me despair. He encouraged
me instead to search for hope. I turned to the *Ensign* and the
scriptures. I looked up *hope* in the Bible Dictionary and read
all the scriptures listed.

By March 1995 I was exhausted and demoralized. In sixteen
months I had not taken any time or thought for myself. All my
mental and physical effort had gone to help Spencer and to
keep up with my family and household responsibilities. But I
knew I couldn't continue at this pace. My most discouraging
realization was that no matter what I did, I could never cure
Spencer. I had believed that if I worked hard enough with him,
I could make the autism "all better." That was a heavy, impossible burden to carry, and I had to put it down. I couldn't let
go of it easily, though. I got into bed and started to cry. Then I
sobbed. I knew that Heavenly Father loved Spencer as much
as I did, and that if it was his will, Spencer could be healed. I
prayed and sobbed to Heavenly Father to ease my burdens,
and I put Spencer's care in his hands. "Let thy will be done," I
said.

Two days later, a national television program featured a
boy with autism who had had normal development but, like
Spencer, had then regressed. A group of physicians in
Philadelphia had treated him, and he was regaining his language. Matt and I had a strong feeling that this information
could be important for Spencer.

The next day I made many phone calls and found the
phone number for the physician in Philadelphia. I called over
and over, but the number was always busy. My strong feeling
that I needed to speak with this doctor persisted. That night I
prayed that I would be able to get through to the doctor and
that, if this was important for Spencer, everything would come
together. I woke up the next morning and continued to feel an
urgency to pursue this information. Again I phoned, and again
I could not get through. Finally I tried another phone number

in the neurology department. I got through to a secretary, Cathy Butler, and explained my situation. She said that their phones had been jammed for two days with more than ten thousand calls. The doctor she worked with was also part of the team that had treated the boy featured on the program. She promised to give my name to the doctor but couldn't promise that he would call me. Nevertheless, I felt calm throughout the day. At 3:30 P.M. the phone rang; it was Dr. Kollros from Philadelphia. We spoke for more than half an hour as I explained Spencer's medical history. I knew thousands of people were wanting appointments, and I was worried that it would be a year or more before I could get in. Dr. Kollros told us what to do to expedite the visit. Within three months, Spencer and I were in Philadelphia. The treatment has been very helpful for Spencer. He is now saying some words, and his language continues to improve.

Let me share with you some words that gave me hope when it seemed there was no hope. Elder Richard G. Scott, in his April 1994 conference address, said: "Recognize that some challenges in life will not be resolved here on earth. Paul pled thrice that 'a thorn in the flesh' be removed. The Lord simply answered, 'My grace is sufficient for thee: for my strength is made perfect in weakness' (2 Corinthians 12:7–9). He gave Paul strength to compensate so he could live a most meaning-ful life. He wants you to learn how to be cured when that is His will and how to obtain strength to live with your challenge when He intends it to be an instrument for growth. In either case the Redeemer will support you. That is why he said, 'Take my yoke upon you, and learn of me. . . . For my yoke is easy, and my burden is light' (Matthew 11:29–30).

"It is important to understand that His healing can mean being cured, or having your burdens eased, or even coming to realize that it is worth it to endure to the end patiently, for God needs brave sons and daughters who are willing to be polished."[1]

Elder Boyd K. Packer had this to say in his April 1991 conference address: "You parents and you families whose lives must be reordered because of a handicapped one, whose resources and time must be devoted to them, are special heroes. You are manifesting the works of God with every thought, with every gesture of tenderness and care you extend to the handicapped loved one. Never mind the tears nor the hours of regret and discouragement; never mind the times when you feel you cannot stand another day of what is required. You are living the principles of the gospel of Jesus Christ in exceptional purity. *And you perfect yourselves in the process.*"[2]

These words gave me hope. I prayed for strength and guidance in finding a way to help our son.

Doors started opening up for Spencer, though we had to expend a great deal of effort and perseverance to access the opportunities. We discovered the TEACCH Program, which helps parents work as co-therapists with their children at home. In an eight-week training session, I learned to do daily educational exercises with Spencer to help him gain the skills that come to most children normally, such as teaching him how to point to something he wanted. I began to feel more comfortable being Spencer's mom. Knowing how to work with him gave me a self-confidence I had not had before, and I began to better understand what autism is all about.

We were able to get Spencer into a speech therapy program with a therapist who had experience working with autistic children. This therapist taught our family sign language, which has enabled us to communicate more easily with Spencer. We also discovered a preschool program (CBTU) in Salt Lake City that specializes in educating children with autism, and we enrolled Spencer in it.

All of these discoveries changed my life dramatically. Before I had an autistic child, I had been majoring in interior design and had nothing in my life that I was passionate about.

I felt very unfulfilled. Now I feel intense passion about autistic children. I have found work that makes a difference in people's lives and gives me great satisfaction. This past year I have been actively involved in getting special-education services for autistic children. Until last year, the only specialized program for children with autism in Utah was in Salt Lake City. In September 1995, through a cooperative effort with the district, parents, and local businesses, an autism kindergarten classroom was started in the Alpine School District in Orem. This past legislative session, I worked with a few other parents and obtained increased state funding for the autism preschool program. In September 1996, a preschool classroom will open in the Alpine School District. Autistic children in Utah County can now attend school close to home. No longer will their parents have to drive to Salt Lake City every day. I am also serving on a state task force, the RAINMAN committee, to develop a state plan to better serve individuals with autism and their families. I also served for a time as executive director of the Autism Society of Utah.

What I have learned from all my experiences is that none of us will escape tragedy in our lives. We will feel despair, sadness, and grief. It's important to allow ourselves to feel those emotions. Then we each need to find a way to move on, to pass through the pain, and to find happiness again. I originally had a plan for my life, but the plan was changed. The change wasn't my idea. But with the Lord's help, I have been able to move forward with faith.

Spencer is doing well. He's learning to talk—gradually. He still has autism and will for the rest of his life. But I worked through the grief and have found joy in my life again. We feel so happy to have him in our family. Our elder two children are kind and loving to him. The devastation that I felt at first has been replaced by hope and happiness.

One day, not long ago, Matt and I were driving together, reflecting on our lives and our feelings about what has happened with Spencer and our family. Matt commented that we must know pain and sorrow to experience joy. "Imagine," he said, "the two of us standing in the next life, watching Spencer walk towards us with open arms. 'Mom and Dad,' he will say, 'Mom, Dad, I love you,' and he will be whole again."

NOTES

1. Richard G. Scott, "To Be Healed," *Ensign,* May 1994, 7.
2. Boyd K. Packer, "The Moving of the Water," *Ensign,* May 1991, 9.

"AWAKE, MY SOUL": AWARENESS AND TREATMENT OF DEPRESSION

JUDY NORMAN

Abby was a nineteen-year-old college sophomore who reported difficulty sleeping, trouble concentrating in school, withdrawal from friends, constant fatigue, and thoughts of "giving in" or "just giving up." In addition, Abby described at times feeling trapped in a black hole or as if dark clouds were closing in around her. She had not always felt this way. Family and social relationships had usually meant a great deal to her, her grades had been excellent, and she had felt purpose and direction in life.

At age sixty, Elizabeth found her life had changed dramatically. "My world was suddenly darker," she noted. "I found I couldn't see very well. I was constantly cleaning my glasses and adjusting the lamp to shine better on what I was reading. I couldn't seem to understand what I was reading and had to go over everything at least twice, sometimes more." Elizabeth had returned to school three years earlier at age fifty-seven and had been enjoying learning, but when she turned sixty, something changed. "I had always enjoyed staying up late to read or study. Now staying up required energy I no longer seemed to

Judith Norman is associate professor of social work at Brigham Young University. She practices as a licensed clinical social worker and is involved in research, training, and treatment related to depression. She serves as a Relief Society teacher in her Salt Lake City ward.

have. I worried constantly about getting enough sleep. . . . I was so tired all the time. School was difficult. I sat against the wall and hoped no one would notice me. I just wanted to get through, go home, close the blinds, and shut out the world."

Confused and fearful, both Abby and Elizabeth suffered from depression. Fortunately for both of them, they sought and received help. As Elizabeth noted, "One Friday morning I awoke and found my bedroom was *light!* The darkness had gone. I knew the depression had lifted, but a total 'coming back' took a little while." Though some symptoms and sources of their depression varied, both women experienced many similar symptoms.

The term *depression* covers a wide spectrum of problems from feeling sad to long-term negativism to severe chemical imbalances. Part of the problem in discussing depression is that a single term is used for everything from mild mood disorders to severe, suicidal despondency. Another difficulty is our own lack of ability to assess readily the type or severity. The person experiencing severe depression—feelings of hopelessness and deep despair—may not recognize how different her experiences are from depressions that don't require medical intervention, partly because a depressed person's thinking is usually distorted.[1]

One sure resource in dealing with depression is counseling with the Lord and with priesthood leaders. President Ezra Taft Benson, in a classic general conference address, identifies twelve activities the Lord has provided to help us overcome "despair, discouragement, depression, and despondency," namely, repentance, prayer, service, work, health, reading, blessings, fasting, friends, music, endurance, and goals.[2] If acting on these resources does not lighten the blackness of despair, the sufferer might consider seeking medical assistance as well. She may be dealing with a clinical depression that needs medical intervention along with these spiritual measures.

Understanding the causes of depression may help individuals avoid blaming themselves for conditions that are often beyond their control. Depression is no respecter of age, gender, race, socioeconomic class, culture, or religious affiliation, although women are treated for depression almost twice as often as men. It is a common, complex, but very treatable illness. Unfortunately, studies indicate that only one in five individuals who suffer with severe mood disorders ever seeks help. Some are not aware of what is wrong with them, or they think it is normal to feel the way they do. Others equate depression with weakness, as something they should be able to conquer alone. Seeking treatment is regarded as another sign of weakness or spiritual failing. Not only is that untrue, but the layer of guilt it adds can actually deepen already painful feelings of despair. When symptoms of depression are sufficient to warrant a clinical diagnosis, depression should be regarded as an illness, even when individual weakness or transgression complicate the picture. The chemical imbalance needs to be addressed as well as the spiritual.

It's important to recognize that depression may be a medical condition. Treatment may need to include medicine as well as therapy and spiritual counseling. From 4 to 8 percent of United States citizens experience at least one clinical depression, and depression is a common cause of suicide. Over their lifetimes, approximately 21 percent of women and 11 percent of men in the United States can expect to experience a significant depression. Once depression occurs, it will likely recur. Research has found that 50 to 80 percent of those experiencing depression, even these properly and effectively treated, will experience another episode.[3]

The common and core features of clinical depression include biological symptoms (sleep and appetite changes, physical agitation or retardation, decreased sexual drive); psychological symptoms (reduced ability to concentrate, indecisiveness, feelings of worthlessness and self-reproach,

249

excessive guilt, and feelings of helplessness and hopelessness); and environmental or interpersonal symptoms (loss of interest, social withdrawal). It is the complicating interaction of these biological, psychological, and environmental symptoms that makes depression so difficult to battle.

Research has shown that recurrent depressions have strong familial or genetic pathways. One woman reported that nine of her fifteen first cousins had suffered from various forms of anxiety or depression. Life experiences—often outside the control of the individual—also trigger depressive episodes. For example, the unexpected death of a close family member, unemployment, a serious illness such as cancer, or troubling relationships may lead to depression through no fault of the individual. Not all women experience depression similarly. Each case should be diagnosed and treated individually.

Some factors that can precipitate serious depression are avoidable. Drug and alcohol abuse both have high physical and psychological costs. Alcohol is a depressant and will further fuel other potential sources of depression. Lying, cheating, and betrayal will eventually damage relationships, resulting in psychological anguish and related physical symptoms such as headaches, stomachaches, fatigue, and nervousness. Choosing wisely and choosing well can foster, though not completely ensure, more healthful biological and psychological functioning.

Women are particularly vulnerable to depression. This well-established fact may be related to reproductive issues, including childbirth, birth control, adoption, and postpartum depression. Some speculate that women's higher vulnerability may have to do with women's social roles and expectations conflicting with personal goals or personal values. Women also suffer higher rates of victimization—rape, assault, sexual and physical abuse—and higher rates of poverty and powerlessness. To their benefit, women are also more likely to acknowledge problems and to seek help.

Latter-day Saint women may face many problems common to women in the population at large: divorce, abuse, limited financial resources, victimization, and discrimination. In the late 1970s, a controversial Salt Lake City television special conjectured that Mormon women were more likely to be depressed than women of other religions. That is false. Numerous subsequent studies found "Mormon women to be no more or no less depressed." The studies did find that women in general "were more prone to feel guilt and shame [than men], though this is not specific to being either religious or Mormon. It may have more to do with women's greater moral sensitivity to disturbances in relationships."[4] In other words, a wife may feel greater unhappiness over marital conflicts than her husband does, more troubled by a disagreement with a friend, or more anxious over disapproval from a mother-in-law.

Skewed perceptions and a self-imposed burden of expectations may also promote and maintain depression. Many people struggle with the ideal of "perfection" and feel guilty, unworthy, and unacceptable when they recognize that the reality of their own lives and families doesn't match their ideals. "Sunday is my most difficult day," says one struggling mother of five. "My children complain about attending church, my husband always finds an excuse to go to the grocery store, and NBA play-off games are never-ending. I seem to be the only one worried about where we are headed." Latter-day Saint doctrine and principles, however, allow for gradual, paced progress in our endeavors. Elder Neal Maxwell reminds us to "contemplate how far we have already come, . . . look neither back or around, comparatively, . . . make quiet but honest inventories of our strengths," and "allow for the reality that God is still more concerned with growth than with geography."[5]

But depressed individuals often have trouble reaching that kind of perspective. Despite good advice, they are often unable to see the temporariness of their experience, predicament, symptoms, or situations. And failed efforts to change are likely

251

to deepen their feelings of hopelessness and depression. A person with depression is very different from the same person free of depression. Yet, in the midst of a depression, a person may believe the symptoms of depression are personality traits. A depressed woman may believe, for instance, that she is inherently indecisive, worthless, sluggish, incapable, friendless and a poor companion, guilty, and prone to failure. When setbacks, temporary declines in performance, or particular disappointments come, depressed individuals frequently blame themselves, feeling they are failures, without looking at past successes or even current accomplishments.

Among high-achieving women, the sense of not doing it all or not doing enough, provokes much guilt; and guilt (often manifest as self-criticism, self-blaming, and self-reproach) is a common experience for the depressed. Guilt may not cause depression, but it may compound other depressive symptoms or may follow in the wake of depression. Whereas a healthy conscience beckons individuals to evaluate and possibly modify behavior, excessive guilt suppresses an individual's ability to be honest, open, and repentant. As one clinical social worker pleaded: "I wish we were more open. . . . Then we could talk about our pain, understand it better, and move toward acceptance of whatever we are dealing with. *Acceptance does not mean we give up*. It means we accept where we are and start making changes, finding solutions—no longer paralyzed by guilt, denial, depression, or anger."[6]

Everyone involved with a depressed individual—including anxious spouses or friends, well-meaning visiting teachers, and the person herself—must remember to be patient. When energy, appetite, sleep, and mental functioning are still significantly impaired, suggestions for more physical activity or social contact can lead the person to feel more helpless, more guilty—yes, even more depressed. Reminding her how blessed she is may well have the same effect. We can listen, and we can encourage her to do what she is able to do. Balanced meals, appropriate amounts of sleep, and modest exercise should be goals.

We can look to the Savior's life for balance. At times Jesus went to "a desert place" to pray and meditate (e.g., Mark 6:30–31), sometimes sent his followers away so he could be alone (e.g., Matthew 14:23; Luke 5:15–16), prayed (e.g. Matthew 26:39, 42), sought the support of friends—"watch with me" (e.g., Matthew 26:36, 38, 40), regularly walked, and let Martha care for some of his physical needs (Luke 10:38–40). The depressed person will benefit from similar activities.

For individuals whose symptoms indicate they may have clinical depression, professional assessment is paramount. Doctors or therapists will look for contributing medical conditions and should evaluate symptoms and sources of depression. Help for individuals with clinical depression comes through treating as many of the psychological and biological symptoms as possible. A combination of medications and counseling has proven to be an immediately effective means of alleviating acute clinical depression. Excellent, nonaddictive antidepressants are widely available. Addressing the overwhelming biological and psychological conditions will get the individual to the point of being able to avail herself of sustaining spiritual help, such as prayer, fasting, scripture reading, priesthood blessings, and a "doing whatever you can from where you are" attitude. "Sometimes the crisis is one of personal survival," Ann Madsen said in this women's conference. "God also hears self-centered prayer, when survival is all that matters. As we work our way out of depression, we move thankfully from focusing on our own coping to noticing once more the needs of others around us."[7]

In 2 Nephi 4 Nephi records his awareness of personal weaknesses and afflictions, yet rests secure in the knowledge of a loving, caring God: "Rejoice, O my heart, and give place no more for the enemy of my soul" (v. 28). Despair and depression are clearly enemies of the soul. There are many things we can give up or give away or do differently when we have the health and emotional energy to do so.

Family, community, church, and national education about depression can benefit us all. Dispelling myths about depression, early intervention, and interpersonal support can add to our arsenal against this particular enemy of our spiritual powers. With a willingness to seek treatment and increased understanding of the illness, many so afflicted can awake one morning and see that the room is light once again.

NOTES

1. A good article to help assess the degree of depression a person may be dealing with is David G. Weight, "Why Is My Wife (Or Husband) Depressed?" *Ensign,* March 1990, 27-29.

2. Ezra Taft Benson, "Do Not Despair," *Ensign,* October 1986, 2–5

3. See, for example, *Severe Depressive Disorders,* ed. Leon Grunhaus and John F. Greden (Washington, D.C.: American Psychiatric Press, 1994), 23, 111–35, 251; *Depression and the Social Environment,* ed. Philippe Cappeliez and Robert J. Flynn (Montreal and Kingston: McGill-Queen's University Press, 1993), 262; *Diagnostic and Statistical Manual of Mental Disorders,* 4th ed. (Washington, D.C.: American Psychiatric Association, 1994), 340–42; *Depression Is a Treatable Illness* (Washington, D.C.: U.S. Department of Health and Human Services, 1993); *Depression in Primary Care: Detection, Diagnosis, and Treatment* (Washington, D.C.: U.S. Department of Health and Human Services, 1993).

4. Allen E. Bergin, I. Reed Payne, Paul H. Jenkins, and Marie Cornwall, "Religion and Mental Health: Mormons and Other Groups," *Contemporary Mormonism: Social Science Perspectives,* ed. Marie Cornwall, Tim B. Eaton, and Lawrence A. Young (Urbana and Chicago: University of Illinois Press, 1994), 142–43, 145.

5. Neal Maxwell, *Notwithstanding My Weakness* (Salt Lake City: Deseret Book, 1981), 9–11.

6. Marian S. Bergin, "It Takes More Than Love," *Ensign,* August 1990, 21; emphasis added..

7. Ann N. Madsen, "Pray with All Energy of Heart," this volume, 102.

HORIZONS

SYDNEY S. REYNOLDS

An energetic musician in our ward once assembled all those
who had ever played in a band to perform at the ward talent show. The audience members were good sports, the ama-
teurs sounded pretty good, and one trumpeter was truly out-
standing, but the man standing next to me joked, "Do you have
any idea how many thousands of dollars in music lessons are
represented here?" His comment implied "wasted here," but
that is wrong. Whether in the fine arts or the sciences or sports,
learning is almost always more important than a one-time, tangible result. What a person learns, for instance, about music,
about discipline, about playing in an ensemble, about learning
a part, being prepared, and associating with other musicians
makes lessons a worthwhile investment even though few students ever approach concert level.

A 1996 *Newsweek* article reported that "a baby's brain is a
work in progress, trillions of neurons waiting to be wired into
a mind. The experiences of childhood . . . help form the brain's
circuits—for music and math, language and emotion. . . . Once
wired, there are limits to the brain's ability to create itself. Time
limits. Called 'critical periods,' they are windows of opportunity

Sidney Smith Reynolds received her bachelor's degree from Brigham Young University and
did graduate studies in history and educational psychology. She and her husband, Noel B.
Reynolds, are the parents of eleven children. She has served on the organizing committee
of the Brigham Young University–Relief Society Women's Conference and is a member of
the Primary General Board.

that nature flings open, starting before birth, and then slams shut, one by one, with every additional candle on the child's birthday cake."[1] Even if we are not interested in rearing a John Stuart Mill, who could read Latin at age three, we are interested in training up our children in the way they should go and in seeking learning, even by study and also by faith (see Proverbs 22:6; D&C 88:118).

To find out how parents can best do this, I called, wrote, and interviewed many friends and associates. Several things were mentioned again and again. Here, then, is a "top five" list of things some families are doing to help their children expand their horizons, things that most of us can do, too. One or more might work for you.

READ

We're probably all familiar with the couplet: "Richer than I you can never be— / I had a mother who read to me."[2] Reading to our children doesn't take dollars or advanced degrees, but it does take time. It is probably the single most important factor in encouraging your children to be lifelong readers themselves. But even if you don't read to your children, and I didn't always, it helps if they see you reading. Studies claim that if a child's parent just held a book (right side up and as if reading) for thirty minutes a day, that child's interest in books, stories, and reading improved dramatically. Other studies indicate that if you have a critical number of books in the house—about fifty—your children are much more apt to be readers than those from homes in which books are not available.

The families I talked to shared experiences of reading at bedtime, reading aloud in the car, scheduling when the TV would be off, or requiring reading hours for TV hours. Parents ordered magazines from *National Geographic World* for children to *Scientific American* for teens. They all were well acquainted with their public libraries.

TRAVEL

Mentioned most often after reading was travel, whether for work, vacations, or planned learning adventures. Parental consensus seemed to be, "If you have the chance to travel, it's almost always worth the effort." Some parents had family members write up reports on different points of Church history before traveling to Nauvoo or other sites. Whoever had written the report on an area was the expert "guide" when they arrived at each place. Jerusalem Center students take turns giving similar "site reports" as they visit in the Holy Land. A greater depth of understanding and appreciation can result from knowing something about what you're going to see. But just a willingness to keep eyes and ears open accomplishes much.

Living abroad helps family members understand a different culture, promotes family cohesion, helps children appreciate the plight of the "new guy in town," and develops understanding that people are people and "different" doesn't mean "wrong." One couple who lived in Great Britain for a time quickly realized that explaining to their children that the British drove on the "other" side of the road, rather than the "wrong" side, set a tone with their family that carried through most of their years there.

One relative of mine, who said good-bye to his twenty-one-year-old son in Cairo one summer, remembered feeling that he really wasn't sure he would ever see his son again. But he and his wife had always encouraged their children to follow their dreams, as his mother had encouraged him. (His father had died when he was young.) It was a formative family value. The son traveled down the Nile River, through the Sudan on public transport, and on into Kenya. When he returned home he decided to get a master's degree in public health and is pursuing a medical education, hoping to do something about the serious health problems he saw in those developing nations. Dreams open doors.

If you can't travel far, there are ways of letting "far away" come to you. Books, of course, are a great way. As Emily Dickinson pointed out long ago: "There is no frigate like a book, / To take us lands away."[3] But, you might also consider some of the following ideas. Many people talked about the influence of having others in their home—for dinner, to visit for family home evening, to live. Some regularly invited returning missionaries to share experiences with their children. Others invited business associates or foreign-exchange students from their children's schools. Just having a mix of people in the house lifts the conversation level, changes the awareness level, and exposes children to relationships that encourage development of social skills and understanding. Many commented on learning from house guests—cousins for a summer, students for a term, friends for a weekend.

TALK

Many people consider dinner table conversation a decent index of broad horizons. Three of our oldest children once had the good fortune to be invited to dinner at a friend's home after an afternoon of skiing. The table was lovely, the food was savory, and as the meal began, the distinguished father said something like, "I would like to propose for our topic of conversation tonight, the impact of political neutrality in the latter half of this century." A stunned silence followed. Our son's desperate hope that he might slip under the table and escape unnoticed only underscored the fact that this sort of thing rarely happened at our house! But the host and hostess graciously included everyone, opinions were respected, and my children had fun after all. I love this story and wish dinner table conversations like that happened more often at our house.

The year my husband attended law school as a visiting professor, he brought home "law cases" for the children to debate and discuss. That was fun. But good talk can happen without a resident law or philosophy professor to provide topics. One

258

family pulls out *The Kids' Book of Questions* at least once a week. Questions range from number 53, "What is the biggest difference between what happens on television and what happens in the real world?" to number 182, "Have you ever—without telling anyone—let someone beat you at a game you could easily have won? If so, why?"[4]

Another friend said that in desperation to curb the ongoing contention at their dinner table, she brought cards with American history information to the table. The cards included questions that became the focus of attention. "I had to do something," she said. "And sometimes it worked." Even though eliminating contention was her purpose, all her children learned to enjoy debate, all are notably well educated, and some are pursuing careers in history and political science.

Another stimulant to good learning can be the experiences a mother has volunteering. One good friend started out telling stories to her children and enjoyed it so much she volunteered to tell stories at the Children's Hospital. She ended up traveling to Jonesboro, Tennessee, for the National Storytelling Festival and organizing a story festival in her hometown to benefit the local library. It's no surprise that two of her children have won local storytelling contests. "Tell me a story" can be successfully requested of almost anyone at their house, but more important, the children are learning something about the blessings that come from helping others. Whether in the public school, the children's hospitals, the homeless shelter, or the local library, our experiences spill over into good conversation and new horizons of learning.

BE THERE

"Be there" means at least two things: traveling in your own area and keeping your eyes and ears open for significant events wherever you are—especially in your hometown. One woman I talked to, a world traveler herself, was grateful that her daughter, a young mother with limited means, was taking her children around Utah for the Centennial Celebration, visiting each Utah county and getting their "passport" stamped. At a minimal cost, her grandchildren are getting many of the advantages of travel, and they are able to do most of it on Friday-to-Saturday stints. We've all heard of New Yorkers who've never visited the Statue of Liberty, people from Cody, Wyoming, who know little about the Buffalo Bill Museum; and Salt Lakers who haven't bothered to tour Temple Square. It is important to put down your roots; respect for your own cultural heritage enhances your appreciation for others'.

Bev Plester, an American friend now married and living in England, wrote, "Believing the family tradition that a Plester was chief of the archers at Banbury Castle several hundred years ago and that a Plester was blacksmithing at Banbury till early this century, it's enticing to imagine that a Plester forged the weapons used by the rebels in the Battle of Edge Hill [in the English Civil War]. Every year we can, we go on October 23rd to Edge Hill outside of Banbury, less than one hour away, hoping to see or hear ghostly soldiers. This past year, I took John's brother Alan, his daughter and her friend, and my son, Sam, and his friend at 1 P.M. to observe. The four children were quickly into the spirit of things, finding artifacts and seeing shadows in the hedgerows, hearing noises that were unbovine in the middle of the cowfield, hearing the crackle of fires where they couldn't see any. . . . If it gets them into history, why not? I will never tire of living so close to so much history."

The corollary to visiting historical spots is to be there when history is being made. My mother took me out of school to watch President Dwight Eisenhower's motorcade drive through our town. In recent years presidents Reagan and Bush have visited Utah Valley, and Margaret Thatcher was also here not long ago. If you can expose children to world figures and do some explaining about who they are, it brings history out of the books and into their everyday lives.

Another way to be there is to encourage exploring. Open

your doors and close the books. There's a whole beautiful world out there. One family mentioned having learned through backpacking not only a love for nature and the mountains but the joy of "making it to the top of the mountain" in whatever they were doing. Environmental consciousness became their heritage, but the desire to "go the distance" became ingrained. Our missionary son wrote that his father, a university professor, raised his horizons by running a farm and raising a large variety of fruits and vegetables.

Don't limit learning to academics. A child's tastes and abilities may run to carpentry, mechanics, building, and gardening, not to mention theater, dance, music, and art. Learning these important skills will give them immediate rapport with people who have similar skills. For example, friends of mine who are quilters find common ground and new friends among other fabric artists wherever they go.

ENCOURAGE GOOD MANNERS

Good manners allow us to move comfortably in any situation and are an important part of raising our children's horizons. Many of us were taught and now teach the old rhyme, "Politeness is to do and say / The kindest thing in the kindest way." In the past, women, especially mothers, have been responsible for the civilizing of society. The April 1996 *U.S. News and World Report* cover laments "In Your Face" attitudes and asks, "Whatever Happened to Good Manners?" The article suggests that we need to strengthen our commitment to civility in the family, the neighborhood, the community, the world. The box office success of *Little Women* and the Jane Austen movies indicates new interest in an era when "manners and restraint played a dominant role in society."[5] Unfortunately, high-tech violence and low-budget blood and gore still predominate in the theaters.

So what can we do? Last month our home teacher gave a fun back-to-basics lesson about respect for others. We

261

discussed standing when being introduced or when an older person enters the room, opening doors, saying "excuse me," and so on. A parent can also stress the practical value of social graces. Understanding good manners has future benefits in the world of work. "Manners are the new status accessory," says Marjabelle Young Stewart, an etiquette consultant for corporations, "pricier than a Rolex, more portable than a Day-Timer, and shinier than handmade shoes. Polished graces can get you where you're going faster than a speeding BMW."[6]

Good manners are a matter not just of which fork to use but of civility and respect for all our Father's children.

So there's a list of five ways to start to expand our children's horizons—obviously not an exhaustive list, but perhaps it may be helpful in giving you an idea or the courage to try something that others have found useful. Let me conclude with a true story.

Virginia Noel was the middle child in a family of fourteen children who grew up on a farm in Vernal, Utah, during the Depression. Few of her family were interested in pursuing an education, but Virginia was. For a year after high school, she worked hard raising turkeys. The next fall, with one suitcase, twelve dollars, and a new hairbrush, she was off to the Agricultural College in Logan to become an elementary school teacher. She worked her way through college, graduated, started teaching, and married a handsome young man who, after the death of his mother, had dropped out of high school to help support his family. After serving in World War II, he homesteaded in Wyoming. There they reared a family of seven children with lots of work, no running water or electricity for years, and very little money but with regular trips to the library, the purchase of a piano, and high expectations. The children in that family were bilingual—they spoke "cowboy" and, because of their mother, they spoke grammatically correct English. All seven children attended college. I will always be grateful that my mother-in-law helped her children lift their sights to the horizon beyond the metaphorical haystack.

President Gordon B. Hinckley emphasized: "It is not enough simply to provide food and shelter for the physical being. There is an equal responsibility to provide nourishment and direction to the spirit and the mind and the heart."[7] As we look at ways to stimulate learning in the home, it is important to recognize that we can't start too early. The opportunities for learning are there whatever our circumstances. The need is obvious, the implications are eternal, and the home is the best place for us to begin.

NOTES

1. Sharon Begley, "Your Child's Brain," *Newsweek* (19 February 1996): 55–56.

2. Strickland Gillilan, "The Reading Mother"; quoted in Ezra Taft Benson, *The Teachings of Ezra Taft Benson* (Salt Lake City: Bookcraft, 1988), 516.

3. Emily Dickinson, "There Is No Frigate like a Book," *Modern American Poetry*, ed. Louis Untermeyer (New York: Harcourt, Brace, World, 1964), 97.

4. Gregory Stock, *The Kids' Book of Questions* (New York City: Workman Publishing, 1988), 56, 144.

5. John Marks, "The American Uncivil Wars," *U.S. News and World Report* (22 April 1996): 71.

6. Ibid., 72.

7. Gordon B. Hinckley, "Bring Up a Child in the Way He Should Go," *Ensign*, November 1993, 59.

LOOK TO THE WANTS

CAROL LEE HAWKINS

Not long ago a Relief Society assignment took me to visit a sister in her home to learn who she was, what her circumstances were, what her challenges and needs were, and what she wanted in life. It was a fairly typical visit for any Relief Society president or counselor, visiting teacher, just plain friend, or family member. As I drove up to this sister's home, I felt a bit uneasy being in an unfamiliar neighborhood. Next door, music was blaring and teenagers were shouting. In the driveway stood a rusty car with a flat tire. The front lawn displayed numerous bald spots. I saw no evidence of shrubs or flowers. A single dented pop can served as a bird feeder. The paint on the front door was chipped. By the time I reached that front door, in my mind I had quieted the noisy teenaged neighbors, repaired the car, reseeded the lawn, chased away the birds, and redecorated the front porch. My list of things that needed doing around this house grew by the second. I worried about this sister's visiting teachers; I hoped that they wouldn't be completely overwhelmed with the number of things that needed to be repaired and refurbished. What a job they had on their hands!

A moment later I was greeted by a well-groomed child with

Carol Lee Hawkins has served as chair of the women's conference at Brigham Young University and is a member of the Relief Society General Board. She directs special projects in the David O. McKay School of Education at BYU. She has lived in various parts of the world with her anthropologist husband, John P. Hawkins, and their four children.

obvious severe physical and mental disabilities. Her smile was broad, though her words were unintelligible, and her gesture welcomed me into her home. A brother and two sisters joined her. "Have a seat. Mom will be right with you," the little boy said. I glanced around the room. The only furnishings were a sofa and a bookshelf. On the wall hung a family photo and a picture of the Savior. The bookshelf was crowded with numerous books, Church magazines, and five sets of scriptures.

In a few moments the mother came out and greeted me warmly. I relaxed and began my interview. I had in mind a list of suggested questions. "Tell me about your life," I began, "your family, your conversion to the Church." Out poured an incredible story of faith and gratitude for a Father in Heaven who loved her and her family. Tucked in between the lines of thanks were tidbits that wove a story of poverty, a struggle to gain an education, the birth of a severely handicapped child, and a husband who had recently left her.

In light of this, I worried about asking the final questions: "What are your challenges? Your problems? Your needs?" I feared the list would be overwhelming. She replied simply, "The only thing I need and want is to have more time with my children. They are the most precious thing I have, and the greatest gift I can give them—especially right now—is my love and my time."

Her answer took my breath away. Here was a woman of enormous faith with a peace and happiness not dependent on temporal circumstances. The list of what *I thought* this sister needed was long, detailed, and very specific. Just by walking to the front door, I had compiled an enormous mental to-do list based on my own cultural biases, values, and assumptions. How grateful I am that my assignment was to listen, to interview and ask questions.

I have reflected over and over on this experience. Was exploring the needs of this sister an easy process? Not for me, it wasn't. The process forced me to discover another's strength

265

and confront some of my own deficiencies. When the Relief Society was first organized in Nauvoo in 1842, the Prophet Joseph Smith said that its purpose was to help "in looking to the *wants* of the poor—searching after the objects of charity, and in administering to their wants."[1] I had been busy assessing *needs*—as defined by myself—when I should have been discovering *wants*.[2]

As I sat on her frayed but serviceable sofa that day, a flood of shame washed over me. I took a good hard look at myself and didn't like what I saw. I found a self riddled with prejudice and biases, a self quick to judge and criticize, a self who viewed the world with too many unimportant and temporal "shoulds" and "oughts." The self I found needed to change; and the sister I had come to help ended up helping me. Through reflection and repentance, I am a different person, a better self because of that experience.

NOTES

1. *Relief Society Handbook* (Salt Lake City: The Church of Jesus Christ of Latter-day Saints, 1988), 2; emphasis added.

2. My eyes have been opened by this experience to note how often the scriptures talk about administering to the *wants* of the poor. See, for example, Mosiah 4:26; Mosiah 18:27–29; Alma 35:9; D&C 42:33; D&C 84:112.

JOURNEYING TOWARD HOLINESS

MARGARET BLAIR YOUNG

*Seek ye out of the best books . . . seek learning, even by study
and also by faith.*
—*Doctrine and Covenants 88:118*

W hen Deseret Book published my first novel, *House without
Walls,* my loyal mother bought literally hundreds of
copies and presented them to anyone who ventured to her
home—including, I suspect, the Avon lady and the mailman.
House without Walls didn't sell particularly well, despite my
mother, but one copy went to a Russian woman—Nina—
who, as a foreign language expert, spoke fluent English. As
it happened, my novel touched somebody clear across the
world and helped set in motion a series of God-directed con-
versions. That, to me, is a testimony of the power art can
have—sometimes even holy power.

My father met Nina in Russia on a six-month teaching
assignment. My mother had taken along a box of my novels to
give away as thank-you gifts. Nina tells the story herself via e-
mail: "I write to you about the special role of Dr. Blair in the
life of my family. He was the first who told me about Joseph
Smith and Mormons and the Church. He also gave me a book,
and even though it was not one of the book of Scriptures, this

Margaret Blair Young is a part-time instructor on the creative writing faculty at Brigham
Young University. She and her husband, Bruce Wilson Young, are the parents of four children. She has served in the Church as stake cultural arts chair, choir director, and ward
music chair.

book opened my eyes on the people who called themselves 'the Mormons.'

"Speaking about his family, Dr. Blair mentioned his daughter Margaret, who was a writer. In response I asked him if he could give me a book written by her. Thus it happened so that the Book of Mormon and the novel *House without Walls* by Margaret Blair Young got into my hands at the same time. I remember, I looked through the Book of Mormon and put it aside: it seemed too strange and foreign to me. Let me try something easier, I thought to myself. So I opened the *House without Walls,* read the introduction, and I could not stop till I turned over the last page of this book. The same world Dr. Blair told me about, which seemed so unusual and obscure, appeared real and alive. I saw the world of the real missionaries with their troubles and joys. I wanted to know more about their life and their religion. I desperately wanted to understand what made them sacrifice, leave their homes, and go to a foreign country to teach the Gospel. So I took the Book of Mormon again. This book led the missionaries over the world; it made them sacrifice their time and money. Evidently, there was something in this book which I missed. I had to understand the wisdom it contained, and I began to read it once again.

"It was the beginning of my way to the Gospel."[1]

Eventually Nina and her son joined the Church; a year later her husband was also baptized.[2]

President Spencer W. Kimball, speaking to the artists of the Church, encouraged them to raise their standards above the mediocre. "Our writers," he said, "our motion picture specialists, with the inspiration of heaven, . . . could put into [a work of art] life and heartbeats and emotions and love and pathos, drama, suffering, fear, courage."[3] His words encourage me not to gauge success by sales alone.

Several years ago, my daughter Kaila, now sixteen, got her teeth into some Sweet Valley High books. As you picture my darling little girl reading about the frenzied traumas of twin cheerleaders, remember that my husband, Bruce, is a professor of Renaissance literature, specializing in Shakespeare, and that I am an English teacher and a lover of great books. Where any number of parents would be pleased to see a child reading anything at all, we felt a need to raise our daughter's sights.

A few days later, Kaila and I chatted about the lives of the Sweet Valley High twins. I read some passages with her. And then I took another book—a fine young-adult novel by Utah author Margaret Rostkowski called *After the Dancing Days*. I suggested to Kaila that we compare the writing of the Sweet Valley High book with Margaret Rostkowski's. We read some of each book, comparing language and characters, after which I asked her which one she thought was better written. Of course, she knew my opinion. But whether she agreed with it or not, Kaila was able to provide the reasons why *After the Dancing Days* simply outclassed the other book—which was a lovely prelude to our reading *After the Dancing Days* together. For Kaila, our chat initiated a new era of "Great Expectations" for the literature she chooses to read. We were anxious for her not simply to read but also to appreciate good literature.

Should that matter? It is possible, and sadly easy, for writers to create simplistic work that provides stereotypes rather than distinctive characters; shallow plots with easy resolutions; clichés rather than rich, original language; "tear-jerking" as a counterfeit for earned emotion.

Contrast such work with that of "Gentle Will" Shakespeare, so called by his peers, who was genuinely fascinated by his fellowmen and women and observed them so well that four hundred years later, we still love the characters he created: Cordelia and King Lear, Hamlet, and Beatrice and Benedick, to mention a few.

Surely the first hallmark of worthwhile literature, then, is its characterization, followed closely by the book's complexity, both in thought and in plot. Of course, there is a place for simplistic literature with easy problems, easy resolutions, and easy tears. But we want to move beyond such milk to the meat that great art can provide.

Next, we need a love of language. We can focus on the language of the scriptures, for example, as we try to raise our artistic standards and those of our children. We can inundate ourselves with the poetry of Isaiah and the allegories of Jacob and the symbols of Lehi. But inundating means pondering, not skimming.

It's easy to fall into quick interpretations of the scriptures without really paying attention to the language. Think of the metaphors in Lehi's vision, for instance. Think of the rod of iron. It's so simple to identify it as "the word of God" that we may not pay further attention to Lehi's figurative language. But where else is the same image used? Note Psalm 2:9: "Thou shalt break them with a rod of iron." Is Lehi suggesting that we cling to the "word of God" so we can be prepared for some hard-core Bible bashing? Not likely! Or how about Revelation 2:27: "He shall rule them with a rod of iron."

So what is a rod? For one thing, it's the insignia of authority—something a king (or even a shepherd guiding his sheep) might carry, and it's also something that might be used to whip someone into shape (see Proverbs 13:24). And why a rod of *iron?* What characteristics does iron have? How is God's word like iron? I'll leave the answer up to you and suggest only that rushing too quickly to the symbol's interpretation cheats us of the implications of the rich figurative language Lehi has given us. Much more is suggested by an iron rod than an easy, fill-in-the-blank answer. The iron rod is the word of God, but that word is conveyed with an image of sovereign power, even priesthood power.

Another characteristic of truly worthwhile literature is the author's sense of verisimilitude. We can guess the meaning of that word from its components: *veri-* (from *veritas*, "truth") and *similitude* ("similarity to"). We want literature that's like truth, like life. I get concerned over formula fiction that resolves difficult questions in a prayer and a paragraph. Such resolution is not only unfair to the reader but simply untrue—inconsistent with the plan of salvation. Novels that participate in this rather common deception, this lack of verisimilitude, suggest inadvertently that it is all right to answer somebody's pain with a cliché instead of with heartfelt empathy. The great writers, on the other hand, will always take us on wonderful, sometimes horrifying journeys, which we experience with their characters who are so well drawn that we can feel what they are feeling. Such journeys not only help us understand and empathize with our fellow beings but ultimately teach us about the plan of salvation. For the plan of salvation is not based upon quick answers and quick resolutions but upon hard journeys—which we thank God we are able to make. Remember, we shouted for joy when the opportunity to do so was presented to us in the premortal existence.

Let me return briefly to Lehi's vision—which, too, is full of journeys. Lehi is making his own journey across a wilderness when he has the dream and in the dream is likewise in a wilderness, or (to use his own wonderful language) a "dark and dreary waste" (1 Nephi 8:7). When Nephi desires to know the interpretation of the vision, he simply asks, "What is the meaning of the tree?" (see 1 Nephi 11:11). The angel does not give him a list of all the symbols from Lehi's dream and a pencil to identify each symbol's meaning. He doesn't give Nephi a direct answer. No, the angel provides him a vision of the Savior's life—another journey, the greatest and hardest yet made, from his birth to his death and beyond the grave. When the vision closes, the angel asks, "Now do you know the meaning of the tree?" And Nephi answers, "Yea, it is the love of God" (1 Nephi 11:22). Though Nephi has not lived the Savior's life, he has seen and felt it. He has, in a way, accompanied Christ on his earthly mission and sensed the magnitude of the Atonement. He understands the meaning of the tree with his whole soul.

In the spirit of heeding President Kimball's admonition, I use these visions from the Book of Mormon as metaphors for what artists attempt and for what the best artists in "the best books" will accomplish (D&C 88:118). Just as Nephi learned the full meaning of the tree of life by experiencing the Lord's earthly sojourn in vision, so too can a reader learn something about guilt and grace by letting Dostoyevsky act as a sort of angel in opening up a vision—fictional, but true in the deepest senses—of Raskolnikov's sad pilgrimage in *Crime and Punishment*. Similarly, a reader can learn something about love and loyalty by accompanying Shakespeare's Lear as he rages into wilderness where the winds howl and "crack [their] cheeks."[4]

As I make my own way—often skinning my knees—in the mortal world and in the world of art, I come to understand the depth and beauty of the plan of salvation and the necessarily difficult journey each of us makes in mortality. I find that "the best books" let me follow others on their journeys and feel what they are feeling. The best artists—like the angel in Nephi's dream—open my mind to their visions as I open their books and let their characters open my heart and their language teach me something about myself, my own possibilities, and even about the love of God.

NOTES

1. Personal communication with Dlora Dalton, 6 September 1996, in possession of the author.

2. At the time of this presentation, I was unaware that Nina had come to Provo for the 1996 BYU–Relief Society Women's Conference. After my presentation, LaRene Gaunt of the *Ensign* asked me if the woman I had referred to was the one who had addressed the women's conference earlier that day. I told her I didn't know. The more Sister Gaunt described Nina Bazarskaya to me, the clearer it became that she was indeed the woman my parents had met in Russia. I was able to meet Nina later that day. As soon as I introduced myself, she held open her arms and, weeping, said, "Your parents brought us light when all we had was darkness."

3. Spencer W. Kimball, "The Gospel Vision of the Arts," *Ensign*, July 1977, 5.

4. *King Lear*, act 3, scene 3, line 1.

WRITING IS BELIEVING

MARILYN ARNOLD

One of Moroni's endearing character traits is his very human concern for how latter-day Gentiles would receive the record he and his predecessors had prepared for them. Specifically, he worries that stylistic deficiencies will persuade skeptical Gentiles to dismiss the record out of hand. Moroni takes his concern to the Lord: "Lord, the Gentiles will mock at these things, because of our weakness in writing. . . . Thou hast also made our words powerful and great, even that we cannot write them; wherefore, when we write we behold our weakness, and stumble because of the placing of our words; and I fear lest the Gentiles shall mock at our words" (Ether 12:23–25).

Even the first Nephi, powerful and able as he was, had a similar concern: "And now I, Nephi, cannot write all the things which were taught among my people; neither am I mighty in writing, like unto speaking; for when a man speaketh by the power of the Holy Ghost the power of the Holy Ghost carrieth it unto the hearts of the children of men" (2 Nephi 33:1).

As these two early prophets see it, those present and spiritually attentive when the Lord speaks through his prophets participate actively in the event. They can be touched

---

Marilyn Arnold, professor emeritus of English, Brigham Young University, has served as dean of graduate studies and as assistant to the president of BYU under Dallin H. Oaks. She is the author of many articles and several books.

simultaneously by the same Spirit that moves the speaker. Centuries down the line, however, cold words on hard metal plates or paper might not enjoy the same reception. I would argue with Moroni; I would insist that he and his predecessors *were* mighty in writing as well as in speaking and that the Spirit touches their latter-day readers just as it touched their contemporary listeners. But I also know, as do most of you, the discomfort of feeling unequal to a task. I cannot help but think, however, that *writing* their faith—and more particularly in the case of Moroni and Mormon, writing their revelations and the revelations of others, abridging a record, putting the teachings of the Lord into their own words—greatly enhanced their personal understanding and their faith.

I say this about them because something similar, though on a much reduced scale, to be sure, happened to me. I am no prophet, but I know from personal experience how attempting to understand scripture by writing about it can change one's life for the better, change it infinitely and lastingly.

This is not a new idea. In 1988 noted writer, editor, and educator William Zinsser published *Writing to Learn,* in which he argues that "writing is a form of thinking, whatever the subject."[1] "We write," he continues, "to find out what we know and what we want to say. I thought how often as a writer I had made clear to myself some subject I had previously known nothing about by just putting one sentence after another—by reasoning my way in sequential steps to its meaning. I thought of how often the act of writing even the simplest document—a letter, for instance—had clarified my half-formed ideas. Writing and thinking and learning were the same process."[2] In fact, writing is simply "thinking on paper."[3]

Zinsser summarizes his position this way: "Finally, in the national furor over 'why Johnny can't write,' let's not forget to ask why Johnny also can't learn. The two are connected. Writing organizes and clarifies our thoughts. Writing is how we think our way into a subject and make it our own. Writing enables us to find out what we know—and what we don't know—about whatever we're trying to learn. Putting an idea into written words is like defrosting the windshield: The idea, so vague out there in the murk, slowly begins to gather itself into a sensible shape. Whatever we write—a memo, a letter, a note to the baby-sitter—all of us know this moment of finding out what we really want to say by trying in writing to say it."[4]

Very likely all of us have made notes in the margins of our scriptures, to capture some insight, to remind us next time around of what we thought, or what someone else said. We may have gone beyond that, writing about an insight for a talk or a lesson, perhaps. Some of us may have made journal entries exploring certain scriptural passages. Others may even have written about scripture for an article or a book. In this essay I intend to describe what happened to me when I moved beyond simply reading scripture to writing about it. I hope, thereby, to plant a seed in your minds that will expand into an irrepressible desire to reach new understandings and to reach them by writing about scripture. I hope you will begin honing your thinking by making good notes in your journals about scriptural passages, deepening your belief by including scriptural insights in your letters to friends and family, and sealing your testimony by shaping your thoughts to the Lord's words.

The story behind this essay begins perhaps ten years ago, when I was prompted by President Ezra Taft Benson's urgings to reread the Book of Mormon. Only this time, I wanted my reading to be more than a mechanical, X-number-of-pages-per-day thing. Up to then, though I was a loyal and active believer, my adult life had been focused on a career. As an English teacher at Brigham Young University, I naturally studied and wrote, but most of it centered on the secular literature I taught. Not that that was bad; people do have to earn a living, and working with literature is a lovely way to do it. It was simply too one-sided. I decided that it was high time I take whatever gifts the Lord had given me, combine them with the training he blessedly assisted me to acquire, and use them in the study of scripture. More than that, I was fired through with a new desire to turn those same gifts and acquired abilities to service in the kingdom.

The two desires merged into one as I began to study the Book of Mormon with new eyes, or more accurately, with an eye single to someone's glory besides my own. By the time I was midway through, the book had gripped me with such force that I felt very nearly consumed by it. I wanted to be with the Book of Mormon all the time; I hated to leave it for other things. I know, too, that I spent more time on my knees in those days than ever before. And in that process, I learned what it meant to submit my heretofore sometimes careless and stubborn will to the Lord's will. As I reread Alma's discourse describing the great change of heart that must happen for each of us, I wanted that more than I wanted any other earthly necessity or pleasure. Maybe for the first time in my life, I brought to the Father a broken heart and a contrite spirit. And in doing so, I felt the burden of countless mistakes, sins, and weaknesses lifted from me—and knew his love in a way I had never known it before.

It is a highly personal thing, this rebirth of the self as a spiritual child of Christ (see Moroni 7:19), and it is not easy for me to talk about. I only regret that I was so long in coming to it. In conjunction with this rebirth, or true conversion, came another desire: to write about the Book of Mormon. It seemed the only thing I could do, the only thing I wanted to do, the only gift I might somehow return to him who had so blessed me. It was more than a wish, more even than a strong desire. It nagged at me and gave me no peace. And so, I turned from Moroni 10 back to 1 Nephi 1 and started again. But this time I began trying to write as I read, to understand, to formulate distinct perceptions about the narrative and its teachings and people.

I thought that if I had any hope of creating a worthwhile manuscript, I ought to try to make a focused work of it—center on a theme or themes, trace an idea, follow a defined course. Though it sounded like a workable plan, I seemed to get nowhere. The Book of Mormon resisted me; and finally, I wound up simply writing about the books, one by one, from Nephi to Moroni. As I did that, I came to understand why I had to do it that way. I was not a Book of Mormon scholar, I had not spent my life in deep study of it, I had not read extensively in the work of scriptural scholars. I could come to know the Book of Mormon—to make it mine—only by writing about it chapter by chapter.

Struggling to put insight into words—and sometimes just working to get the narrative straight once the multiple complications entered—was the process that gave the book to me. It was in that struggle, to do all I could to understand, that the Spirit taught me as never before. I had previously been aided in the preparation of lessons or talks; I would not want to devalue those precious experiences. But this was different. Always before, the task was defined and had limits—usually time limits. And once the lesson or talk was over, the insight was shelved and largely forgotten. It never became part of a larger whole, was never assimilated into a meaningful design.

Now, however, the study had a larger purpose, and the idea could not simply be a jotted note. The idea had to be in complete sentences, submitted to the rigors of purposefully written language: it had to be precise, it had to make sense, it had to be true to the text. It seemed that I could discover what I really thought about a passage only by framing written language to convey it. At times meanings eluded me. But there were other times—only a few—when the Spirit was so strong that the words seemed to be placed in my mind, phrase by phrase. And those moments were so lovely that the tears flowed along with the words.

Another thing happened in this process. Not only did I come to know the book as the undeniable truth, as the greatest text I have ever encountered, as the most authentic record ever

277

published, but I also came to love the doctrine. It grew to be so sweet to me that I began to hunger for it. I saw value in every part and aspect of the Book of Mormon, but the doctrinal discourses thrilled me in a way that I would not otherwise have thought possible. Coming to grips in writing with some of the doctrinal complexities was the most difficult part of the work, but it was the part I liked most—perhaps because of how much I learned as I labored to put the prophets' and the Lord's teachings into my words and to understand beyond the obvious.

The Book of Mormon, and the writing it inspired in me, became incredibly precious. Going to it became the reward I allowed myself after meeting other demands of the day. And then when I could give an entire, glorious day, or even several days, to uninterrupted work with the book, I grew, as Thoreau said, like corn in the night. I have never known such happiness. This phase of the work stretched over several years. And now that the writing is finished, I miss it terribly. There is another problem, too: every time I go to the Book of Mormon, I spot something I missed, I think of something I should have said, I see places where my thinking was shallow or ill-conceived. That is the way with scripture. Because we learn line upon line, precept upon precept, we can never be finished with it. As we change or need new instruction in our personal lives, scripture rises to meet our earnest inquiry, our changing needs, our growing capacity to understand.

Good as reading scripture is, writing about scripture is better. Let me just share a few insights I gained from putting my thoughts into black words on white paper. I'll begin with an obvious example, one of the most quoted sentences in Mormondom, from 2 Nephi 2:25: "Adam fell that men might be; and men are, that they might have joy." Now, taken by itself, that passage does indeed speak truth and offer hope. But perhaps like me, you have been inclined to isolate such passages, lift them from context to make a particular point—in this case, to suggest that the Lord wishes us to live joyfully. He does, yes, but that is not the only point of the discourse from which this passage is taken. What writing about the Book of Mormon compelled me to do was to consider every passage in context. I simply could not move through the book, one sentence at a time, without considering the surrounding territory of thought.

The passage takes on added significance when we examine where and when it occurs and what else is being said. Here, an aged Lehi is pronouncing a patriarchal blessing upon his son Jacob, a son born in the wilderness, who never knew the comforts and amenities of his father's home in Jerusalem. Moreover, as a tender youngster, Jacob experienced the deprivations of wilderness living and the demands and dangers of a long sea journey. Furthermore, on that journey he witnessed the murderous ill-treatment of one brother at the hands of two other brothers—and the severe suffering of his parents because of it. Lehi begins his blessing by acknowledging what Jacob has suffered: "And now, Jacob, I speak unto you: Thou art my first-born in the days of my tribulation in the wilderness. And behold, in thy childhood thou hast suffered afflictions and much sorrow, because of the rudeness of thy brethren. Nevertheless, Jacob, my first-born in the wilderness, thou knowest the greatness of God; and he shall consecrate thine afflictions for thy gain" (2 Nephi 2:1–2).

Lehi then moves toward his principal subject, the necessity for opposition in all things, a subject Jacob had experienced in a highly personal way. The Fall and its broken law, which require punishment, Lehi explains, stand in opposition to the Savior's atonement, which answers the law's requirement. It is the principle of opposition that makes agency operative and mercy necessary. We could scarcely exercise agency—choice— Lehi declares, unless we had opposing alternatives to choose between. Lehi expands on the principle, explaining its broad application and the necessity of the transgression and Fall. The

279

pattern was established in the Garden with Adam and Eve. Without the Fall "they would have remained in a state of innocence, having no joy, for they knew no misery; doing no good, for they knew no sin" (2 Nephi 2:23). This passage precedes (with one short comment between) and generates the familiar one: "Adam fell that men might be; and men are, that they might have joy."

The context for that well-known passage, then, is the doctrine of opposition, in conjunction with the doctrine of agency. Without opposition, there would have been, first, no fall and no mortal experience. And second, there would have been no redemption and thus no *reason* for joy, nor any *capacity* for joy, nor any way to *choose* joy. Even as I revisit this passage and write about it again, I see beyond what I saw when I put my book to bed. And now I want to go back and rewrite that section.

Let me give you another example of something that might not have occurred to me if I had not been writing about the Book of Mormon. The text is so dense that it is difficult to keep details straight. Writing about them tends to plant them in the mind a little more solidly; it enables us sometimes to see echoes of earlier situations and circumstances in later events. One such "echo" experience occurred for me as I was writing about the brother of Jared's requests to the Lord for help with the eight vessels he was instructed to build. We are all familiar with that story, and we have rightly taken a valuable lesson from it: we are to pray for guidance, but we are also to exercise our own ingenuity in solving problems rather than simply presenting them to the Lord (or to our leaders) for solution.

Jared's brother had previously built some "practice" barges for local maneuvers and excursions before undertaking the long voyage to the new world. And when the work on the long-distance vessels was completed, he took three problems to the Lord: how were the vessels to be lighted, ventilated, and steered? The Lord readily answered the questions about ventilation and steering, but he required his prophet to solve, at least partially, the lighting problem himself: "What will ye that I should do that ye may have light in your vessels?" (Ether 2:23). Two verses later, the Lord asks the brother of Jared again what he wants Him to do. And, as we know, the prophet comes up with a workable scheme.

As I wrote about this, I recalled Nephi's response when the Lord similarly commanded him to construct a boat, and I returned to that passage. It is true that Nephi received much instruction from the Lord in building the ship, but Nephi was also prepared to exercise personal initiative in the project from the beginning. We see his initiative and assumption of responsibility even in the manner in which he answers the Lord's first injunction on the matter. Nephi is apparently asleep when the Lord speaks to him, saying, "Arise, and get thee into the mountain. And it came to pass that I arose and went up into the mountain, and cried unto the Lord" (1 Nephi 17:7). Nephi did not merely take himself to the mountain and then passively wait for instruction. Rather, he made earnest, and probably immediate, supplication—he "cried unto the Lord." In answer to Nephi's prayer to know his will, the Lord tells him to build a ship. Nephi's response is instructive. He is clearly ready to apply himself and all his capacities to the task. He does not ask the Lord to provide tools and building materials for him. Rather, he asks, "Lord, whither shall I go that I may find ore to molten, that I may make tools to construct the ship after the manner which thou has shown unto me?" (1 Nephi 17:9). He asks for guidance in finding ore so that he can make tools. The brother of Jared became one of the greatest prophets ever to walk the earth, but at this juncture in their somewhat parallel ministries, it appears that Nephi already knew something his early predecessor had not yet learned.

Let me share one more quick example of how writing about the Book of Mormon opened my eyes to new understanding. This one has to do, in particular, with awareness of language. Recall Lehi's marvelous vision of the tree of life, and remember also that Nephi, in answer to his great desire, was blessed with a vision of the tree—and of other things, too. Lehi's book was lost, but Nephi, fortunately, had included in his record on the small plates an account of his father's vision. He tells what his father said, representing Lehi's words: "And it came to pass that I beheld a tree, whose fruit was desirable to make one happy" (1 Nephi 8:10). And that is all Nephi records of Lehi's description of the tree.

As I was writing a little later about Nephi's vision, I was struck by the difference in tone—in energy, really—between the two passages. The one I just read was Nephi's reporting of a secondhand experience—in rather plain, straightforward terms. But there is a marked difference when Nephi is telling his own firsthand account of a similar experience. Note the lilt of the language, the joy that leaps off the page: "And it came to pass that the Spirit said unto me: Look! And I looked and beheld a tree; and it was like unto the tree which my father had seen; and the beauty thereof was far beyond, yea, exceeding of all beauty; and the whiteness thereof did exceed the whiteness of the driven snow" (1 Nephi 11:8).

By the same token, I notice now (for the first time) that Nephi does not say whether or not he tasted of the fruit. It is the tasting of the fruit that spurs Lehi to eloquence: "And it came to pass that I did go forth and partake of the fruit thereof; and I beheld that it was most sweet, above all that I ever before tasted. Yea, and I beheld that the fruit thereof was white, to exceed all the whiteness that I had ever seen" (1 Nephi 8:11).

Let me emphasize that it is not necessary to write an article or a book, or even to prepare a lesson or a talk, to come to scripture with new eyes by writing about it. Thoughts given expression in a journal or a letter can do the same thing for us. I don't do this nearly often enough, but occasionally I overcome inertia and write a thought triggered by scripture reading in my sporadically kept journal. Often, such thoughts occur when I am studying in preparation for a Relief Society lesson. Let me take an excerpt from my unpolished scribblings dated "6/25/95—Monday" and "6/29/95":

"Started preparing my next R.S. lesson last night—subject: the fast. . . . As I was reading Doctrine and Covenants 59:9–19—a wonderful passage—vs. 13–14 seemed to introduce a new dimension to the concept of fasting. Curiously, v. 13 speaks of preparing food in such a way ("with singleness of heart") "that thy fasting may be perfect, or, in other words, that thy joy may be full." We generally think of fasting as abstinence from food, so why would the passage give instructions for food preparation? The footnote suggests something that had not occurred to me. The note attached to the word "fasting" in v. 13 says, "IE hungering and thirsting after righteousness." Fasting, then, is equated with *spiritual* hungering. . . . I take it to mean that we are to reach beyond physical hungering entirely and transform that physical sensation (of desiring or requiring food) into a spiritual one. After all, how could we know what hungering and thirsting after righteousness means unless we have something to associate it with?

"Since the subject of section 59, from v. 9 on, is the *Sabbath Day,* not specifically 'fast day,' the text implies that we should "fast," that is, spiritually hunger, *every* Sabbath day, not just one Sabbath a month—and, in fact, 'all days and at all times' (v. 11). Our Sabbath focus should be *not* on filling our stomachs— nor on any 'other thing'—but on filling our souls. And we can't stuff spiritual food into a soul that is not hungry. Unless the soul is hungry, it will turn away from spiritual feasts just as a full stomach has no interest in temporal food. . . .

"The focus of the Relief Society lesson, then, the only one I can settle on and teach, it appears, is this: Fasting is much more than abstinence from food and drink, though it may begin there, as a preparation for true observance of the principle of fasting, that is, of hungering and thirsting after righteousness."

If I had not written these ideas down as I worked with the pertinent scriptures, they would be as lost to me as countless other insights—surviving only in some virtually irretrievable state among a file of scratched notes from long-ago lessons. These entries I had made less than a year ago, and already I had forgotten them. But, because I wrote them down, I have now been able to repossess them and then share them with you. Whatever we write down can be recaptured. What we do not write is likely to be lost.

I have found, too, that these moments of insight, when scripture seems to open a door in my mind, when I am being taught by the light of Christ, or by the Holy Ghost, are the most joyful moments of my life. None of us lives on this kind of spiritual high continually. We have exceptional moments, and then we lose them in the busyness of everyday life. But if we formulate them in writing, we have not lost them. We can retrieve those moments and be lifted and renewed by them. They reinforce testimony and remind us of what we thought and felt when truth touched us on the shoulder. It is not enough simply to note that we experienced insight and joy. We must at the very moment write out, give words to, the insight itself. Otherwise, we will be retrieving only the confetti and empty plates of the celebration.

Let me suggest, also, to anyone who does not yet have an abiding testimony of the power and wonder and truth of the Book of Mormon, or any book of scripture—writing about it is a surefire way to get one. Encourage your children or grandchildren to work out the meanings of scriptural passages in their journals and share them with you or with the family. Knowing that they intend to write about what they are reading will change the way your children read and study scripture. It will also change the way you read scripture. Your reading will, I think, become more deep and attentive and less mechanical and superficial. Your appreciation will grow, and your life will take on new purpose.

To illustrate, let me share one more extract from my journal, this one recorded last November 28: "I just finished the final revision of the last chapter of my Book of Mormon manuscript. I will send it off to the publisher tomorrow. As I read the conclusion, I was overwhelmed with gratitude for the great blessing the work has been in my life. . . . It is easy to see why Joseph Smith, having received this book through the power of the Spirit, endured everything for his faith. He must have been so full of it, and his knowledge of the truth of it, that he felt like shouting 'Hosanna!' every day of his life."

Let me conclude with my witness that the Book of Mormon "is indeed a holy work, priceless, saving, comforting, lifting, and immeasurably dear. To read it is to find a still center of truth in a world spinning with confusion. To study it is to be blessed by the choicest gifts of heaven. To write about it has been to discover the illuminated chambers in my own soul. Sweet, indeed, is the word. And none sweeter than this word."[5]

NOTES

1. William Zinsser, *Writing to Learn* (New York: Harper & Row Publishers, 1988), vii.

2. Ibid., ix.

3. Ibid., 11.

4. Ibid., 16.

5. Marilyn Arnold, *Sweet Is the Word: Reflections on the Book of Mormon—Its Narrative, Teachings, and People* (American Fork, Utah: Covenant Communications, 1996), 359–60.

INDEX